The Quest for Service Quality: R_Xs for Achieving Excellence

The Quest for Service Quality: R_Xs for Achieving Excellence

by

Phillip S. Wexler
W. A. (Bill) Adams
Emil Bohn, PhD

Maxcomm Associates, Inc.

1333 East 9400 South, Suite 270
Sandy, Utah 84093

ISBN 0-9632471-2-3

LCCN 92-60518

Printed in the United States of America

10 9 8 7 6 5 4 3 2

Dedication

To our children,
Chase, Kasse, Ashley, Dana, and Laura

Acknowledgments

The authors wish to thank Garry Schaeffer for his assistance in writing this book. In addition, our thanks to Gregg Baron, Robert Coates, Joe Pepe, R. Richard Bastian III, and Marjean Daniels for their contributions to and invaluable feedback on the manuscript. Finally, we wish to acknowledge Stephen E. Ewing, Alfred R. Glancy III, William (Kes) McCrackin and our clients and friends who have contributed to our work.

Phillip S. Wexler
W. A. (Bill) Adams
Emil Bohn, PhD

Preface

How does your company rate in terms of service? What's the best way to position your company for the future? What philosophical changes must be made to achieve that positioning and to create a high-performance, market-focused organization? These are the basic questions answered in this book. This book also describes the management philosophies and service practices that will influence the future of American corporations.

This book has many unique features. First, throughout the book you will find a number of pages from the authors' prescription pads. These Service R_xs, which appear in boxes, are major points that express philosophies, principles, and practices. In fact, we believe the Service R_xs are important enough that we reiterated them in an appendix at the end of the book. You may use them as a quick reference to refresh your memory after you've read the book.

Unlike most customer service books, this one does not center on case studies. Instead, there are brief examples and anecdotes from the authors' personal experiences—stories they share with thousands of people each year in their speeches and consulting efforts.

Within these pages you will read about the Zones of Service Quality concept. This is a process for qualitatively and quantitatively determining the level of service your company is presently providing. Knowing where you are is the first step in developing a clear vision of where you want to be.

Lastly, the authors' background and experiences make this book unique. Just as there are many ways to consult with clients, there are many ways to write a book. In their consulting work, the authors look at a business from three diverse perspectives. Three of America's quality service experts share their insights into the components of service excellence.

The authors, Phil, Bill, and Emil—got together and posed the question, "What is happening in the marketplace?" From their three perspectives came the same answer: The need, as always, is for differentiation. Twenty-five years ago differentiation was achieved through technology. Today, however, technology is a given. Service has become the differentiating factor of the 1990s.

There's more to differentiating your organization than just motivating employees to smile and say, "Thank You." That may be the "form" of service. However, the "substance" of service goes much deeper. As service quality is a direct reflection of the quality of management, top executives and managers must transform their organizations into service cultures if they intend to be competitive in the future. It is that all important cultural transformation that this book will help you create.

Most companies implement customer service programs by "shooting from the hip." Instead of taking the time to find out what their customers really want, they assume they know. It's all-too-common for companies to make the wrong assumptions.

As organizations try to accomplish more with less and customers become more demanding, companies can't afford to expend resources that do not guarantee a return on the investment. Many companies that measure "service" in terms of response time think the important service issue is how quickly their people answer the phone, not the outcome of the call. Even though response time is important, it is not as important as a quality interaction with a service provider. This book will share proven techniques (R_Xs) for achieving service excellence in the never-ending quest for quality.

About the Authors

Phillip J. Wexler is a much sought-after keynote speaker and customer service trainer whose talents are threefold. He has the ability to 1) quickly understand diverse businesses, 2) apply broad philosophical concepts to different businesses and 3) teach the philosophies in ways that people will understand and use them.

In the past 14 years, Phil has addressed over 1,500 audiences throughout the world for clients that include Westin Hotels, AT&T, IBM, Budget Rent-A-Car, Northwest Airlines and United Airlines.

Phil sees things from a marketing perspective, which gives him a bottom-line approach to the subject of service. And let's face it, if service is going to be championed by busy corporate executives, it must have an impact on the company's bottomline.

Phil is the author of *Non-Manipulative Selling*, *Selling by Objectives*, and *The Art of Professional Serving*. He was also a contributor to *The Art of Managing People*.

W.A. (Bill) Adams is a principal in and founder of Maxcomm Associates, a Salt Lake City-based international management consulting firm. As a top ranking management consultant, Bill works with CEOs and high-level executives around the world. One of his strengths is the ability to design practical methods for motivating employees to take responsibility for producing results. Bill is a human resource advocate; he sees people as the means to increased bottom-line performance.

Bill has worked with diverse businesses and industries, including Michigan Consolidated Gas Company, American Express, Tupperware Worldwide, and First National Bank of Rockford, Illinois.

Emil Bohn, PhD, is a co-founder and principal in Maxcomm Associates, Inc. He is a management consultant with a gift for taking theoretical concepts and transforming them into timely, practical strategies. Before founding Maxcomm Associates with Bill in 1984, Emil was a tenured professor of organizational communication, a consultant, and an extensively published author.

Emil designs many of Maxcomm's customer service, team building, and leadership development programs. He's a pro at asking the right questions to uncover the data needed to determine where a company stands and where it needs to go. He also has a gift for getting people to commit to change and perform at their best. Over the last 15 years Emil has worked with companies in Europe, Latin America, and Japan. His clients include Tupperware Worldwide, Gannett, American Express, Honeywell, Michigan Consolidated Gas Company, First National Bank & Trust of Rockford, Illinois, Cigna RE, Snowbird Ski and Summer Resort, Citicorp Mortgage, and Quality Service Institute.

Table of Contents

Introduction 1

Part I Creating a Competitive Edge

Chapter One
Differentiation in the 1990s 27

Chapter Two
Marketing as a Philosophy,
Not as a Department 51

Part II Assessing Service Quality

Chapter Three
The Four Zones of Service Quality 75

Chapter Four
The Rigid Zone of Service Quality 83

Chapter Five
The Safe Zone of Service Quality 93

Chapter Six
The Progressive Zone of Service Quality 99

Chapter Seven
The Indulgent Zone of Service Quality 111

Part III Achieving Service Excellence

Chapter Eight
  Selling Quality With Service 119

Chapter Nine
  Encouraging Demanding Customers 141

Chapter Ten
  Nurturing Complaining Customers 175

Chapter Eleven
  Managing the Recovery Process 205

Chapter Twelve
  *Fostering Moments of
  Magic, Misery and Truth* 225

Part IV Building a Quality Service Organization

Chapter Thirteen
  *Creating the Vision-Driven
  and Values-Guided Organization* 239

Chapter Fourteen
  Implementing a Quality Service Change Effort 261

Chapter Fifteen
  Managing the People Systems 285

Appendices

Appendix One:
  Service R_Xs 315

Appendix Two:
  Nine Phrases to Avoid at All Costs 337

Notes 339

Index 341

Introduction

HI & LOIS   BY MORT WALKER & DIK BROWNE

Back to Basics

Start a book with a cartoon? A little unconventional? Not really. Being treated badly is no fun.

Customer service is a serious topic. Witness the proliferation of books, articles, training programs, executive rhetoric, advertising hype, and other cultural indicators that scream, "Pay attention. This is the trend of the future!" But as a serious business topic, it doesn't measure up. There are still too many companies providing lip service rather than quality service.

Too many companies see quality customer service as a fad, not as a management philosophy that sets a standard for the way to conduct business. They think service is the "ultimate weapon"—as one book referred to it—to increase marketshare. There is no denying that outstanding customer service will give a competitive advantage, but it is *not* a short-term strategy. Strategies have beginnings, middles, and ends. They are the "flavor-of-the-month" approaches that employees and managers have grown to abhor. Customer service is as much of a goal as is making a profit. Service is the basic modus operandi of doing business. It is something you do all the time—a philosophy more companies need to rediscover.

SERVICE R$_x$:
Make quality service a core value, not a marketing ploy, because that is what quality service is.

Fads, Fads, Fads

As management consultants and customer service trainers, we're tired of trying to create buzz words that will motivate corporate executives to adopt service philosophies. Even if we could, we wouldn't want to create a new fad. Fads are short-lived. Ken Blanchard, co-author of *The One Minute Manager* once said, "People keep asking me what my next book is going to be about. I keep asking them if they've used my last book yet." More often than not, the answer is no. Unfortunately, that's the American style of managing: discover a new fad, jump on the bandwagon, (maybe) practice the principles for a couple of months, and then move on to the next "flavor-of-the-month."

Corporate thinking is chronically short-term and short-sighted. What actions do Americans typically take when the economy slows down? They close factories and lay off employees. How do the Japanese respond in similar circumstances? They negotiate with their employees—ask them to work fewer hours or accept a lower wage for a time. Instead of shutting down, the Japanese use their people to repair or maintain the facilities during periods of decreased output.

What happens when the economy begins to accelerate again? The Americans, who have laid off their work forces and let their plants fall into disrepair, have to start virtually from scratch. They have to invest heavily in hiring and training new employees and then repair their machinery. The Japanese, however, rebound more quickly. Their start-up expenses are significantly less because they didn't let their assets—people and machinery—deteriorate during the lull. Not only is their work force in place, it is also well trained and committed to the long-term success of the company.

Commitment is modeled from the top. If the CEO and president lack a long-term commitment to quality service, so will everyone below them. Top executives lack commitment for any number of reasons. The average tenure of most American corporate presidents is less than six years. During those six years they concentrate on making their companies as profitable as possible so stockholders will enjoy high returns. Accomplishing this, they are then in the ideal position to move on to the next company where they can command even higher salaries. All of this means the top executive is giving a higher priority to short-term goals, which may undermine the long-term strength of the company. Financing through junk bonds is a perfect example.

American CEOs and presidents are the highest paid executives in the world. However, their six-figure salaries discourage them from taking risks. They would rather be conservative than chance losing their places in the sun. Between playing it safe and focusing on the short-term, they are hesitant to embrace changes that would improve customer service. Those changes demand long-term commitment.

Another aspect to this short-term thinking is the structure of executive compensation. Many executives are rewarded with stock options. These incentives motivate them to make decisions that impact quarterly earnings and stock prices. Marketshare, technology, and service end up taking a back seat to financial performance. Financial performance can be improved three ways: by cutting overhead (the safe way), by increasing sales (the risky way), or a combination of the two.

Most executives cut overhead—the path of least resistance and risk—because increasing sales means they have to spend money on training, support, and so on. Is it any wonder that American business executives have an insatiable appetite for management fads that purport to *quickly* bail them out of any dilemma and turn a quick profit?

The truth is *there are no new fads*. There are no quick fixes for the problems American businesses face. Personal experiences and formal research have revealed that every management fad is just a repackaging of concepts that have been around for generations. The problem is corporate executives don't want to pay attention to the basics until a management guru renames them and wraps them in a sexy package. If you're going to read this book and think of it as just another management fad, you're wasting your time. If you really want long-term organizational health through differentiation, this book will show you how to accomplish it.

One of the reasons for so much management failure—and a never-ending market for new fads—is that we're working with people. Any time you try to do something with people, you encounter innumerable stumbling blocks. And let's face it, most managers are promoted by virtue of their technical skills, not their communication or leadership skills. So when people-problems don't improve overnight, managers become impatient and move on to the next highly-touted quick fix.

We all know the theories—Quality Circles, MBO, Managing by Wandering Around, excellence this, the One Minute that, and now customer service. These management concepts have been circulating for a long time (Quality Circles have been around since 1917, when they were called Shop Committees), but how many people are practicing them today? Very few.

One reason for our fickle nature is, like most people, most companies don't have a picture of themselves in the future. They have failed to create visions and long-term philosophies for themselves and, as a result, lack a commitment to planned and controlled growth. There are exceptions. Exxon, Xerox, Michigan Consolidated Gas Company and Belron Corporation are a few companies plotting where they want to be in ten years and committing the resources to achieve their visions. The common denominator among these companies is a commitment to define and remain true to their vision and core values.

Values Are Everything

You may be surprised to learn that service improves when you attend to people's basic social needs—the need to be included, wanted, competent, and in control. This is possible only when you share and live by a set of well-articulated corporate values.

SERVICE R$_X$:
Treat your people like responsible adults.

Every company has values, explicit or implicit. They are the attitudes, policies, procedures, and expectations for daily decisions and behaviors. Some companies have well-defined values spelled out in policy manuals; others have never formulated or articulated their values, but they do exist.

SERVICE R$_X$:
The behaviors exhibited by managers and the way they treat their employees speak volumes about corporate values.

The attitudes and philosophies of the person at the top play an important role in the dissemination of corporate values. That person also plays an essential role in shaping the culture of the organization and raising its service awareness. In fact, consultants and customer service trainers have found that the organizations achieving the most success are those in which changes are championed by top management. Whenever there is a failure to implement service improvements, it is invariably due to a lack of commitment and support from the president, CEO, or top executives.

In some ways a customer service training program is similar to the treatment of an illness. A weak drug can cure if the patient has faith in the remedy. Conversely, a powerful drug will be ineffective if the patient doesn't take it as prescribed. A mediocre customer service training program can be highly successful if it has a tremendous amount of management support; an excellent training program can fail miserably if it lacks commitment from the top.

Some companies, in an attempt to stimulate service awareness, launch an internal campaign to promote the "right" attitudes. They use banners, buttons, slogans, hats, T-shirts, and every other kind of pep rally gimmick. There is nothing inherently wrong with this type of enthusiasm, unless the changes are superficial and are expected only of front-line employees. This is usually the case. Again, that is the *form*, not the *substance*, of service. It just won't play. The behaviors expected of front-line people must be modeled consistently throughout the organization. Supervisors, managers, and executives cannot ask front-line employees to treat customers courteously unless, internally, people are also being treated courteously.

SERVICE R$_X$:
Management has to model what they advocate—
"Walk the talk."

The need for consistency ties into the need for values in a company. It isn't enough to teach employees the technical skills required for their jobs; management must also impart values. One of the very basic principles which must be defined is: "how we treat people around here."

Our society is evolving in such a way that there are few moral or ethical anchors for people. We have a schizophrenic sense of things. On one hand, we espouse honesty and respect for others. On the other, we worship money and create pop heroes out of fabulously wealthy people, regardless of how they achieved their wealth.

There is evidence the greed of the 1980s has, unfortunately, shaped the values of young people. According to a pair of studies, high school seniors and college freshman have become much more materialistic since the mid-1970s. The surveys revealed that more men and women desire lifestyles focusing on cars, clothes, stereos, vacation homes, high-paying jobs and prestige. The studies reveal that few people think it is important to help others, correct social and economic inequalities or develop a meaningful philosophy of life.[1]

A company's image and reputation are shaped "one person at a time" as employees interact with the public. It is crucial, therefore, when organizations take on the role of educator—as they will in the 1990s—that education in ethics is not overlooked. For that education to be meaningful, companies must also promote ethical behaviors and consistently practice what they preach.

Values come in many shapes and sizes and serve many functions. Among other things, a company's core values shape its image, competitive posture, working environment, and service quality. The core values present in every business are comprised of three different levels: ethical values, philosophical values and operational values.

Ethical Values

Ethical values are the most lofty and sacred principles that guide people, and companies, through life. They are a code of conduct—a set of behavioral standards that dictate how people are to be treated, both internally and externally. As such, they create corporate rules that cannot be violated by anyone—not even the president or CEO. Ethical values include such ideals as honesty, maintaining individual integrity and self-esteem, respecting diversity, and protecting the environment.

An example of an actual ethical value is the Sierra Club's guideline that prohibits the acceptance of donations from corporations that are major polluters or makers/vendors of environmentally damaging products.

The ethical value of honesty is one that is "bent, folded, and mutilated" every day of the week. You have to assume that, if asked, most companies would claim to advocate honesty. The problem, however, is that not all companies strive to live up to their ideals.

A good example is the traditional automobile dealership. Their sales techniques are an insult to customers. It's virtually impossible to walk onto an automobile showroom and purchase a car without investing two to three hours in stressful negotiating time. The process is replete with manipulative games designed to wear down customers and extract the highest profit from the transaction. It's a system in which management violates its ethical values by training salespeople to use coercive sales tactics.

Superior service grows out of a company-wide respect for the dignity of everyone—employees and customers.

> **SERVICE R$_x$:**
> **A company's level of service is a mirror-image of the way management treats employees. That treatment is, in turn, a reflection of the ethical values and corporate culture created by top executives.**

Does your company treat everyone as equals worthy of respect and courtesy or do you think some people deserve better treatment than others?

Emil: *I attended a meeting at a very big telecommunications company with some high level executives. At one point, a secretary came in and whispered something to the gentleman at the head of the table. When she left, he said to us, "You've just witnessed something that you should see in every corporate meeting. That was my secretary telling me my boss was on the phone. I had her tell him that I would call him back."*

Unusual? Quite. Most people defer to their bosses because the majority of companies are still operations-focused. In fact, the message at virtually every level is that there is always someone more important than you. Furthermore, at every level, the value of an individual's time is determined by what the boss wants, not by the demands of the marketplace.

This is gradually changing. More companies are becoming market-focused and employee-focused. They are realizing and acting on the fact that employees are their most valuable asset. In such cultures, everyone is equal because everyone serves the customer. It would be inappropriate, therefore, to interrupt a meeting with anyone—employee or CEO.

How does your company treat people? Is there a difference between the way you treat customers and the way you treat noncustomers? Do you treat customers like royalty, but then turn around and treat noncustomers rudely? Such a dichotomy is common, as is the inconsistent treatment of people in general. Many of us were raised with prejudices that range from mild to extreme, so we have become accustomed to categorizing people and acting differently towards different people. There's no place for that in business. Quality service, ethical values, and professionalism all dictate that you treat everyone well, and do so sincerely. People are human beings. A filing clerk deserves to be treated with dignity just as much as the company president.

SERVICE R$_X$:
Compassion is an ethical value.

This cartoon illustrates Aristotle's concept of virtue. He believed you cannot be virtuous in just part of your life. You are either 100% virtuous or you're not. Life can't be compartmentalized. A man who appears to be an excellent manager at work, yet goes home and beats his kids, is probably not really an excellent manager. People of excellence are consistent. They do *everything* well.

Consistency is important in business. Inconsistency confuses customers and undermines credibility. A company cannot remain credible if it only has ethics part-time.

Phil: *In 1975 I wrote a book called* Non-Manipulative Selling. *In my speeches and seminars on the subject, I admitted to having been a traditional, manipulative salesman early in my career. But I wasn't content. So I began practicing and preaching the nonmanipulative, consultative sales techniques that developed into my book.*

One day a prospective client called and said, "Phil, we want to hire you to train some of our salespeople. The thing is, we

*want you to teach traditional closing techniques—you know, the
stuff you used to practice before you wrote the book."*

*How should I have responded? I could have accepted the
work. After all, why turn down $10,000 for a full-day training
session? On the other hand, I had ethical values to uphold. One
of my values is that I will not teach something I do not believe
in; I do not believe in manipulative sales techniques. So I turned
down the work.*

*If my client's request had been different, I would have had
more options. If he had said, "Phil, we want to hire you to teach
us Non-Manipulative Selling, but we want you to leave out the
part on goal setting," I wouldn't have had a problem with that
request because it wouldn't have violated my ethical values."*

Philosophical Values

Philosophical values are the broad, strategic definitions given to a
business that help position it in the marketplace. As such, they can also
be called strategic values, although there is a minor distinction between
the two. Philosophical values pertain to a company's internal culture.
Strategic values relate to the company's customers; they help the
marketplace understand what to expect from a company.

One of Phil's philosophical values is to speak or train only in his
area of expertise: sales, customer service, or management. (Many
speakers will talk about any topic a client requests.) If a client were to
call and ask for a speech on stress management, Phil would refer them
to someone else. By focusing his expertise on a few areas, Phil has
clearly defined his business and gained a reputation as an expert.
Granted, he has also narrowed the number of prospective clients who
might hire him. However, if he were to give speeches on any requested
topic, he would dilute his credibility in the marketplace and fail to
differentiate himself from thousands of other speakers in the United
States.

An example of a set of corporate philosophical values comes from
Perot Systems, a computer systems and communication company
founded by H. Ross Perot.

- *We will have only one class of team member—each member will
  be a full partner.*

- *We will recognize and reward excellence while the individual is
  still sweating from his efforts.*

- *We will build and maintain a spirit of one for all and all for one.*

- *We will encourage every team member to take risks, make decisions, exercise initiative, and never be afraid to make mistakes.*

- *We will hold team members accountable for results, with great flexibility in deciding how to achieve results and the clear understanding that ethical standards must never be compromised.*

- *We will eliminate any opportunity for people to succeed by merely looking good.*

- *We will promote solely on merit.*

- *We will ensure that our ethical standards with our customers and suppliers are impeccable.*

Perot Systems also has a code of conduct that they make explicit: We will not tolerate anyone who . . .

- *acts in a manner which will bring discredit to the company;*

- *discriminates against another with regard to race, religion, sex or any other reason;*

- *looks down on others;*

- *becomes a corporate politician;*

- *tries to move ahead at the expense of others;*

- *uses illegal drugs.*

Strategic values affect the marketplace directly and help define the company's target market. Every company has the right to define with whom they will or will not do business. For example, there are companies that align themselves with Christian values and choose to limit their business relationships to other Christian companies. Along the same lines, there are printers and publishers who refuse to print pornography. There are landlords who will not rent to drug dealers. There are defense attorneys who will not serve as public defenders. The list goes on and on.

Hotels and restaurants make their strategic values apparent by their prices, locations, physical appearances, features, and reputations for service. This is basic positioning, and with it come other philosophical values. For example, the Rancho Valencia is a luxurious hotel in San

Diego, California. One of the philosophical values of its gourmet restaurant is to require men to wear jackets in the dining room. This standard of dress positions the restaurant in the marketplace and creates an ambiance diners have come to expect.

Ethical values are inflexible, but what about philosophical values? Imagine a man without a jacket entering the restaurant one night and requesting to be seated. If you were the *maitre d'*, how would you handle this situation?

First, here's what should not be done. Never enforce a rule by saying, "It's company policy." Customers don't object to a company having rules, but they do object to being treated like children when someone says, in effect, "you have to do this because I say so." Think back to how you felt when you were 15 years old and one of your parents ordered you around and gave you that meaningless reason, "because I said so." How did you feel? Angry. Frustrated. Rebellious. Well, people don't change much. We resent hearing that reasoning at any age. When you're given an explanation, you may not be satisfied with the rule, but at least you're not offended by it.

SERVICE R$_x$:
Treat your customers as adults. When you uphold company policies and procedures, do it by intelligently explaining the reasons to your customers.

So how should you resolve the dinner jacket problem? The most obvious solution is to have a supply of jackets on hand to use as loaners. If your guest does not want to wear a jacket, however, your explanation should sound something like this: "We have a formal ambiance we guarantee all our guests and it's often one of the reasons they choose to dine here. We like to maintain that ambiance for everyone. If you wish, I have a jacket I can lend you."

Group Rights Versus Individual Rights

There will be times when you can't cater to the whims of a customer because your action will adversely affect the rights or needs of a group. One of the dilemmas of customer service is that you strive to give the best possible service to everyone, but sometimes a situation will arise in which bending the rules for customer A will prevent customers B, C, D and E from being satisfied.

If you look at it from the company's point of view, you're better off losing one customer due to a lack of flexibility than giving poor service to a large number of people.

The opposite holds true for hotel clerks making reservations. When the phone rings, they deal with people one at a time. However, they're often pressured to rush the customer on the phone because there are five blinking lights waiting to be answered. To rush the call would be to give poor service in the interest of serving a larger number of callers. Again, that's operations-focused thinking. The incoming calls—all those blinking lights—are not the reservationist's responsibility; they're the responsibility of management. It's management's job to hire enough people to manage the phone traffic. The reservationist should give the best possible service to the person at hand.

> **SERVICE R$_x$:**
> **Never make an exception for one customer if it hurts your ability to serve other customers the way they expect to be served.**

Inasmuch as flexibility is an important ingredient in customer service, it is a business owner's right to dictate philosophical values that may preclude doing business with disreputable people. That's part of positioning. Virtually every business decides who its customers are going to be and how to appeal to them. Flexibility, however, is the key when it comes to operational values.

Operational Values

Operational values are the policies and procedures that serve as guidelines in the day-to-day running of your business. As such, they should be handled with sensible flexibility when customers have special requests. Unfortunately, that isn't always the case.

Bill: *One night my wife and I went to a restaurant. After being seated, we were approached by a waiter who said, "Can I get you something from the bar?" I told him we were famished and would like to order our meal. He said he was only the beverage waiter and couldn't take our food order. He said he could bring us our drinks and tell our regular waiter to come right over. I asked him what would happen if we wanted our drinks with dinner, rather than before dinner. He said they didn't do it that way; it was easier for them to divide the duties between food waiters and beverage waiters.*

It's obvious that this restaurant had an inflexible set of operational values designed to make the employees' jobs easier. But what about the customer's dining experience? What values do they have to maximize that? All too often companies design operations and make decisions without taking their customers into account.

Who Gets to Break the Rules?

How sacred are a company's values? Who should and should not be able to break the rules? Starting at the top, ethical values are the most sacred and cannot be violated by anyone. Philosophical values are also important, but exceptions can be made by the people who created them—owners, CEOs, presidents, and upper managers. Operational values are also important, but more flexible. Anyone can violate an operational value if doing so will benefit a customer without violating the company's ethical or philosophical values. For example, in Bill's story above, would any harm have been done if the beverage waiter had taken a food order to the kitchen? Of course not. No ethical values would have been violated nor would the restaurant's image in the marketplace have been hurt.

What about the gourmet restaurant that requires men to wear jackets in the dining room? Which employees can violate that philosophical value and why would they chose to do so? Owners and managers are the only people empowered to change philosophical values, and they generally do it only when there is a very good reason. What would be a very good reason?

A very good reason would be a guest who has good intentions, but is unable to conform to the restaurant's policy. Imagine a large football player entering the restaurant, unaware of the jacket requirement. The alternative, lending him a jacket, is not possible due to his size; there are no 52 regulars in the coat room. So it wouldn't be inappropriate for the manager to allow the maitre d' to seat him without a jacket. Granted, violating this policy would affect other diners—the most important consideration—but the manager could reasonably assume that most people would understand the situation and not object.

Look at it from the customer's point of view. You are dining in an exclusive restaurant and see the *maitre d'* seat a man without a jacket. You call the *maitre d'* over and say to him, "One of the reasons I come to your restaurant is that I enjoy being in a formal environment. I'm wondering why you allowed that man to be seated without a jacket."

The *maitre d'* politely says, "I understand how you feel. We do have a dress code and we keep a half-dozen jackets on hand for such occasions, but unfortunately we don't have one large enough to fit that gentleman. Due to the fact that he came all the way here with good intentions, we made an exception for him."

Most people would understand and not object. People would object if the *maitre d'* had said, "Oh, that's the owner's brother." That type of exception is an inappropriate violation of the jacket policy. The owner's brother is fully capable of wearing a jacket and his relationship to the owner does not entitle him to preferential treatment. If the *maitre d'* wants to treat him like a VIP, let him seat the man in a private dining room. When he's seated with other guests, however, he has to abide by the same rules as everyone else. People will make exceptions for truly special cases, but not for people who only think they are special.

We've just given you two dilemmas with solutions. What would you do if the Denver Broncos walked in without jackets and wanted to be seated? Would you make an exception for 25 big guys? We have no answer for you. There's no way to address every possibility, but this is what you are up against every day. There will be innumerable situations in which you have to decide which rules to bend or break. The important thing is that you think it through. Ask yourself how important the philosophical values are. Ask yourself who might be hurt if you violate a philosophical value. Make a decision and learn from your experience. If you use core values as parameters, your decisions will more often be right than wrong.

How would you handle the following situation?

You are the general manager of a hotel and have recently hired a woman to clean rooms. She is a poor, single mother of two young children and you want to give her every break you can. One day you find out she has taken some cans of food from the kitchen. When you confront her, she claims she had no money and needed something to feed her kids until her first paycheck arrived. What would you do?

The only answer—and it's not an easy one—is to fire her. She violated one of the company's ethical values, honesty. Case closed. What about compassion? Of course there's a place for compassion, so you may give her a week's pay to help her buy food for her kids until she finds another job. Should your compassion move you to make an exception to one of your company's ethical values? No. The moment you make an exception, that value ceases to be an ethical value. It then becomes a philosophical value that can be violated depending on the situation. That won't work. Top management must create and articulate ethical values and determine the consequences of violating them.

SERVICE R$_x$:
Operational and philosophical values are strategic and situational. Ethical values are absolute.

The Philosopher General

Just as the United States has an Attorney General to oversee legal issues and a Surgeon General to oversee public health issues, every company should have a Philosopher General who oversees philosophical issues.

The Philosopher General is someone high on the corporate ladder—the president, chairman, or CEO—who is responsible for ethical consistency throughout the organization. People come to them and ask if their plans pose a potential conflict with the company's mission statement, ethical values, or philosophical values.

Articulating a set of core values is analogous to adding an autopilot to a yacht. It helps the ship steer itself. The autopilot doesn't eliminate the captain's job, but it obviates the need for constant surveillance, thus allowing someone to keep half an eye "on the road" while tending to other tasks.

Look at what can happen when your company doesn't have a Philosopher General. A major airline spent millions of dollars to set up a customer service program that would train all 25,000 of their employees within one year. At the same time, someone with an operations focus was analyzing how to save money. He looked at the number of seats in some of their planes. Let's say there were 150 seats. The FAA has a regulation requiring a certain ratio of flight attendants to the number of seats on the plane. This number-crunching analyst figured that the average flight has 25 empty seats. If those seats are physically removed from the plane, then the airline could legally fly with one less flight attendant. Think of the money they would save! Smart?

Well, it should be obvious what the outcome was. With one hand the airline was training its people to provide better service. With the other it was taking away the resources to provide that service. Employees knew it, passengers soon realized it, and the effort to cut costs back-fired, wasting the millions of dollars spent on service training.

This inconsistency was made possible by divergent interests and a lack of vision and values throughout the company. Different people were trying to accomplish different goals without taking the time to check on consistency. Hence, the need for a Philosopher General.

If a Philosopher General had existed, the operations-focused person could have said, "Here's a cost-cutting idea I'm considering. Is it consistent with what we are trying to accomplish in terms of service and as a company in general?"

Another cogent example of how a Philosopher General could have saved jobs, money, and headaches occurred when Bill and Emil put together an in-depth consulting and training package for a large ski resort. This multi-faceted, two-week-long management and customer service program cost around $50,000. After the program was completed, the president of the company laid off 70% of the people who had been trained because poor snow conditions were affecting business. This layoff was temporary, for only two weeks, so the company could save $4,000 in overhead during a slow period! Of those people who were released, 80% went to work for the competition. The president of the ski resort ended up spending $50,000 in order to save $4,000. On top of that, he paid to train his competition's employees!

George Bush is a good example of a leader who has operated without a vision or set of values. A painful example is the way he responded to the violent repression of the pro-democracy student demonstrations in China, the massacre in Tiananmen Square. President Bush quickly condemned the action and imposed trade sanctions. Six months later, however, with no change in the Chinese hard line, he sent a secret delegation to Beijing to try to normalize relations with the Chinese government. A little over a year after the incident, Bush fought to restore China's most-favored-nation trade status, despite the objections of both Democrats and Republicans in Congress. There was no ethical or philosophical consistency to his actions.

A positive example of upholding ethical values was an incident in 1990 at CBS. Sports commentator, Jimmy "The Greek" Snyder was deemed by them to have made a blatantly racist remark. Consistent with CBS's ethical values, they fired him.

The journey from being an operations-focused organization to a market-focused organization must be planned and managed. Without a vision, a course of direction and someone at the helm, there are no guidelines by which to judge certain behaviors in relation to the company's goals. If you don't know where you're going, any road will get you there. If you know where you're headed, but don't have a plan to get there, you will never know where you are. If you know where you're going and have a course to get there, but no one manages the journey (inspects what they expect), then you'll wander off-course.

SERVICE R$_x$:
Service should be everyone's responsibility . . . and someone's accountability.

SERVICE R$_x$:
You can't shoot an arrow and then draw the target.

Service Versus Services

It is important to digress here to define a few terms. First, let's draw a distinction between service and services. Using a hotel example, *services* are features of the hotel—what they offer to do for you. Some of the services offered by hotels are room service, valet parking, an airport shuttle, dry cleaning, a concierge, and a bellman.

Service requires a value judgement. It is how well a hotel does what it does. So the Westin, by virtue of its higher prices, provides more services than Super 8. That does not necessarily mean the *service* at Super 8 is inferior. They simply offer fewer *services*. When we talk about customer service, we are referring to the judgement of how well a company does what it does. If the world were comprised only of excellent people, everything would be done with excellence and there would be no need for customer service books, consulting, or training.

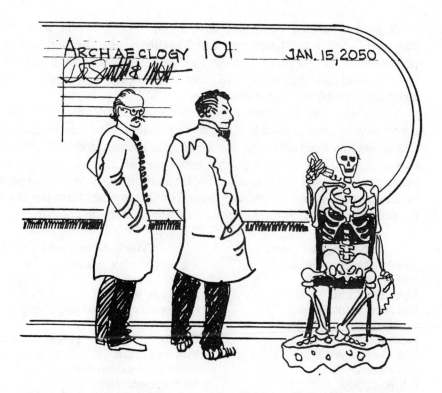

"A common cause of death in the late 20th Century was something called 'Hold.'"

SERVICE R$_x$:
Services are the things you do for your customers.
Service is how well you do them.

Two other terms need defining: Operations-focused and Market-focused (also referred to as customer-focused). These are two ways to run a business, and there are many shades of gray. An operations-focused company is one in which the needs, policies, and procedures of the company hold a higher priority than the needs of customers. The attitude of an operations-focused company is that policies and procedures are hard-and-fast rules with which employees must comply to prevent the company from losing money (and avoiding chaos). An operations-focused company is interested in customers who are willing to do business the way the company wants to do it.

A market-focused company, on the other hand, makes sure that customers' needs are taken into consideration in its decision-making process. Policies and procedures are flexible guidelines rather than hard-and-fast rules, so employees have more freedom and authority to solve customers' problems creatively.

The difference between operations-focused and market-focused companies is more than skin deep. In fact, there are so many facets to this dichotomy that most companies end up in the gray area between the two extremes. The following table lists some of the many ways that operations-focused and market-focused companies differ. These characteristics are mostly philosophical, but philosophies form the bases for practices and, therefore, affect every behavior in the company.

Operations-Focused	Market-Focused
Strictly adheres to policies	Practices sensible flexibility
Internal focus	External focus
Short-term focus	Long-term focus
Dictatorial (authoritarian) Management	Employee involvement/empowerment
Employees viewed as tools	Employees viewed as resources
Risk discouraged	Risk encouraged
Bureaucratic structure	Enlightened management
C.Y.A. attitude	100% responsibility
Out of touch with markets	In touch with customers
Discourages complaints	Encourages complaining customers
One-way communication	Two-way communication
Primary focus: financial	Primary focus: market
Responsibility without authority	Authority with responsibility
Hierarchical management	Self-management
Industrial Age	Information Age
Service viewed as expense	Service viewed as investment
Organizational structure is vertical	Organizational structure is horizontal
Managers act like police officers	Managers act like coaches

Money Equals Power

One of the most salient reasons many executives do not adopt a service or market-focused philosophy for their companies is that they just don't see the bottom-line impact. Too many CEOs are guilty of saying, "I don't see how spending money on customer service is going to increase our bottomline."

Let's look at a hypothetical situation that illustrates the far-reaching ramifications of poor service and the importance of quality service.

You are a car dealer. You call your dealership the O-F (Operations-Focused) Company. You run a tight ship with little flexibility. A customer comes in and makes an unusual request. He says, "I'm Mr. Jones. I own a computer repair service and have a fleet of cars my field technicians drive around town. I'm interested in buying one of your cars. The thing is, when I bring that car in for service, I'm going to need another one for a loaner; and my field tech is probably going to put about two hundred miles on the car in one day. If you'll promise me that service in writing, I'll buy a car from you today and probably another one three months from now." Being a truly operations-focused company, your salesman reflects management's rigidity and then invokes the excuse, "I'm sorry, I can't do that. It's against company policy." (See Appendix Two regarding this phrase.)

By uttering those fateful words, your salesman has, in effect, communicated: "You're not an important customer." "I don't want to put forth the effort to accommodate you." "I don't even want to ask my manager if we can accommodate you." The result is that your dealership is willing to lose a customer rather than bend a rule or devise a workable solution.

There are many consequences to losing a customer—particularly this customer who needs several vehicles for his business. Later in the book we will discuss other consequences, but for now, let's just look at the big picture. The Technical Assistance Research Program has determined that over the lifetime of a loyal customer, an auto dealer can expect $150,000 in business from just that one customer. That's the average. For a business with a fleet of cars, the figure is much higher.

There are other, more far-reaching ramifications. Given the opportunity, this customer would have bought your $12,000 car. Instead, he walks off your lot and buys the $12,000 car from your competitor, M-F (Market-Focused) Motors. They bend over backwards for their customers.

The myopic way of looking at this is as follows. The car cost your dealership $8,000. The net profit after expenses and commissions is about $2,000. So your company loses $2,000 and M-F Motors makes $2,000. The narrow point of view might also concede that your dealership has lost some goodwill and M-F Motors has created some.

If those were the only loses, you could live with yourself for having been so inflexible. That, however, is just the tip of the iceberg. The real loss is not in terms of dollars and cents. Money is only the concrete representation of the far more important concept of power. When Mr. Jones gives his money to your competitor, he gives them power; and that power will enable them to win more business from you in the future.

You see, M-F Motors will take that $2,000 profit and invest it. There are a myriad of things they'll buy with the money—a paint job to improve their building, a bigger and brighter sign to attract more attention, more effective advertising, sales training, customer service training (of course) . . . the list goes on and on. These are all things you could have done, but, by refusing your customer's request, you have given your competitor more power to compete with you.

Six months later a customer is listening to the radio and hears M-F Motors' ads. (They can afford to buy air time; you can only afford newspaper ads.) Perhaps this customer is driving down the street, on the way to your dealership, when he sees M-F Motors' big new sign. He'll be more attracted to M-F Motors' bright, clean building and may very well turn into their lot instead of yours.

SERVICE R$_x$:
Every time you lose a customer you strengthen your competitor's position. The gains and losses are not about money, they are about power.

Unfortunately, too many companies think quality customer service is not important. It's not a joke or a fad, especially if you take business survival and success seriously. We joke and laugh about poor service when we are its victims, but humor is only a defense mechanism for the way we feel.

To be or not to be a market-focused organization is a weighty decision which will affect profits, marketshare, and the overall competitive strength of your company. As consultants, we have seen clients make vast improvements in service and reap tremendous financial rewards in a very short time. We have also seen companies refuse to change and regret it later.

For your company, making the transition to being market-focused must be a question of when, not if. Making customer satisfaction your first priority is as basic to business as buying low and selling high. If you disregard one of these fundamentals, you're destined to fail.

SERVICE R$_x$:
  Make superior service the reflection of a market-focused philosophy that is a permanent, cherished, company-wide culture. Service must be deep in the foundation of your company, not a glossy new facade.

Part I

Creating a Competitive Edge

Chapter One

Differentiation in the 1990s

Since the days of the Neanderthal Man, when cave dwellers were in the business of selling clubs, drums, pottery, and square wheels, there has been a need for product differentiation. In those days, the location of a business was a major differentiating factor. Regardless of the quality of their products, cave people would buy from a local *McCaveman* who was right down the canyon rather than walk ten miles to a *Caves R Us*.

Two things caused the decline of location as a differentiator: competition and developments in transportation. Buying decisions became more complicated when cave dwellers had a choice of a club from Mr. Neanderthal or Mr. Rosenthal, both of whom were a short mule ride away. When proximity disappeared as a decision-making criterion and failed to guarantee a captive market, something else had to take its place.

Throughout history the need to differentiate hasn't changed, but the means for achieving it have. This need will, of course, continue into the future. Where technology once set one company apart from another, service is now taking over. What the differentiating factor will be 100 years from now is anyone's guess. One thing is clear. Companies that fail to meet market demands, which in the '90s is for service, will lose a significant portion of their marketshare or go out of business.

The Evolution of Customer Service

"Technology is turning every product into a commodity."
—Phil Wexler

"There is no such thing as a commodity because every product can be differentiated by people and service."
—Ted Levitt, Sr. Marketing Fellow, Harvard

Who is right, Phil Wexler or Ted Levitt? Actually, they're both right. In a nutshell, technology has turned every product into a commodity, which is why customer service must be used as the differentiating factor in a company. A commodity is a product or service that is indistinguishable from other similar products or services. For example, two red delicious apples from different growers are commodities. You don't care who grew the apples; they are identical. And since they're identical, price becomes the only differentiating factor.

A differentiated product, however, has unique features that make it preferable to similar products. For example, Haagen-Dazs is not just ice cream. It's a differentiated product known for its extraordinary flavor.

An easy way to remember the difference between a commodity and a differentiated product is this: if you seek out an item by name, it's a differentiated product. If you look for the generic item (e.g., a scoop of ice cream), it's a commodity.

Sometimes advertising, not technical features, will differentiate one product from another. Public perceptions of things like aspirin and cold medicines are shaped by prime time television commercials. In this case, it is indoctrination and familiarity, rather than first-hand knowledge, that steer consumers toward a product.

Customer service has gone through an interesting evolutionary cycle in the last 35 to 50 years. The cycle illustrates the role of technology in the destruction and then return of service. The cycle illustrates three stages of technology as it has affected product differentiation.

"The Customer Is Always Right."

Before the 1950s, how did people determine where they would buy a product? It was a *relationship* decision. Every neighborhood or small town had a butcher, a hardware store, restaurants, a drug store, and so on. When you walked into the corner butcher shop, the owner's name was on the door; he greeted you personally and responded to your requests with sincere attentiveness. He knew you well and asked about the family. While trimming your T-bone, he listened to your problems and told you his. You had a relationship with him that was more important than what he charged for lamb chops or the fact that he was located next to the shoemaker.

You chose where to shop based on service. Conversely, if you ran a business, you knew you had to treat your customers like royalty to keep them coming back. After all, people did business with those they liked. (To a large extent, this is still true.) You practiced the philosophy, "The customer is always right," which said, in essence, that even if the customer is wrong, it doesn't matter; future business is worth more than the just resolution of this problem.

"They'll buy whatever we make."

Between 1950 and 1955 two things happened. Technology began to have a profound impact. Advances in technology turned products that were once commodities into differentiated products by virtue of their new features. For example, all television sets were no longer the same. When GE developed the technology to make a television with advanced features, people bought GEs. Years later, when Magnavox came out with an even more advanced television, people bought them for their advanced features, whether they were real or perceived.

When product differentiation was achieved through advances in technology, there came a shift in the consumer's perception of what was important in the buying decision. Their preferences for specific products changed shopping habits. If a customer wanted the features of a Magnavox and only one store in town sold Magnavoxes, he would shop at that store regardless of who owned the shop or the level of service given.

As technology began differentiating products, the nature of American business began to rapidly change. The small Mom and Pop stores gave way to large corporations and conglomerates. Companies such as IBM, Xerox, RCA, GE, Ford, GM, Chrysler, and others began to grow by leaps and bounds. As the "corporatization" of America grew, the distance between top executives and their customers increased. Owners were thousands of anonymous stockholders. Presidents, CEOs, and Executive Vice Presidents were insulated from the buying public by layers of managers and supervisors, all of whom aimed to please their bosses rather than their customers.

Corporatization of America helped cause the collapse of the customer-focused philosophy, "We'll sell what the customer wants to buy," and fueled the R&D and operations-focused philosophy, "The customer will buy what we sell." Companies no longer catered to their customers. Instead, they lived or died by the innovation of their product's features—technology.

The price the consumer paid for technology and corporatization was a decline in service and that decline has yet to significantly reverse itself (although the awareness of the need for service has increased).

As a result, there are one or two generations of Americans—children of the sixties and seventies—who, as consumers, have very low service expectations. They were raised in a self-help world of fast-food restaurants, ATM banking, and self-service gas stations. To them, service is not important because they have no sense of how things could or should be. People who have rarely experienced excellent service are also at a loss as to how to provide it.

> Phil: *I overheard a young person in a shoe store talking to a clerk. The clerk offered to take back a pair of shoes that had split a seam. The young person looked at her and said, "You can do that?"*

"You Have a Right to Service."

Here we are at the beginning of the 1990s. In the '50s and '60s, technology was the differentiator. Today that same technology has become the great equalizer, turning virtually every product into a commodity. This has happened because the technology of one company becomes available to others virtually overnight. Just as one company thinks it dominates a market, another comes along to vie for its share. Competition in the marketplace has never been more formidable—and it will only become more so.

The intensity of technology is so great and its cycle so short that the top selling products of 1995 have not even been developed yet. The top selling products of the year 2000 have probably not even been imagined yet!

Products that once achieved differentiation due to technology have lost that competitive advantage forever. For example, ask yourself, based on their respective features, does it make much of a difference if you buy an Hitachi, Toshiba, Mitsubishi, GE, RCA, Magnavox, or Sanyo VCR? Not really.

Consumers have more choices than ever. There was a time when television viewers had the choice of three major networks. The advent of cable television in the 1980s increased that offering to more than forty channels, and satellite dishes gave viewers their choice of over 100 channels. If you have recently bought a camera, fax machine, VCR, television, or stereo system, you know there are more brands than ever. So many, in fact, that it is often difficult to make a decision.

"Today's specials . . . we have soup *du jour*, a catch of the day, and a chef's special. Any other questions?"

Alvin Toffler predicted this dilemma in his book, *Future Shock*, and called it "over-choice." You may have experienced it yourself—the stress of too many choices. The more choices there are, the more products look the same; distinctions begin to blur. When all the brands look the same, it doesn't matter what you buy, *price* becomes the differentiating factor.

This is bad news from a business standpoint. Companies don't like to compete on the basis of price for many reasons, not the least of which is that price is the least reliable basis on which to create loyal customers. When you win customers on price alone, you risk losing them to a competitor who lowers his prices by a few cents. When you win customers with quality service, however, they remain loyal because your service cannot be duplicated elsewhere (especially if it's Progressive Customer Service, which will be discussed in chapter six.)

Given the modern dilemma of product homogeneity, how do people in the 1990s decide where to do business? To answer the question, let's finish Ted Levitt's statement from the beginning of the chapter. "There is no such thing as a commodity *because every product can be differentiated by service and people*." Service is now the criterion by which people judge businesses. And this issue, customer service, is forcing Corporate America to go back to the basics.

Notice the answer to the question "How do people in the 1990s decide where they will do business?" It isn't some revolutionary new marketing strategy, although many companies are treating customer service as such. On the contrary, the answer is the common-sense practice of doing the best you can to take care of each and every customer, something corporate America should have been doing all along.

The familiar, often-cited example of outstanding customer service is the Nordstrom company. In a world full of department stores, Nordstrom has made itself stand out above the rest by virtue of its obsession with customer service. It is setting a trend that a few smart businesses across the country are emulating. Some are making the attempt and some are catching on slowly.

Here's an example of how differentiated Nordstrom has become. A friend of ours was shopping at another department store. He found a pair of shoes he liked, but there were none in his size. He asked the salesperson to call some of their other stores to find his size. The salesperson looked at him incredulously and said, "What do you think this is, Nordstrom's?"

One industry that is changing its focus slowly is the American automobile industry. For 75 years it was strictly operations-focused; that is, it decided what cars the public would buy. It built the cars it wanted to build and then, with advertising, convinced consumers to buy them. The "take it or leave it" attitude was apparent in Henry Ford's famous answer to a customer asking if his cars would soon be available in different colors. Ford said, "You can have any color you like, as long as it's black." Obviously, the Ford company changed that policy; otherwise, it wouldn't be one of the top car manufacturers today.

The Germans (with the VW Rabbit) and the Japanese, later put an end to the U.S. auto makers' "take it or leave it" attitude. Foreign dominance in the U.S. market caused Ford, GM, and Chrysler to significantly lose marketshare. Previously, the Americans had had a lock on the market, but within three years, they lost almost 20% marketshare. It was only then that they began to listen to consumers and give them what they wanted—smaller cars with better gas mileage. Ford even went as far as having a woman design a car with women in mind (the Ford Taurus). Chrysler, in a series of television commercials in 1989, acknowledged their customers' inherent right to service. The president of Buick, at an annual convention in 1989, said, "For the first time in the history of GM, we're going to build cars that people like rather than trying to teach them to like the cars we build." Only time will tell if this and other industry-wide changes are too little too late.

In the early 1990s, we're still facing increased corporatization. Multinational conglomerates are growing, turning their efforts from national marketshares to global marketshares. Competition still has its roots in products rather than service. But that trend must change, especially in saturated markets such as the United States and Western Europe. Security is not to be found in products. It's the human factor that is needed in this high-tech world to make it, as John Naisbitt predicted, more of a high-*touch* world.

The same technology that killed quality service in the '50s and '60s (by differentiating products through features) is now turning those same products into commodities that require *service* to differentiate them.

The Cost of Acquiring New Customers

Unlike advertising, which pays off only once, customer service keeps people coming back time and again. It is, literally, an investment that pays annuities.

What roles do advertising and service play? Jack and Mary Consumer are sitting in their living room watching football on a Sunday afternoon. They see a commercial for a furniture store. What effect does that ad have? It motivates Jack and Mary to put down their munchies, get dressed, and drive across town to the store. Once they step into the store, the television commercial has done its job.

Advertising doesn't sell anything. It motivates the customer to respond by either calling or coming to your business. Every year companies spend millions of dollars to get people to respond. Once the prospect has responded, however, it's up to the sales staff to take the next step and make the sale. For this reason, millions of dollars are also spent to hire, train, motivate, and pay inside and outside sales representatives. All this, just to acquire new customers. The exception to this rule is the highly sought-after product such as a breakfast cereal in which the advertising actually does the selling.

Once a new customer has made a purchase, if he was treated well, you can expect future returns on the cost of the advertising that brought him in. To illustrate how service is an annuity, we will create a simplified model to calculate the cost of acquiring one new customer. The cost is the sum of your advertising budget and your sales budget (including salaries, commissions, and support) divided by the number of new customers you acquire during the year.

For the sake of easy numbers, let's say you're the proprietor of a ladies' boutique that spends $20,000 per year on advertising. You gain 1000 new customers per year. Your cost for attracting a prospect and turning them into a customer is $20.

Once advertising has worked and you've made the sale, there can be two outcomes: you either keep your new customer or lose them. If Ms. Jones received poor service, but bought something anyway, you will only have gotten a one-time return on your $20 investment. If, on the other hand, you treated Ms. Jones well, you can expect her to come back. Keep in mind that when she returns, it will not have been the original advertising that brought her back; it will have been her satisfaction with the service she received during her first visit.

So the first time Ms. Jones came into the store and spent $50, you recovered the cost of acquiring her as a customer and made a profit on the sale. The next time she comes in and spends $50, you will receive another return on your original $20 investment.

SERVICE R$_x$:
The best sales presentation is delivering excellent service.

Effective advertising and quality service are the cornerstones of repeat business. It is virtually impossible to maintain or increase a marketshare and remain profitable if you constantly have to find new customers to replace the ones you've lost. You need to keep the existing ones *and* add new ones.

Customer service must be seen as an investment in the long-term growth of your company. It's the key to differentiating from the competition. If customer service is responsible for repeat business, logic would dictate that it be given as high a priority and budget as advertising and sales. Is it? We all know it isn't, and that's one of the injustices we hope to change with this book.

Customer service is more than a complaint desk where people return items or air their grievances. It's a company-wide philosophy—a vision and a set of values and behaviors—designed to help you get more customers, keep the customers you have, and get both to spend more money. If service didn't accomplish these things, no one, including Nordstrom, would spend a nickel to raise service standards.

The Cost of Losing a Customer

Based on the following story, you be the judge. John Barrier of Spokane, Washington went into his bank, cashed a check, and asked to have his parking ticket validated. Mr. Barrier was dressed a bit shabbily because he owned a construction company and was on the job that day, but he *was* a customer of the bank nonetheless. The teller refused to validate his parking ticket because *company policy* dictated that cashing a check was not a sufficient reason to validate a customer's parking stub. When Mr. Barrier approached the branch manager with his request, the manager turned him down as well.

Foolish? Petty? You're not going to believe how foolish and petty it was, in retrospect. Mr. Barrier was angry. In fact, he was so irritated he decided to teach these bank officials a painful lesson in customer service. That 50 cent parking validation cost the bank plenty. Mr. Barrier pulled his $1 million account out of the bank and put it elsewhere. As if that weren't bad enough, the story of the bank's unprofessional behavior probably made every newspaper in the country. For all we know, the bank manager may now be an entry-level carpenter working for Mr. Barrier.

Fortunately, extreme customer service blunders are being publicized more and more these days. Hopefully, publicity will serve to educate and pressure companies to improve service.

How Much DO Lost Customers COST YOU?

There is a more customized way for you to compute the cost of poor service.

Figure 1.1 shows a formula developed by the Forum Corporation. Plug in your own numbers and you'll be surprised how costly it can be to lose customers. The percentages on lines C and E (dissatisfied customers and those likely to switch) are averages the Forum Corporation has derived from its research. Figure 1.2 shows the same formula with a hypothetical company. Losing 18% of its customers will result in an 18% loss in revenue.

Calculating the Revenue Lost Through Poor Service Quality

Lost Revenue

A. Annual Revenue $ _____

B. # Customers   _____

C. % Dissatisfied Customers   X _____ **.25**

D. # Dissatisfied Customers (C x B)   = _____

E. % Dissatisfied Customers
   Likely to Switch (60-90%)   X _____ **.75**

F. # Dissatisfied Customers
   Who Will Switch (D x E)   = _____

G. Revenue/Customers (A ÷ B)   = $_____

H. Revenue Lost Through
   Poor Service Quality (F x G)   = $_____

Figure 1.1: Losing customers from poor service quality can be very costly.

> **SERVICE R$_x$:**
> Keep your customers. It costs six times more to acquire new customers than to keep existing ones happy.

Sample Costs of Losing Dissatisfied Customers

Lost Revenue

A.	Annual Revenue	$	240,000,000
B.	# Customers		6,000
C.	% Dissatisfied Customers	X	.25
D.	# Dissatisfied Customers (C x B)	=	1,500
E.	% Dissatisfied Customers Likely to Switch (60-90%)	X	.75
F.	# Dissatisfied Customers Who Will Switch (D x E)	=	1,125
G.	Revenue/Customers (A ÷ B)	= $	40,000
H.	Revenue Lost Through Poor Service Quality (F x G)	= $	45,000,000

Figure 1.2: Even though only a small percentage of dissatisfied customers are likely to switch, the cost is still significant.

Service and the Law of Supply and Demand

The law of supply and demand affects customer service the same way it affects products in the marketplace. When a company doesn't have to compete for customers, it becomes independent and operations-focused. As soon as competition appears, the company must differentiate itself with service.

Businesses think they can afford to be operations-focused when the demand for their product or service is significantly higher than the supply. Of course, this is a short-term outlook, as you will see when we discuss the divestiture of AT&T.

Theoretically, if you have the supply of a product and the demand is high, your service is not going to affect sales. In real life, however, service always matters. Take the case of Company A that sells something no one else offers. They treat their customers rudely. While Company A's customers are buying its exclusive product, they are also looking around for an alternative source. Sooner or later an entrepreneur will spot the need for better service, form Company B, and start competing with Company A. How will the marketplace respond? They will gladly abandon Company A and buy from Company B, even if B's prices are higher! So Company A's good fortune and independence will have been short-lived.

By the way, after Company B comes on the scene, even if Company A decides to give good service, it will be futile. Customers don't forget. Once they've decided not to do business with Company A, they will stick to that decision. It will take Company A a long time to change its reputation.

The Marketplace Always Gets What It Wants—Eventually

The marketplace always gets what it wants, even if what it wants is not in its best interest. The perfect example is the break-up of AT&T. Consumers were dissatisfied with the phone company's monopoly. Until relatively recently, however, there was no way for another company to compete, even though the need existed. AT&T owned the phone lines they had laid when copper wire and labor were inexpensive. It was impossible for another company to start stringing a new copper wire system. The issue of regulation was moot because the technology to make competition viable did not exist.

The need for an alternative opened the door for competitors and created an incentive to further develop satellite communications technology. In time, satellite communications became a relatively inexpensive technology which allowed competition in long distance phone service. The dissatisfaction in the marketplace was about to be answered.

What was the discontent due to? Not a poor quality product—the American telephone system was the best in the world.

> Phil: *Most people, when they return from an overseas trip, kneel and kiss the ground at the airport because they are so happy to be back on U.S. soil. The first time I traveled overseas, I returned and kissed a pay phone.*

The dissatisfaction wasn't due to a lack of service. When you called for a repair, someone usually showed up the next day—the phone company was responsive.

The phone customers' irritation was a result, in part, of a lack of choice. AT&T was a monopoly. Even though Americans are monopoly-phobic, the lack of choice wouldn't have been fatal if it weren't for AT&T's poor attitude. Their fatal flaw was that they were operations-focused to the bone. They were a monopoly and acted like one. You could almost hear them saying, "If you don't like it, go to the other phone company." There was no other phone company! That is what started the consumer revolt.

It is not unreasonable to speculate that if AT&T had had a market-focused philosophy and attitude, they might still be the only phone company in the United States.

When the government ordered the breakup of Ma Bell, everyone expected prices to decrease and service to increase. Unfortunately, that never happened. Prices continued to rise and service got worse. Hundreds of small new phone companies sprang up and lured customers away from AT&T with lower long distance prices. But the quality of their product was inferior. Before they could say "Please hold," customers were returning to AT&T for the quality of their phone transmissions. A lot of small long distance companies went out of business.

MCI and US Sprint survived because they had more to sell than a low price. They realized early on they needed to invest in the technology to improve their transmission quality. After developing fiber-optic and satellite networks, they were close to or on a par with AT&T in terms of quality. So they adopted a new tack in promoting themselves. Instead of trying to capitalize on low prices, they positioned themselves *alongside* AT&T. This strategy put them in a different league than the bargain basement phone companies. It would not have been possible if they hadn't been able to compete on the basis of quality. Now these three major players have to compete in terms of service.

The AT&T example serves to illustrate that when a need exists, the technology—and competitive companies—to serve it come racing into existence. There are warehouses full of technology waiting for the need to arise. Bell Laboratories is a good example. Its research has been so prolific that it has received a patent for every day it's been in existence. In other words, take the number of years it has been in business, multiply it by 365, and that's the staggering number of patents it holds! Yet much of this technology doesn't even have a market yet.

Why Is Service So Bad?

When you encounter bad service, you blame the company. There are a million excuses: they hire low-wage employees; they don't have the money for better training; they're unaware of the importance of customer service; and so on.

A fact of American business life is that customer service is not catching on quickly enough. Books, articles, management training films and videos, professional speakers, management consultants, and seminar leaders are all talking about improving the service climate in this country. Audience members by the hundreds of thousands at customer service seminars are shaking their heads in agreement, but then everyone goes back to work and nothing changes. So you could blame corporate America.

You could also blame advertising agencies. They are supposedly the most innovative, aware, and creative people in the business world. Supposedly they are the marketing gurus who know how to increase sales, boost images, sway public opinion, and position companies within a marketplace. Yet, they still have not faced the reality that service is now *the* differentiating factor for every business.

Over a three-month period in 1989, the authors surveyed print ads in five magazines (*Readers Digest, Newsweek, Playboy, US News & World Report, and Fortune*) and four newspapers (*New York Times, USA Today, Los Angeles Times, and the Washington Post*). What they discovered was astounding. In the magazines, 92.4% of the ads were product-oriented, while only 7.6% were service-oriented. In the newspapers, they found 97.5% of the ads were product-oriented and 2.5% were service-oriented. Product-oriented ads emphasized product features, benefits, and price, but never service.

Despite the fact that virtually every marketing expert in America agrees that service is the top differentiating factor, advertising agencies are still designing ads that sell features.

There are always, of course, admirable exceptions, a few of which we have reprinted. In early 1990, Marriott Corporation, Honeywell, and Kaiser Permanente ran full-page ads nationwide that promoted service. The Kaiser ad was especially impressive. It accomplished four purposes at once. It 1) promoted Kaiser as a provider of health care; 2) promoted its service by highlighting people in the ad; 3) served a recruiting function by portraying Kaiser as a desirable place to work; and 4) rewarded some of its employees with public recognition.

While we were writing this book, a friend of the ours saw the Honeywell ad in the Wall Street Journal. He called to ask for permission to use it. Within one week he received not only written permission, but also the camera-ready art from Honeywell's advertising agency. Now, that's professionalism!

Why is service so bad? The truth is, in the final analysis, we have to blame ourselves. Service is bad because we tolerate it. The vast majority of us tend to keep our mouths shut when we are dissatisfied. We leave tips in restaurants even though the service is poor. We put up with impersonal bank tellers. We tolerate plumbers and electricians who don't show up when they said they would. We have grown accustomed to all kinds of businesses that employ young people who haven't been trained to handle customers.

Why don't people complain? One reason is our nature. Most people are just too timid. *The biggest reason, however, is that most people don't believe complaining will do any good.* By not complaining, we help validate the lack of service. For companies to increase their level of service, customers must become vocal.

SERVICE R$_x$:
Be more demanding of the personal service you receive everyday.

We influence the standards of service by accepting or rejecting what we are given. If we were more demanding, over a period of time businesses would be forced to respond with better service.

WE DIDN'T GET TO BE #1 WITH BUSINESS TRAVELERS JUST BY LEAVING MINTS ON YOUR PILLOW.

Those little details are sweet, but it's crackerjack performance that business people savor most. That's why a recent survey in USA TODAY reported Marriott the first choice among business travelers. We believe efficient, warm, respectful service always leaves the best taste of all.

SERVICE. THE ULTIMATE LUXURY.℠

Marriott
HOTELS·RESORTS

It begins the moment you call us at 1-800-228-9290. Or call your Travel Professional.

Kaiser Permanente salutes all of its people, and their commitment to high quality health care.

KAISER PERMANENTE
Good People. Good Medicine.
Southern California Region

During the past year, we've featured some of our many health care professionals in our weekly advertisements. These individuals exemplify the Kaiser Permanente standard of excellence in their specialty areas.

We've tried to give you an idea of just who we are—a collection of GOOD PEOPLE with diverse personal interests and professional specialties—all sharing a common commitment to GOOD MEDICINE and high quality patient care. We are proud to have such valued individuals in our organization. Not only do we recognize these employees, but all of our employees who deliver our services.

We invite you to share the pride we take in delivering high quality health care to our members and join our family of health professionals. For information on employment opportunities, please send or fax your resume to:

Allied Health Care & Administration

Judi Hansen
Kaiser Permanente
Director, Region
Recruitment Services

Dept. NEW-001-12/89
393 E. Walnut St.
Pasadena, CA 91188-8251
Fax #(818) 405-2613
Or telephone the service area
of your choice below.

Nursing

Naja McKenzie, RN
Kaiser Permanente
Director, Regional RN
Recruitment/Retention

Dept. NEW-001-12/89
393 E. Walnut St.
Pasadena, CA 91188-8701
(800)421-0086
Fax #(818)405-6260

Bellflower (213)920-4244	Fontana (714)829-5031	Harbor City (213)517-1628	Los Angeles (213)667-6932
Mental Health Center (800)421-0086	Orange County (714)572-8963	Panorama City (818)375-2614	Pasadena (818)405-3279
Riverside (714)351-4414	San Diego (619)528-3065	West Los Angeles (213)857-2581	Woodland Hills (818)719-4390

We are an equal opportunity employer

"I'M IN THE WALL STREET JOURNAL TO TELL YOU WHAT HONEYWELL PEOPLE ARE SAYING ABOUT OUR CUSTOMERS."

All our employees know that Honeywell's continued success depends on our customers. So above all else, we put customers first. We know customer satisfaction is a fundamental source of our competitive advantage. That's why we remind each other that "Customers control our world."

In fact, Honeywell people worldwide have been reviewing our goals and priorities to make sure everything we do is aimed at putting our customers first.

One result is this written goal in our strategic priorities: "To serve customers to their full satisfaction, by careful identification of customer requirements, measuring our performance, and empowering employees to meet customer needs."

Deep down, this renewed commitment to you is the way all of us at Honeywell know we can serve you best. Because along with our promise of "Helping you control your world," we understand that "Customers control our world."

Jim Renier

James J. Renier
Chairman and Chief Executive Officer

Honeywell

HELPING YOU CONTROL YOUR WORLD

Phil: *I went to the movies and was standing in line for popcorn. The people behind the counter were terribly slow and the line took forever to move. I did what I always do when I'm upset, I became vocal. At one point, the woman in front of me turned around and said, "They're doing the best they can." "That's what I'm afraid of!" I replied.*

The point of this story is that people shouldn't accept poor service. If the candy counter clerks are doing the best they can, then they need to be better trained. How will management know people need more training unless customers tell them? What's the solution?

Imagine this scenario: Everyone waiting for popcorn leaves the line and watches the movie without making a purchase. (That's going to hurt because theaters make their money on the concessions.) After the movie, everyone tells the manager about the poor service at the snack bar. Then they tell the manager that, if it happens once more, they will never patronize his theater again. The manager can either accommodate the request or go out of business. That's how customers motivate a business to provide better service.

SERVICE R$_x$:
There are three things you can do when you are unhappy with your environment. You can leave it, adapt to it or try to change it. When it comes to poor service, you have to change it.

Is Service Getting Better or Worse?

According to a 1988 Gallup poll, the majority (61%) of people surveyed believed service had not improved since 1985. Only one in five people believed companies had become more responsive to their customers.

If service hasn't improved, what are companies doing? Some are improving their service, but others are simply content to talk about it—without changing a thing.

The increase in service-consciousness has, however, led to a copycat syndrome. Everyone has jumped on the bandwagon and is touting their service as if it were unique. Unfortunately, the changes that have taken place are too few, too cosmetic, and too infrequent. Most companies haven't become customer-oriented; they're still operations-focused. The following slogans and ad headlines were around in the late 1980s. They show varying degrees of commitment to the customer:

"GTE . . . Quality Service from Quality People."

"US Sprint Means Customer Service."

"Customers FIRST at Woolworth."

"Continental Savings . . . Service Is Our Business."

"Because You Deserve More." (C&R Clothiers)

"British Telecom: It's *You* We Answer To."

"Service is your right. We intend to see you get it."
(Chrysler)

"There's One Hotel In Newport Beach Where The Staff Outperforms The Weather." (Four Seasons Hotel)

Kay Bee toy stores ran a series of ads that focused on their customer service:

"Buy the Atari Video Games Systems
where good service is not a game."

"Buy Centurions from a toy store
where good service doesn't cost a Cent."

"Buy Parker Bros. VCR Games from a toy store
where you'll be treated like a VIP."

It is nice to see some companies have recognized the importance of promoting service as a differentiating factor and have taken the first step of creating new expectations for their customers. The next step is to deliver on these promises.

The sad fact is that most companies do not know how to create, implement, budget, and manage an effective customer service initiative.

They administer customer service programs by the seat of their pants. The outcome, more often than not, is second-rate.

ATM Machines—A Service Illusion

ATM machines were a service shortcut. In 1979 there were less than 10,000 of them. Ten years later there were over 67,000. Why were they so successful? Why do people prefer dealing with ATM machines? The answer is simple. You receive human-like treatment from machines, which is preferable to the alternative—machine-like service from humans. What we really want is human-like service from human beings, but we're not getting it.

ATMs actually provide better service than tellers. The ATM knows your name and does its work quickly and efficiently. The tellers inside the bank, may not care what your name is. Unlike the ATM, which exists solely to serve you, the bank tellers have other chores to do—operational tasks—so they often regard customers as an interruption. More often than not, their courtesy, if it exists at all, is perfunctory.

There's another point to be made about ATMs. It's obvious that people want human-like service, even if it's from a machine. Proof of this is the continual technological improvements made to the ATMs. The new ones don't just print your name on the computer screen, they have synthesized voices that greet you. They're even given names such as Tally the Teller. Obviously, the ultimate ATM would be a real live person . . . oops, we already have those.

If you still want to call the ATM impersonal and mechanical, that's fine. But our point remains valid. You can forgive a machine for being impersonal because *that's all it can be*, but you can't forgive a person for being impersonal. That, if for no other reason, is why ATMs are so popular—they don't disappoint you. Technology has no favorites. Ken Blanchard relates the following personal experience:

> "I went to my bank—it's one of those with walk-up win-
> dows—and the woman in front of me wasn't quite sure if her
> transaction was finished. But the teller had just walked away, so
> she said through the microphone, 'Are we finished yet?' The
> teller turned around and said gruffly, 'I told you to have a nice
> day, didn't I?'"

It's all a question of expectations. Banks have been trying to lower our expectations of their service for years. The ATM machine is proof of this. They're saying, "Look, we all have ATM machines; service is the same from one bank to another." Some have even tried to gain an advantage by having more ATMs than the competition. Banks have made themselves into commodities because even though customers want convenience and speed, they want it from humans. If given a choice between a pleasant, friendly teller and an ATM machine, we believe people would choose to go into the bank and see a live teller. Of course, there are also people who prefer the speed and efficiency of an ATM machine. So no matter how perfect tellers are, a bank would be wise to keep ATMs as well.

The ATM trend is beginning to change. Wells Fargo led the movement toward 24-hour phone teller service featuring *live tellers*.

Their advertising capitalized on the fact that you could call, day or night, and speak to—believe it or not—a real person, not a computer!

Along the same lines, one bank differentiated itself with a print ad that said, "We will treat you with honor, trust, and respect, but you'll get used to it." By acknowledging the impersonal nature of most financial institutions, this bank promised to be an exception.

Toasters, Crock Pots, and CDs

There was a time when banks didn't think they needed to improve their service because free gifts were their way of attracting new customers.

> Phil: *Many years ago I was trying to sell a customer service training program to a savings and loan in Florida. The head of customer service said to me, "A customer service training program would be a waste of money. If I want more customers, I run an ad offering a crock pot. People will go to the bank across the street, withdraw their money and deposit it here. Six months from now, if the bank across the street offers a toaster, my customers will take their money out of my bank and put it across the street." P.S. That bank is now out of business.*

What do you think it was like to be a customer of that bank? If they regarded their customers as fickle, free gift gluttons, how much courtesy and respect do you think the tellers showed customers when they came into the branch? They were probably treated like numbers.

How can banks encourage customers to be more loyal? They're beginning to find out that a market-focused approach works well. Deregulation has forced banks to take an active rather than passive approach to acquiring customers. These financial institutions have begun to differentiate themselves by adding value and accommodating their customers: staying open later, opening on Saturdays, reducing the time spent waiting in lines, hiring more tellers, and adding services such as in-home consultations for real estate loans.

In every industry there are companies that set examples for the rest. These market-focused companies are at the top of their industries because they provide impeccable service. In the airlines, it's top-ranked

Singapore Airlines. In financial services, American Express. In retailing, Nordstrom. In delivery and air freight, Federal Express. In the mail order industry, L.L. Bean. In office equipment and computers, IBM. You can name others.

Being market-focused doesn't happen by chance. It is an executive decision and an organizational commitment implemented with a concerted effort involving everyone in the organization.

Chapter Two

Marketing as a Philosophy, Not as a Department

What's the function of every business? Take your time, think about it. This is not a trick question.

Is the function to make money? To make sales? To fill a need? To grow? Most people believe the function of a business is to make money. If that was your guess, your answer was the same as a lot of others—but inaccurate. Don't be dismayed. We answered incorrectly the first time we were asked. Making money is the *goal* of every business. The correct answer was proposed by Dr. Ted Levitt, Senior Marketing Fellow at Harvard University. In his book, *The Marketing Imagination*, he said the function of every business is to get and keep customers.

SERVICE R$_x$:
   The function of every business is the acquisition and maintenance of customers.

If you think about it for a minute, you'll see just how simple and yet profound that one sentence is. Dr. Levitt took this principle one step further:

SERVICE R$_x$:
Therefore, the function of *every employee* in every business is the acquisition and maintenance of customers.

This tenet should be an American mantra. If every morning on the way to work, people chanted, "My function at work is the acquisition and maintenance of customers," service would improve overnight. You'd think you were transported to another world—customer heaven. If this philosophy were accepted universally, the impact on decision-making at every corporate level would be dramatic.

The essence of this book, literally, is *"The function of every business is the acquisition and maintenance of customers; therefore, the function of every employee in every business is the acquisition and maintenance of customers."*

Your Job Is Just the Tip of the Iceberg

A very sound business practice would be to rewrite every job description so employees know their functions go beyond their job tasks. Every job description should start with: *"The primary function of every employee in every business is the acquisition and maintenance of customers."* Every behavior that supports this principle—even if it's outside company policy—is acceptable behavior. Any behavior that contradicts this principle—even if it is within company policies—is unacceptable behavior. Your paycheck at the end of every week represents your contribution to "the acquisition and maintenance of our customers."

How many business people recognize the relationship between their behavior and the acquisition and maintenance of customers? Probably very few. Think how differently people would do even routine tasks if they thought they were working for the company's customers rather than for their boss.

Everybody wants to take pride in their work and be recognized for it. Dishwashers in restaurants would be more conscientious if they were made aware of the connection between their jobs and every guest's dining experience. Pride of workmanship is the result of knowing that your work is accomplishing more than simply getting you a paycheck.

SERVICE R$_X$:
Give people a reason to take pride in their work.
Make them customer-focused.

Every day we do business with people who know their jobs, but don't understand their function. The following story illustrates the absurdity (if you think that word is too strong, you've never been a victim of this crime) of becoming stuck in a rule-enforcing (operations-focused) frame of mind.

Phil: *One of my corporate clients hired me to give a seminar in a hotel. I had about half an hour to kill before the 7:30 PM start of the seminar, so I went to the hotel's restaurant for a quick bite.*

This restaurant was a gourmet French restaurant. They were used to people spending lots of time over a meal. I had to think of something to say that would get me in and out relatively quickly. I walked in and smiled at the hostess. She asked me the quintessential mechanical question, "Joining us for dinner tonight?" Whenever I hear that, I always feel like saying, "No, playing golf; mind if I play through?"

Actually, I wasn't having dinner, but I made the mistake of telling the truth. I said, "I don't have time for a big, fancy dinner. I'm a guest in the hotel (a detail I thought and still think should carry a lot of weight), and I'm giving a seminar in about half an hour. I'd like to just have a bowl of your famous lobster bisque."

The hostess told me that company policy did not allow the serving of less than a full meal. The menu was a fixed-price dinner of five courses, one of which was a soup course.

I repeated myself, hoping that a new emphasis would change her mind. I said, "I'm a guest in the hotel. I'm giving a seminar in half an hour. I am famished and would love to have a complete dinner, but I just don't have the time. I heard you have the best lobster bisque. If you give me a bowl, I will eat it as quickly as possible and then come back for dinner after my seminar."

She repeated the restaurant's policy and I began to get hot under the collar. I asked for the manager. While she was gone, I quickly looked around and, wouldn't you know it, the restaurant was empty. The manager came out and played the part of a sophisticated French maitre d'. You've seen the type—a penciled-in mustache, fake French accent—probably born and raised in Brooklyn.

I repeated the whole story to him and could tell by his attitude that he had decided to refuse my request before he even came out of the kitchen. Sure enough, he supported the hostess and recited the company policy.

The function of every employee in every business is the acquisition and maintenance of customers. Do you think the restaurant manager understood his function? Of course, he didn't. He thought his function was to enforce the rules. To whom in our society do we give the authority to enforce rules? The police. But no one wants to eat at a restaurant run by cops!

The lowest form of human communication is quoting company policy. It's precisely the type of nonthinking, rote litany you would expect from children and robots—those who are unable to reason. Adults serving customers should be above it.

SERVICE R$_x$:
Delete the phrase "It's company policy" from your vocabulary. If the reason for the policy is a good one, explain it to people. If it isn't, give your customers what they want.

Company policies are, more often than not, operations-focused rules that exist for the sole benefit of the company. In a truly market-focused company, the only company policy is, "Give our customers what they want."

Nobody likes being told, "It's against company policy," or any other arbitrary rule. For those of us who see it as the meaningless phrase it is, it's even more frustrating. Phil has devised a clever way to combat the company policy dilemma. He wrote his own policy manual, a black leather book that says "Phil Wexler's Policy Manual" on the cover. When someone says to him, "I'm sorry, Mr. Wexler, but it's against company policy," Phil takes out his policy manual and says, "It's against your company policy. Let's see what my policy manual says. It says here on page 38 that I can do it. The only issue we have to resolve now is whose policy manual we are going to use—mine or yours. If we're using my money, we're going to use my policy manual."

Why does this happen? Why do employees treat their customers so poorly? Why do managers allow their line people to frustrate customers when they should be bending over backwards to please them?

The Evolution of a Business

To understand the roots of business insensitivity, it's important to understand the changes that take place as a business grows. Let's take a look at the evolution of a hypothetical business and see how the management priorities change with size.

Once upon a time there was a waiter named Harvey. He loved to serve people and truly enjoyed his job. He was very dedicated to his customers and was the best-tipped waiter in the restaurant. One day his aunt died and left him some money. What do you think he did? He opened his own restaurant.

His new restaurant was very successful. As an owner/manager, Harvey tended to his customers with the same zeal he possessed as a waiter. Six months after his opening, Harvey's banker stopped by and said to him, "I've had my eye on you. I knew you were going to be a success. Let's become 50-50 partners in a second restaurant and we'll really take this town by storm."

They opened a second restaurant and hired a manager for the first one. Harvey scribbled out three or four pages of notes on all the different situations that could arise and told the manager, "Whenever something happens that falls into one of these categories, follow these guidelines. If something else happens, *use your best judgement* and then call me and I'll add it to my notes."

A year later both restaurants were doing quite well. The banker again came to Harvey and said, "Let's open four more restaurants. You put up a little money, and I'll put up the rest." So in a short time they had a total of six restaurants. Instead of hiring four more managers, Harvey had to hire five because now he had to manage the managers.

Harvey, like many managers, was primarily dealing with paperwork and found he had a lot of time on his hands. So he took back his policy manual, which had grown to 12 pages, hired a policy consultant, and rewrote it. He began to get compulsive and covered all the possible situations and operational details he could imagine. With pride, he turned the policy manual into what he thought was a work of art—a 100-page masterpiece! He had it printed and bound and proudly delivered new copies to all his managers.

In the new policy manual, the message to the managers was different. Instead of being encouraged to use their judgement, managers were instructed to call Harvey in situations not covered in the manual. At this point, the restaurant chain made the transition from being a market-focused organization to being a policy-focused or operations-focused organization. With this new focus, the rules were given highest priority and, by default, customers came second. One could even say the rules were so important a customer could be sacrificed for them.

A year later the banker saw more dollar signs before his eyes. He proposed to Harvey that they open 30 more restaurants nationwide. With the banker's help, they secured a multi-million dollar line of credit and soon had 36 restaurants in total. Each restaurant had a manager and an assistant manager. Every five restaurants had a district manager. Every two districts had a regional manager and the company had a national marketing director, operations director, assistant to the president and so on. The policy manual was pushing 250 pages and required a three-day training course to understand.

As president of the corporation, this friendly, former-waiter, Harvey, who went into business because he loved the interaction with customers, was perched in a 17th floor downtown office. With such a large network of restaurants, control and quality diminished. From the top of the corporate tower, however, that was difficult to see because even though each restaurant was less successful than the original, the number of restaurants still made the company successful.

In his plush office, the only time Harvey talked to customers was when they had complaints; and not just mild complaints—those were handled by lower levels of management. Harvey heard from the obnoxious and pushy complainers who really liked to throw their weight around.

At that point in his career, how do you think Harvey felt about customers? He hated them! So he told his assistant to see to it he never had to talk to a customer again. The assistant, wanting to preserve her job, worked hard to keep her boss happy. She, in turn, was kept happy by her subordinates. The same unwritten rule—keep the boss happy—filtered down all the way to the individual restaurant managers. So what

Harvey had was an organization in which everyone was working so hard to keep their boss happy that they didn't care about keeping the customers happy. Sound familiar?

"I guarantee that's the best hot dog you've ever eaten!"

"Yep, and I've got four more just like this throughout the county!"

"George, if another customer gets through to me you're in big trouble!"

Everyone became operations-focused. The commitment to the customer that fueled the growth of Harvey's original restaurant was absent throughout his chain. As a result, each restaurant was less profitable than the original, making the overall company much less profitable than it could be. By becoming a mediocre chain, Harvey's lost the competitive edge they could have had if they'd stuck to their original formula. Eventually Harvey had a decision to make; either go back to the spirit of the original Harvey's or go out of business.

The story of Harvey's illustrates the typical evolution of a company and how it becomes operations-focused. As common as this is, rest assured it is possible for a company to mushroom and still remain market-focused. In fact, in the future, businesses must be market-focused if they are to grow.

There are so many examples of operations-focused thinking that we could fill an entire book with them. To those of us with more than a modicum of customer-consciousness, it seems incredible that so many people can be so obtuse.

Take the retail store that doesn't allow customers to use the parking space directly in front of its door because its delivery trucks need a place to park once or twice a day! The store's trucks use the space for a total of perhaps an hour a day, but for the other seven hours the parking space remains blocked and empty. The owner of the store has his priorities backwards. He has only his convenience in mind, not his customers'. Handicapped people must really appreciate that!

> Emil: *While consulting with Snowbird Ski Resort of Salt Lake City, I heard the most incredible story. Their food and beverage director is in charge of the food and decor in their seven restaurants. Two or three times a year he changes the atmosphere in all the restaurants. Part of these changes includes new artwork, which, for seven restaurants, produces a lot of business for a picture framing store in Salt Lake City. One time the manager was driving down the mountain into town with a trunk full of posters to be framed. He spotted a new picture framing store closer to the hotel and thought, "How convenient. I'll give them a try." It was about 4:55 PM. He went into the store and the young lady said, "Can I help you?" The manager told her who he was and said he had some pictures he would like to have framed. She asked how many pictures he had, and he told her thirty or forty. The woman said, "Gee, it's five minutes to five. We close at five. Could you come back tomorrow?"*

The store clerk thought the important part of her job was closing on time. She never even considered the fact that she could have acquired a new customer—and a big, lucrative one at that! One sale would have paid the rent for six months! She saw her function as the keeper of shop hours, not as someone responsible for the acquisition and maintenance of customers.

> Bill: *I got a letter from one of my banks that said, "Dear Mr. Adams, You are a valued customer and we appreciate your business. According to our records, you have an inactive savings account with us. If you do not activate your account within 60 days, we will assess a $50 charge to the account," and so on. They neglected to consider the fact that there was $3,200 in the account. I agreed with them; the account was inactive. So I closed it and put the money in another bank where it could become active.*

You can just see it—the controller was going through his computer readouts, trying to figure out a way to increase revenues. So he came up with the bright idea of separating the wheat from the chaff among account holders. He assumed inactive accounts were all a bunch of deadbeats, but he didn't have the insight and training to check their balances! No doubt, he lost a lot of customers with that letter. In fact, an inside source revealed that 25% of the customers who received those letters closed their accounts.

The bank controller had a good seed of an idea, but his implementation was faulty. His perspective was short-term. He lacked the big picture perspective and the bank lacked a market-focus. It was sheer operational thinking—looking at numbers rather than the people behind the numbers. If the controller had been communicating with other departments in the bank, especially the marketing department, he would have devised a different plan for stimulating business. Hence, the need for a Philosopher General.

The difference between the way the accounting department sees things and the marketing department's perspective is a matter of focus. The controller looks at the 1000 inactive accounts, multiplies them by $50 and sees $50,000 in service fees. His attitude is, "Get them active or get them out of here."

The marketing department thinks of ways to stimulate business in a positive way. They think in terms of giving customers more and, therefore, enticing them to increase their account activity. Marketing might come up with an incentive such as a half-point increase in the interest paid on the account if certain minimum deposits are made periodically. They can create any conditions they want, but the bottom-line is their focus is on the customer, not on operations. They're used to asking, "How is the customer going to react to this?"

SERVICE R$_X$:
Always include the customer in your decision-making process. If your focus is not on the customer, then change your focus until it is.

There are better ways to stimulate inactive accounts.

Phil: *I received a letter from the CBS Compact Disc Club notifying me that I hadn't placed an order in quite a while. The letter said something like, "We noticed you are no longer a member of the CBS Compact Disc Club and we're really sad to see you go. We're going to make you a special 'Welcome Back' offer that we've never made before. You get eight compact discs* *for only 13 cents! (If you commit to buying six more over the next year.) By the way, if you buy the first of those six now, you can have them for 1/2 price!" It was incredible. Nine compact discs for $6.95. Now that's the way to activate an account!*

Emil: Here's a superb example of market-focused thinking. MCI long distance service has a program in which, no matter how large your account, their computers monitor your usage and establish an average monthly usage for you. If you go below your average usage for two consecutive months, you get a phone call from a customer service representative: "Mr. Bohn, we noticed you haven't been using MCI as much as you used to. We just want to make sure there are no problems."

The contrast between the last three stories is remarkable. CBS and MCI chose to coax their customers into more activity. The bank chose intimidation. The last two strategies were very effective and succeeded in differentiating their companies. What could the bank have done differently?

Obsessed With Your Boss?

Restauranteer Harvey's story also illustrates a common dilemma many employees have—they are subservient to a fault. Most people think they work for their boss. If you believe that, you probably act as if your boss were responsible for your future. So you respond primarily to your boss and run the risk of short-changing your customers with perfunctory service.

As Phil's experience at a McDonald's demonstrates, often in large organizations, middle management is at fault:

Phil: I went into a McDonald's and said, "I want a quarter-pounder cheeseburger with nothing on it except Big Mac sauce. Instead of ketchup or mustard, I just want Big Mac sauce." The clerk replied, "I'm sorry, we can't put Big Mac sauce on a quarter pounder, only on a Big Mac." I said, "Come on, you can do it, what's the big deal?" "I'm sorry, we can't do that," he responded. We went back and forth on this. The guy was very nice and saw my point, but he had rules to follow. I inquired, "Can you give me a little container of Big Mac sauce on the side?" He answered he couldn't do that because it was against health regulations to serve open containers. I asked him what he would do if someone ordered a Big Mac and asked for extra sauce. He said he would put it on for him. I suggested, "So take the extra sauce you're not putting on someone's Big Mac and put it on mine."

At one point I asked him, "Haven't you ever heard the saying, 'The customer is always right'? Did they teach you that?" He answered, "Yes, the customer is always right, except when he's asking me to break the rules." We went on and on about this and the only thing that kept me from getting angry was that the guy was genuinely nice about it.

He continued, "If the regional manager walked in and saw me do it, I'd lose my job." I said to him, "If Joan Kroc walked in and saw you do it, what would she do?" He deferred, "I don't know." I told him, "I know! She would praise you! That's what serving the customer is all about." He countered, "That may be, but Joan Kroc doesn't come in, the regional manager does. At that point, a young kid who was mopping the floor came over and whispered to the clerk, "The Thousand Island sauce for the salad is almost the same as the Big Mac sauce." The clerk realized I had overheard this. He just smiled, handed me some packets of Thousand Island and said, "I'd be happy to give you some Big Mac sauce, Sir."

The guy was sharp. And the message is clear. Some line personnel want to serve their customers as best they can. The top brass of the company also understand what customer service is all about. In between, however, there are layers of number-crunching managers who look over the shoulders of line people and turn them into penny-pinching, inflexible robots.

As an employee who is serving the public, you have to fight that. You do it by treating your customers like royalty, which means giving them what they want. Good service doesn't mean giving them everything they want for free. You have to strike a balance between accommodating your customers and driving your company into bankruptcy.

People often say the worst thing that can happen to them is to lose their boss, especially one that they just figured out. Now they have to figure out a new boss—think of all the energy that will take away from your real function at work.

The reality is this: You and your boss work for the same person—your customer. Both of your futures with the company depend on the strength of the company, which is based on how well you acquire and maintain customers.

What do Harvey's story and the McDonald's incident have in common? Why do so many companies make the all-too-typical transition from being market-focused to operations-focused? There are two reasons. The first is it's easier to run an operations-focused company—recruiting is easier, training is less stringent, employees don't have to be as resourceful and independent, and there is little risk of losing money due to poor service decisions. The reason most companies become operations-focused is short-term thinking.

Short-term vs. Long-term Thinking

Short-term thinking is generally caused by ignorance, greed, or fear. Corporate executives feel enormous pressure to show shareholders the company is profitable. A rising stock price is also advantageous to executives whose bonuses are in the form of stock options. So short-term strategies are given priority over long-term investments. This short-term approach is often taken at the expense of the long-term needs of the company, its customers, and society in general. Short-term thinking at its worst leads to things like insider trading, defense contractor overcharging, environmental pollution, and government scandals, to name a few. Long-term thinking can lead to industry dominance. Just look at the Japanese.

Short-term and long-term thinking are also related to the scarcity versus abundance mentality. Some people think there will never be enough to go around. Long-term thinkers are more relaxed because they believe there will always be enough for everyone.

Short-term thinking is operations-focused. It's the philosophy that doing something extra for the customer must have an immediate return. But that makes no sense, because good will is never short-term; yet no one would deny the value of good will.

Long-term thinking sees the customer as someone with whom you have an ongoing relationship. Thus the long-term philosophy dictates your company should *never* have a customer transaction that may jeopardize the business relationship. Everything is geared toward maintaining customers.

Trusting Your Customers

In late 1989, Ford Motor Company launched a new program affecting the performance of warranty work at Ford's 5,600+ dealers across the U.S. In the past, if a customer came into a dealership with a car that was slightly over its warranty period/mileage and requested warranty work, the dealer had to fill out a lot of paperwork to get permission to do it. Ford changed all that. They told their dealers to start using their best judgement in those situations. If the dealer thought the request for warranty work was fair and the repair was necessary, he could commit Ford's money to doing the job.

Ford's shift toward long-term, market-focused thinking had an important implication regarding trust. Ford told their dealers, in effect, "Look, you guys are *our* customers and we trust your judgement. Now we want you to trust *your* customers. When a customer comes in with a story, *assume the story is true*, unless you have some evidence to support that it isn't."

There's a message here for every company and every employee.

SERVICE R$_x$:
Don't make policies that punish good customers to protect you from those who might cheat you.

Conduct business with the attitude that most people are *not* out to take advantage of you. See your function as finding ways to fulfill customers' desires, not thwart them.

Phil: *The day after I heard about Ford's new policy, I was giving a customer service seminar to a group of hotel managers. I told them about the Ford concept and gave them an example of how the hotel industry distrusts its customers. I then related a personal experience.*

I had checked into a hotel in which I had a barter account that included rooms, meals, everything. I showed the desk clerk my reservation, on which was stamped "Bill to Barter Account." He said, "Our barter accounts only cover the room. I'll need a credit card for the incidental expenses." I told him my barter account covered everything. He answered, "Well, you'll just have to wait a second," and went into the back room. Implicit in his actions was the accusation that I was lying to him and that he would have to check to see who was right. He returned a minute later and apologized for being wrong.

What would have been the appropriate way to handle that situation? The desk clerk should have taken Phil's word for the barter account, smiled, and sent him on to his room. Then, once Phil was gone, he could have checked out the validity of Phil's story. Phil would never have known the clerk was double-checking and, if the clerk had found Phil to be wrong, he could have called up to Phil's room and asked for the credit card. That would have been the tactful way of handling things.

SERVICE R$_X$:
TRUST your customers. It's little things like trust that make a big difference in a business relationship.

Phil: *The ironic part is this: about an hour after I told this story to the hotel managers in my seminar, they saw first-hand what I was talking about. I went to check out of the hotel. Now, I hadn't checked into the hotel. The association that hired me checked me into the room, and when they picked me up at the airport, they gave me my room key. When I checked out I just told them I was leaving and that everything went to the association's master bill. The clerk said, "No, Mr. Wexler, we need you to pay for it." I assured the clerk that it went to the master bill. We went back and forth on this until I said, "Why don't you just take my word for it?" He told me to wait a minute and went into the back room. Meanwhile, some of the folks from the seminar were behind me in line, laughing hysterically.*

The classic example of distrust is the store you walk into and immediately see 10 or 15 signs that proudly state all the reasons customers should take their business elsewhere. You've seen them, signs that say, "No returns without a receipt." "Absolutely no checks." "All returned checks subject to $10 fee." "Not responsible for items left over 30 days." "If you break it, you bought it." "Keep your kids on a leash." "We reserve the right to refuse service to anyone." "If you don't see it, we ain't got it." "You want it when! Hahahahaha!"

Many companies create rules that encourage customers to play games with them. A friend, George, tells an interesting story:

George: *I was flying somewhere and due to a schedule change, I had to change flights from Delta to American. Now I'm an*

American Airlines Gold Frequent Flyer. I called American reservations 24 hours before the flight and the conversation went like this:

George: "I'd like to upgrade to first class."

Reservationist: "One of the requirements of a Gold first class upgrade, to get it 24 hours in advance, is that your ticket is already issued."

George: "Yes, I know. I have a Delta ticket."

Reservationist: "We can't do that because it's issued to another airline."

George: "So what you're telling me is that you don't want me to fly American. You want me to take the Delta flight."

Reservationist: "No, no. We want you to take the American flight, but you can't upgrade to first class until you get to the airport. We just can't give you an upgrade guarantee at this time because you must have an American ticket issued at the time you do the upgrade."

George: "Let me ask you a question. If my ticket was issued by a travel agent, you wouldn't have a way of knowing, would you?"

Reservationist: "That's correct."

George: "I'd just tell you I have a ticket for an American flight."

Reservationist: "That's right."

George: "So what you've done is establish a set of rules that force me to lie to you. And actually you have no way of proving me wrong, so I'm going to tell you I already have an American ticket issued. Now, can you do my upgrade?"

Reservationist: "Well, I could, except for the fact that our calls are occasionally monitored and if I upgraded your ticket I could get in trouble. After all, you already told me you didn't have an American ticket."

George: "Okay, so what you're telling me to do is hang up the phone, wait two minutes, call back and tell the next person that I already have an American ticket issued."

Reservationist: "Yes."

And that's what I did.

It's absurd that any business is encouraging customers to lie to them. Instead, they should give their people the authority to make decisions on the spot. Then reservationists could accept the fact that the spirit, if not the letter, of a rule had been satisfied.

With short-term, operations-focused thinking, any spirit of generosity gets squelched in favor of law enforcement. Rigid thinking takes over where flexibility should be. With long-term thinking, everything is geared toward maintaining the customer, so short-term losses can be justified and condoned.

The Operations-Focused Model

One of the primary differences between operations-focused and market-focused organizations is their top priority. Figure 2.1 shows the direction of priority within an operations-focused company. Most of the focus is directed internally toward profits. Every department is cost-conscious, short-term oriented, and concerned with the bottomline. Company policies are sacred and take priority over individual managers' discretion. As a result, the mind-set of virtually everyone in the company is rigid. No one wants to rock the boat.

Operations-focused companies often have an "us versus them" mentality between departments. They're all competing for budget dollars; they also represent separate profit centers. So interdepartmental or interdivisional cooperation is given begrudgingly, if at all. There's a lack of team spirit because people are only interested in doing *their* jobs or making a profit for *their* division.

In a large company with many divisions, it's not uncommon for a management decision to be bad for the parent company but good for the division. Marriott Corporation, besides owning hotels, holds a company called Fairfield Farms Kitchens. Fairfield Farms Kitchens produces, among other things, frozen pecan pies. Marriott sells pecan pie in its hotel restaurants. Instead of automatically buying pecan pies from Fairfield Farms Kitchens, Marriott solicited bids for the pies. Believe it or not, another company underbid Fairfield Farms Kitchens, and Marriott awarded the contract to the lowest bidder. A myopic decision? Indeed.

The justification for that decision was that the restaurant division of Marriott is a profit center and, therefore, is pressured to save every penny it can to be as profitable as possible. What the company failed to see was that all the revenues flow into the same pot—the parent company's. Buying pies from an outsider cost the parent company more money in the long run.

Operations-Driven Organizations

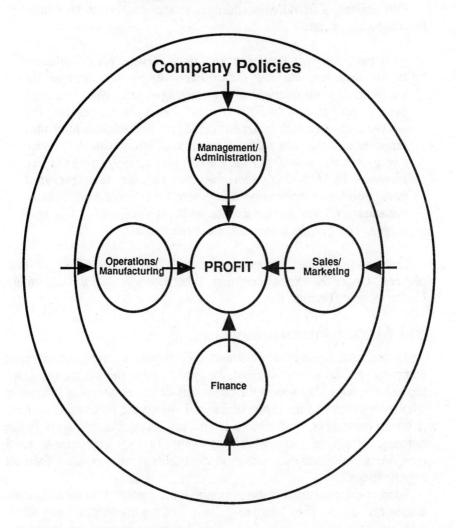

Figure 2.1: Organizations that are internally focused often forget the "acquisition and maintenance of customers" is the ultimate reason for being in business.

Go back to figure 2.1. Can you see what's missing? Where is the customer? In an operations-focused company, customers are secondary. It's not that operations-focused companies don't question where their profits come from; they just come up with the wrong answer. They think profits come from products or services when, in fact, profits really come from customers.

Phil Steffen, a friend, was sitting in a restaurant when he witnessed the following scene:

> *A customer was receiving very poor service. He complained to his waitress, but she didn't improve. Finally he told the waitress, "I want to speak to your manager, and when he comes over, I want to talk to both of you." The waitress snorted and walked away in a huff to get her manager. Two minutes later they returned and the man said, "I am very unhappy with the service I've gotten this morning. I think I can sum up my feelings in one sentence. And I think it's something that you, Mr. Manager, must understand. But more importantly, you have to see to it that she understands." He looked at the waitress and said, "It's very simple. You are the overhead; I am the profit."*

Look at the ledger for any business. Where do you find the employees? Under the expense column. Where do you find the customer? Under income. Enough said!

The Market-Focused Model

In contrast, figure 2.2 illustrates the priority of a market-focused company. As the arrows suggest, everyone within the company—from top to bottom—either serves the customers or serves someone internally who serves them; so the thrust is external. When the focus of a business is on its customers, profitability is still important, but it's seen as the outcome of giving them what they want. In fact, customer-focused companies are generally much more profitable than operations-focused organizations.

Market-focused organizations exhibit more creativity in meeting their customers' needs. They adapt to the wants of the marketplace and allow employees to be flexible and use their discretion in applying company policies. In fact, policies are actually guidelines rather than hard-and-fast rules. That flexibility and cooperative spirit flourishes within the company as well. Interdepartmental team spirit says, "Let's work

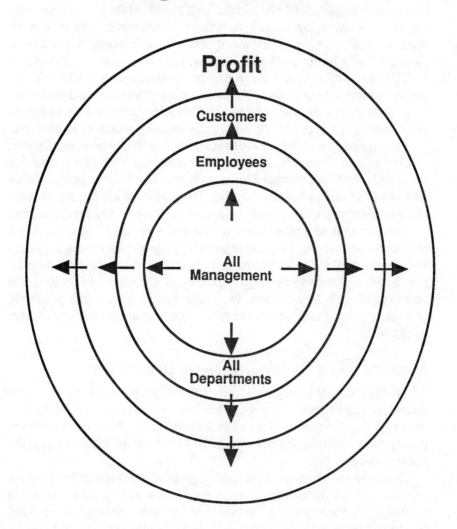

Market-Driven Organizations

Profit

Customers

Employees

All Management

All Departments

Figure 2.2: When organizations focus on the customer, the profits take care of themselves.

together to give our customers what they want. If it weren't for them, we wouldn't have jobs!"

The market-focused approach is long-term. It sees quality customer service as an investment, not as an expense. (An investment gives you a return on your money; an expense does not.)

A good example of being market-focused is the restaurant chain, TGI Friday and its affiliated restaurant, Dalt's. For years TGI Friday was known as a swinging singles restaurant where the emphasis was on drinking and mingling. That image changed after management took a close look at who its customers were and made appropriate changes.

TGI Friday's customers are young professionals with children. These people want restaurants where children are accommodated and where the food is a higher caliber than McDonald's or Denny's. They want an atmosphere that isn't a zoo, like the restaurants catering primarily to children.

So TGI Friday and Dalt's have begun accommodating families. They've added balloons, customized high chairs (ones that look like animals or cars) and children's menus that also serve as coloring books. Other restaurants are being equally creative. They serve meals in toys children can take home or provide coloring placemats, crayons, and animal crackers.

There are innumerable ways to meet the needs of parents. Some restaurants are making it easier for them by putting diaper changing tables in the restrooms. Peter Sachs, owner of Spangles in Los Angeles, says he puts a rush on food orders for young children. The idea is to get them fed and keep them happy—before they raise havoc. This trend is gaining popularity, with upscale and moderately-priced restaurants learning to cater to children.

Marketing Is a Philosophy, Not a Department

Traditionally, the only customer-oriented people were those in the marketing department. They were involved in sales and promotion, so naturally they thought in terms of customers' needs. Now companies are raising their customer-consciousness and making an effort to provide better service.

One mistake often made is the creation of (and dependence on) a customer service department. Sometimes a senior management position is created solely for improving customer service. The problem with this kind of specialization is that it's created in lieu of, rather than in addition to, a company-wide drive for service quality. The outcome is that everyone else slacks off. They figure customer service is being handled by the customer service department. Unconsciously, people think, "It's someone else's responsibility."

The right way to transform your company into a market-focused organization is to create a vision of how the company should be. This vision and a set of core values will provide everyone—from the CEO to the switchboard operator—with the understanding that they play a role in the acquisition and maintenance of customers. We will discuss the vision and values-focused organization in chapter thirteen. For now, the point is that everyone's focus must be external—everything you do is for the customer. You could be a mailroom assistant or the director of marketing—it doesn't matter—you are doing your job for the customers.

One of the most remarkable examples of a customer-focused managerial style comes from an apartment management business executive in Atlanta, Georgia. This man's instruction to his employees is simple: "If one of your tenants wants something and your answer is 'Yes,' you don't need to get management approval. If you're wrong, we'll work it out. If your answer is going to be 'No,'—even if it's in the policy manual—you need management's approval. You never need my approval to say yes."

SERVICE R$_X$:
Be a customer advocate. Find ways to say yes to your customers' requests.

You Have To Have an Obsession

Every book, magazine article, and speech on customer service mentions one store as the shining example of service excellence—Nordstrom. And one word is always associated with Nordstrom—obsession. Nordstrom is obsessed with quality service. Everyone in the company is obsessed with quality service. In fact, you can't work there if you don't have an obsessive-compulsive personality. Its reputation in the industry is so powerful that it affects other department stores as well. When Nordstrom is due to open a new store in a city, the nearby department stores get nervous and start improving their service, which proves that people are motivated more by potential loss than potential gain.

Clearly, the market-focused way of thinking—that traditionally characterized only the marketing department—must now spread to every department in the company, including engineering, and especially management.

A dramatic example of this is the fiasco that befell General Electric in the mid-1980s. Determined to regain marketshare in its sagging refrigerator business, GE engineers designed an innovative compressor—the heart of the cooling system—and a modern factory to manufacture it. The price tag was $120 million. The wager? Their entire $2 billion refrigerator business. In 1983 GE chairman Jack Welch gave the go-ahead and set the wheels in motion.

From the beginning operational pressures took priority over the needs of the marketplace. Engineers made some poor design assumptions and failed to correct their mistakes. Managers, eager to cut costs, forced engineers to speed up reliability testing, curtail field testing, and rush into production. The outcome? GE's new compressor failed so miserably that, as of May 1990 the company had voluntarily replaced almost 1.1 million compressors with units manufactured in Japan and Italy. In the beginning, GE was replacing 5,000 per week! In 1988 they wrote off a $450 million pretax charge.

Ultimately the blame must be attributed to poor corporate communication and an operations-focused mentality. During the preproduction testing phase, several technicians suspected the new compressor might be defective. They told their superiors. Senior executives, however, six levels removed, heard only *good* news. The pressures of regaining marketshares, increasing profits, and meeting production schedules outweighed what should have been the *only* priority—giving customers a quality product!

Now and then you have an experience as a customer that renews your faith in people as quality service providers and reminds you that service is a philosophy, not a department.

> Emil: *I went to a shopping mall and was standing in front of the directory with another shopper. Along came a maintenance man pushing a cart. He stopped and said, "Excuse me, is there a store I can help you find?"*

We found it delightful to have someone take an interest in us without us having to make a request of them first.

Part II

Assessing Service Quality

Chapter Three

The Four Zones of Service Quality

Just as a doctor diagnoses a patient's illness before starting treatment, it is valuable for you to determine the level of service your company currently provides before you plan changes. Knowing where you are now will help you set a proper course for change.

If you were to step back and objectively diagnose the health of your company's customer service, how would it fare? How would you feel if *you* were a customer? The best way to find out is to actually shop at your company. If you can be anonymous, visit one of your stores, offices, or plants. See how your employees treat customers and each other. You can also learn a lot by calling. The telephone is usually the first point of contact a customer has, so good impressions are everything. If you can't shop anonymously, hire someone to pose as a customer and rate you on service.

Our system of dividing service quality into four zones is a useful tool. It will reveal your service practices and attitudes and show you what quality service looks like. For a quick customer service check-up, take the following self-test. Which zone applies to your company?

The Zones of Service Quality Self-Test

How would you respond in the following hypothetical situations. Choose only one answer per question.

1. In the eyes of many customers, your company provides a highly valued service. This sentiment is often expressed immediately after service. While working near two customers, you overhear them make complimentary comments about the quality of your company. What would you do?

   a) Politely introduce yourself and thank them for their comments.

   b) Mind your own business.

   c) Be especially courteous to them in the future.

   d) Arrange for a special gift as a token of your appreciation for them.

2. At the end of a long day, a customer approaches you and complains that she has been kept waiting without apparent reason. In an angry voice, she demands an explanation. What would you do?

   a) Drop everything else and spend as much time as necessary to appease this customer.

   b) Politely request more information until she has calmed down.

   c) Apologize for the delay and immediately work to solve the problem.

   d) Respond indifferently to the customer and offer an excuse.

3. During a business day, a customer asks to speak to you and then requests special service at no extra cost. What would you do?

   a) Give the customer what he wants as long as, in your judgement, it will not be expensive or excessive.

   b) Agree to the request because you should always give customers what they want.

   c) Consider whether a precedent exists for such a request and agree to it only if one exists (or if company policy allows it).

   d) Deny the request, no matter how small.

4. After receiving service from you, a customer makes a face that indicates she is irritated or annoyed. What will you do?

   a) Ask politely if anything is wrong.

b) Presume something is wrong with the service and ask the customer how you can correct the problem.

c) Pretend not to notice or wait for the customer to say something.

d) Ask the customer if you can be of help and, if possible, offer her something extra to make amends.

5. A customer asks you for personal information about another employee—a request that possibly violates the conventions of good taste. When you resist, the customer reminds you that he has been a loyal customer for many years. What will you do?

a) Tell the customer to get lost.

b) Explain to him that it's unethical and against company policy to release that kind of information.

c) Give the information freely.

d) Weigh the sensitivity of the information sought, the reason given for wanting the information, the appropriateness of the disclosure, and then base your response on your assessment.

6. While leaving work one day, you accidently bump into a customer. The customer, having been almost knocked down, is speechless. What will you do?

a) Quickly say, "Sorry" and walk away.

b) Apologize and help your customer regain her composure.

c) Express regret and show genuine concern for your customer's well-being.

d) Express regret and offer a special service or gift as a way to apologize.

7. Management tells you that a very special group of customers will be seeking your company's service during the next month and you should take extra care to satisfy all your customers during this period of time. You interpret this to mean:

a) You should conceive of ways to pleasantly surprise most of your customers.

b) You should be especially friendly and courteous.

c) You should stage an elaborate show of attention and provide additional benefits for all customers during this time.

d) You shouldn't make mistakes.

8. After receiving a service or product from your company, a customer calls to ask for more information. The customer, a history buff, begins his inquiry by asking you to explain the recent history of your company. You:

   a) Place the customer on hold and ask the service manager to tell you what to say.

   b) Tell him you don't know the company's recent history.

   c) Explain what you know and, if necessary, offer to find out more information and promise to call the customer back.

   d) Ask a senior employee to chat with the customer about the history of the company.

9. An expert in customer service visits your company several times one month to give management an honest appraisal of service personnel. She is most likely to describe you and your fellow employees as:

   a) flexible and professional

   b) impersonal and unknowledgeable

   c) courteous and interested

   d) very generous and eager to please

10. After receiving a product or service from your company, a customer returns, shows you a receipt, and says, "I am totally dissatisfied with this and respectfully request a complete refund." What would you do?

    a) Politely insist on more information and then follow company policy.

    b) Explain that the company wishes to correct any mistakes it may have made and then work with the customer to resolve the problem.

    c) Immediately refund the customer's money and provide an additional service or product at no cost to make amends.

    d) Regard the customer suspiciously and direct him to the service manager.

11. Which metaphor best describes the way you view your company's customers? They are:

    a) Acquaintances

    b) Relatives

c) Strangers

d) Friends

12. Which term best describes how you treat your company's customers? You treat them as:

a) An interruption

b) A necessity

c) Special people

d) Royalty

To score your test, enter the number that corresponds with the letter you selected for each question. Add these numbers to get your total, then refer to the chart below. This chart indicates your company's zone of service quality (assuming your fellow employees or managers would answer similarly).

1.	_____	a = 3	b = 1	c = 2	d = 4
2.	_____	a = 4	b = 2	c = 3	d = 1
3.	_____	a = 3	b = 4	c = 2	d = 1
4.	_____	a = 2	b = 3	c = 1	d = 4
5.	_____	a = 1	b = 2	c = 4	d = 3
6.	_____	a = 1	b = 2	c = 3	d = 4
7.	_____	a = 3	b = 2	c = 4	d = 1
8.	_____	a = 2	b = 1	c = 3	d = 4
9.	_____	a = 3	b = 1	c = 2	d = 4
10.	_____	a = 2	b = 3	c = 4	d = 1
11.	_____	a = 2	b = 4	c = 1	d = 3
12.	_____	a = 1	b = 2	c = 3	d = 4
	_____	Total			

Your Score	Customer Service Zone
12 - 18	Rigid
18 - 30	Safe
30 - 42	Progressive
42 - 48	Indulgent

Your answers may put you within more than one zone of service. This isn't unusual and simply indicates your company has a blurred vision of its service. This, undoubtedly, makes your service inconsistent. Companies that are inconsistent are often in transition, hopefully in the process of improving. Regardless of the reason, inconsistency is confusing and disconcerting to customers.

The Four Zones of Service Quality

The four zones of customer service include two strategically ineffective ways of providing service, a neutral stance, and an excellent philosophy and practice. Figure 3.1 shows where these zones fall on the continuum between 100% operations-focused and 100% market-focused.

Chapters four through seven cover each of the zones in detail. Keep in mind that few companies consistently provide one level of service. Within most organizations there are departments or individuals who work differently than the company as a whole. The perceptions that customers form when they do business with you are crucial. Your company must strive to make those perceptions consistently positive.

The Zones of Service Quality

Figure 3.1: When the focus shifts from internal to external, the level of service quality increases. The ideal is to balance the needs of the customer with those of the organization. Extremes in either direction can be costly.

Chapter Four

The Rigid Zone of Service Quality

Most companies operate in the rigid zone. There is no safety in numbers, however, as lemmings discover after a brief swim. The rigid zone could also be called inferior customer service. As the poorest level of service, it is 99% operations-focused. The attitudes of companies in the rigid zone seem to be, "Here's what we're selling, take it or leave it." "This sure would be a great place to work if it weren't for the customers."

A company in the rigid zone sees service as something the customer isn't necessarily entitled to, but something the company will provide if it must. Customers' expectations are irrelevant and never enter into the company's decision-making process. Rigid service fails everyone—the customer *and* the company—by falling short of customer expectations and damaging the company's reputation.

Rigid service is often provided by employees who have not received enough training, are unhappy with their jobs, or feel resentful toward management. When employees are angry at their employers, they get even—often by taking it out on customers.

This substandard form of service is one-sided; that is, it serves the short-term needs of the company or individual employee at the expense of the customer. Long-term, it serves no one. Service is provided begrudgingly by employees who sometimes show an open disdain for customers. This can be seen in government agencies that have no competitors, such as the Department of Motor Vehicles and the postal service.

Bill: *I went into a department store during the winter to buy a scarf and pair of leather gloves. As I was selecting these items, I heard a salesman on a personal phone call behind the counter. When I was ready to pay for the items, I went to the counter where the salesman was standing. Instead of terminating his phone call to attend to me, he turned his back on me, walked to the other end of the counter, and continued talking. I was furious. I threw down the scarf and gloves and left. The next day I called the store to talk with the manager. I told her what a lousy job they had done of training that employee. Instead of apologizing, she became defensive and told me the employee might have been taking care of another customer."*

Wrong answer. Even if the clerk had been talking to a customer, that was no excuse for turning his back on another customer. Furthermore, the manager should not have been making excuses. Few things make a customer more angry than a manager who defends their employees whether they are right or not.

What should the manager have done? We all know that people make mistakes, and we're willing to forgive mistakes. So sometimes you can't judge a company by the actions of one employee. But you can judge a company by the way it handles its employees' mistakes. The way the store manager responded to Bill's complaint was narrow-minded, rigid, and totally devoid of customer-consciousness. She was dealing with an irate customer. She could have apologized and looked for ways to fix the situation. For example, she could have said, "I'm very sorry and will certainly talk with that employee. What can I do to rectify this situation? If you'd still like the scarf and gloves, as a way of saying we're sorry, I'd like to give you a bottle of cologne with your purchase."

By making amends, she would prove the incident was uncharacteristic of the company. You see, rigid zone service is not always company-wide. There can be individual employees or even entire departments serving customers differently from the rest of the company. The same can be said of all the zones of service. They may be the exception rather than the rule. That's why a company must pay attention to its service quality and strive for consistency.

> Emil: *I have been leasing Volvos for the last five years. The lease company once sent me a mailgram notifying me I was in default on my lease agreement. The mailgram, in very strong language, threatened to take my car if, within seven days, I didn't prove I had insured it. The letter said I must call them and I must not operate the vehicle. The letter said they didn't want my insurance agent to call them—I had to call. So I called my insurance agent and asked him what was going on. He said he'd contacted Volvo three times in the last six months and given them the information they wanted. Then I called Volvo in New Jersey and complained. The Volvo representative said their West Coast office (that handles insurance) doesn't do a good job of communicating with the New Jersey office (that handles leasing and threatening mailgrams). I was annoyed, to say the least. They had made their problem mine.*

This is a good example of an otherwise excellent company with one division operating in the rigid zone. Here was an international automobile company that succeeded in creating high expectations. They made an excellent car and even paid your transportation costs in the event of a breakdown far from home. Unfortunately, they could not communicate internally and, as a result, harassed and victimized their customers.

Customers sometimes tolerate rigid zone treatment in a business with a unique product or service. A restaurant that's *the* hot spot in town can briefly get away with rigid service. But it will slowly alienate its customers, and they will soon move on to the next hot spot where the service, ambiance, and food are better.

Rigid service creates nothing but bad will. The usual reaction is outrage and a determination never to do business with the company again. As we all know, most people also go a step further and tell their friends about their negative experiences. In the case of writers, professional speakers, and consultants, they tell tens of thousands of people about their disappointing experiences—through books and speeches. Phil has used his profession as a leveraging tool. When he encounters someone handling a service problem poorly, he says, "You might be interested in knowing that I'm a professional speaker. And my specialty is customer service. Now I've already decided to use this incident as an example in my speeches. The only question that remains is whether I'll use it as a good or a bad one."

Expectations play a large part in creating perceptions of service. A certain hotel in Dallas makes a magnificent physical impression. Gasps can be heard as first-time guests enter the lobby. Back in 1987, however, this hotel was failing its guests in terms of quality service. Imagine this scenario:

You've checked into this palatial, first-class hotel that's costing you $175 per night. Around midnight you pick up the room service menu and find only three choices: a chef's salad, a tuna fish sandwich, and a hot dog. You order the hot dog. The waiter arrives and gives you a cafeteria-style, plastic tray with a plate in the middle. On the plate is a hot dog wrapped in Saran Wrap, one pickle, and a mini-bag of generic potato chips. Alongside the plate is a pile of packaged condiments. To top it off, the entire tray is wrapped in Saran Wrap. Before the waiter leaves, he mentions that you can leave the tray outside the door when you're finished. He doesn't even offer to unwrap the tray for you.

Now this may be acceptable service in a motel that charges $37.50 per night, but it's an insult in a luxury hotel. Service like this loses more than it saves. The little extra it would cost the hotel to offer a decent room service menu and present the food in a more appetizing way could make the difference between a guest coming back or going elsewhere.

Rigid service is often delivered when the company does not trust its customers. We all know of stores where no refunds or exchanges will be granted without a sales receipt. In effect, their policy says, "We've been cheated before and anticipate being cheated again, so we're not going to trust anyone, including you."

Values In the Rigid Zone

Even though all companies have ethical values, rigid zone companies are more likely to violate theirs. In fact, rigid zone companies are least likely to formulate or articulate a set of core values. Whether they are articulated or not, values are communicated daily through interactions between employees, supervisors, managers and customers.

SERVICE R$_x$:
Spend ten minutes with an employee of any company and you'll have a pretty good idea of what it's like to work for that company.

Rigid companies do not treat their employees well; in turn, employees respond by treating customers poorly. The rigid zone is such a self-centered, short-term way of thinking that unethical behavior can be just a short step away. For example, if the behavior modeled by management is, "make the sale at any cost," then sales people might lie and manipulate to make a sale. The stereotypical door-to-door salesperson is a case in point. It's interesting to note that there is more than one way to make a sale at any cost. Another way is the method used by an employee of an indulgent zone company. That will be discussed in chapter seven. For now, suffice it to say that an indulgent zone employee would make the sale at any cost by giving customers whatever they want regardless of cost.

Rigid zone companies, by definition, adhere to their strategic and operational values at all times. The attitude is, "Let's make doing business easy for us. If a customer doesn't like it, too bad. There are more where they came from." Customers are regarded as commodities.

The inflexibility is company-wide. Even the people who can make exceptions to the philosophical/strategic values—managers and owners—are narrow-minded and won't or don't bend the rules to accommodate a customer. Similarly, operational values are inflexible. A good example is a bank which requires a holding period before cashing or giving credit for an out-of-state check. Most banks will make an exception to this operational value for a long-time customer. A bank in the rigid zone, however, will inflexibly stick to its rules, like a robot programmed with only one response—"I'm sorry, I can't do that . . . it's company policy."

SERVICE R_x:
Never, ever, invoke company policy as a reason for doing or not doing something for a customer. Always give customers what they deserve—an explanation.

We've all seen clerks in stores who derived great pleasure from enforcing the rules, even if it meant depriving a customer of a reasonable request. It's amazing to see such inflexibility. It is also astonishing to see an employee who is forced to give a customer what they want and then gets angry because the customer got it.

" . . . because it's company policy!"

Treatment of People

Rigid zone thinking is best summed up in the attitude, "I don't give a damn." Rigid companies don't care about their customers. They don't care about their employees. Just as customers are regarded as commodities, employees are regarded as expendable tools. When an employee has a problem, termination—rather than training, coaching, or counseling—is the automatic solution. Management's attitude is that one employee is as good as another, so it's easier to hire another warm body than to invest time and money in further training. We know of a company that fired the least productive warehouse employee each month, regardless of his absolute level of performance. That was the company's way of setting an example and keeping everyone off balance.

This "warm body syndrome," in which virtually anyone will suffice, creates an environment where turnover is high. Everyone lacks commitment and the last thing on their minds is the customer. To make matters worse, management sees employees as obstacles to the completion of their paper work. In their minds, life would be far easier if the people they supervised didn't need so much attention.

A second "warm body syndrome" is philosophically different than hiring just anyone, but the outcome is the same. Some companies strive to hire good people, but they have a warm body approach to replacing employees. Here's the situation. You've got six well-paid, high quality employees. You come into work one day to discover that one of them has quit. Your goal for the day is to quickly replace that person, so you do so with a warm body. Six months later the same thing happens. Again, your replacement is a warm body. If this pattern continues, you will replace your entire staff with people from the warm body pool rather than people from the high quality pool.

The better approach is to avoid rushing to hire a warm body. Research has shown that, for a short time, other workers will pitch in and work harder to make up for the loss of a team member. In fact, the new, smaller team will be more productive than they were before losing a member. But their new enthusiasm and productivity will last for only a short time. That's the time you use to recruit the right person.

In every company, employees imitate the behaviors they observe. When the internal attitude is adversarial rather than cooperative, employees treat customers the same way. The cause for this may be the mirror effect ("This is the way we treat people around here,") or it could be an angry reaction ("If they're going to treat me poorly, I'll take it out on their customers.")

SERVICE R_X:
You get what you give. Managers have to treat their employees with respect if they want customers to be treated with respect.

Rigid zone companies treat everyone the same. If they were to give preferential treatment, it would only be to their most important customers. Most of the time, however, it doesn't matter to them if you are a million-dollar-a-year customer or a noncustomer who came in to ask for change for a dollar.

In chapters nine and ten we will discuss the most important customers a company has—demanding ones and complaining ones. Both groups create situations that test the mettle of a company's commitment to quality service. Those tests play an important role in forming a company's reputation. In the rigid zone, the indifferent response to complaining customers is, "So what?" or "Big deal!" To demanding customers, the attitude is, "What you see is what you get." One of the most common examples of an inflexible attitude toward customer requests is a store's policy of "No receipt, no refund." The attitude this policy conveys is, "If you don't have a receipt, we don't believe you bought it here."

Management Style

Rigid companies are perfect examples of short-term thinking that focuses only on profits. Their owners, presidents, and CEOs lack an understanding of the realities of the marketplace and rarely have a vision of corporate growth, longevity, or positioning.

Management is as rigid with employees as employees are with customers. Employees are rewarded for conforming to policies and procedures, not for taking risks in the ongoing process of acquiring and maintaining customers. Take a bank, for example. Imagine two new accounts people. One is meticulous about paperwork and is an operations manager's dream. The other is a whiz at opening new accounts, cross-selling and maintaining customers, but is less disciplined in terms of paperwork. Which customer service employee do you think will be promoted? Typically, the bureaucrat.

There is little freedom and authority given to employees. Decisions of any significance must be approved by higher-ups, slowing the process and making any delivery of quality service more unlikely or untimely. To further exacerbate the problem, managers are isolated and out of touch with front-line people. You could call it "Managing by Memo."

> Phil: *I once did some consulting for a business that had a supervisor who managed by memo. There was a large office and the supervisor's desk was on one side. In front of her, fanned out in a semi-circle, were ten office workers at their desks. When the supervisor wanted to disseminate some information, she wrote a memo, took it to her secretary, had the secretary type it up and make copies to be given to the secretaries. It was absurd! Her people were only six feet away!*

Impersonal management is often due to a lack of trust between managers and employees, and from that lack of trust comes detachment. For example, one company refused to train its employees because it would make the employees too attractive to the competition.

From management's point of view, employees are expected to stay only a short time, so there's little incentive to invest in extensive training. Without training, managers don't believe employees can be trusted to think for themselves, much less make important decisions. It's a Catch-22.

Marketing/Sales Focus

Just as all current customers are treated the same, all prospective customers are treated identically. This doesn't mean they're treated poorly; it simply means they are treated well only if they want exactly what the company is selling at the exact price it's being offered. No flexibility, customization, or extra service is ever offered. No value is added to the sale. What you see is what you get. If price is a customer's sole buying criterion, he may not be alienated by a company in the rigid zone. If a customer expects more, however, he'd better take his business elsewhere.

The sales and marketing attitude of a rigid zone company is "We're the only game in town. We've got the product . . . now let the world beat a path to our door."

SERVICE R$_x$:
The minute you start acting like a monopoly, you're guaranteeing that you won't be one in the future.

This is a technical orientation, one that can only lead to trouble. As we mentioned in chapter one, technology plays no favorites. Technological advantages are usually short-lived. If you have an advantage and treat customers poorly, they'll abandon you as soon as a competitor comes on the scene.

Differentiation

The only way a rigid zone company can differentiate itself is by virtue of a product or service that's high in demand and low in supply. Nowadays, this differentiation can only be a function of technology. Look at the cable TV industry. They're very much rigid zone companies—and their customers are looking forward to the day when there's an alternative. In fact, some people predict that home satellite reception is going to knock the wind out of the cable TV industry.

Company policies and procedures evolve, just like a company's level of service. The rigid zone is the beginning of the evolution and, as such, is a primitive state for a company.

Chapter Five

The Safe Zone of Service Quality

Safe zone service is one step above the rigid zone in that the company acknowledges its customers deserve *some* level of service. That level, however, is the mediocre, run-of-the-mill service that merely meets customers' expectations, but never exceeds them. Safe zone companies provide just enough service to get by.

Smile training is typical of safe service. Smile! You're in Customer Service! Put on a happy face! You've probably heard them before—training programs that focus on smiles rather than improved service, as if smiling would make it okay to say, "I can't do that; it's against company policy." Again, smiles are the form, not the substance, of service.

Smile training is about as effective as painting over rust. It never lasts. Safe service remains risk-free, courteous, and perfunctory. Everyone gets the same treatment, regardless of individual needs. The amount of goodwill created is proportional to the originality of the service—very little.

Like the rigid zone, safe zone service remains within clearly defined parameters and only fixes something when it's broken. In the same way a mechanic repairs your car, safe service handles your problems—with no foresight or preventive maintenance. Nothing extra is volunteered; no added value is offered. In fact, customers' expectations are often *lowered* so the company can more easily live up to them.

"Damn it, Ms. Jones, smile, you're in customer service!"

Safe service usually lacks a sound plan to improve service. It's actually a plan to *maintain* service.

Safe service falls toward the middle of the continuum in figure 3.1. It is mostly operations-focused, with a little market-focused awareness thrown in. Employees believe customers are entitled to service, but management gets in the way by insisting that company policies be followed to the letter. Employees are given no freedom to bend the rules. Safe service ranges from providing the basics with civility to listening attentively to customer complaints. This level of service gets the job done, but it provides customers with nothing more or less than they paid for.

Safe service, which is mediocre at best, often reflects the limited commitment the company made when it decided to jump on the customer service bandwagon. The majority of businesses still don't see quality customer service as an investment that should be taken as seriously as research and development, advertising, and sales. Companies in the safe zone are often trying to change their images and service standards solely through advertising. Unfortunately, few companies fully grasp what is involved in the transformation. The outcome is usually a rewrite of the company policy manual with no real service vision. The company remains operations-focused.

Compare these two levels of service: Imagine you are a guest in a hotel that has electronic room keys. You go up to your room and the key doesn't work. So you return to the front desk and the clerk hands you another key and tells you to come back if that one doesn't work. How would you feel?

There's nothing overtly wrong with this service per se, but there's nothing special about it. It's the thoughtless, unmemorable service most of us have learned to accept, unless we've experienced better service elsewhere.

Now imagine a better response to your key problem. The desk clerk dispatches a bellman to accompany you to your room to make sure the new key works. How would that kind of service make you feel? You'd be impressed by this level of service, which would seem above the call of duty—and worth talking about.

Phil: *I had an amusing experience at one of our ubiquitous fast food restaurants. I asked the clerk for a root beer float. He stopped dead in his tracks and said, "A what?" "A root beer float." He said they didn't have root beer floats. I told him, "You have root beer and you serve vanilla ice cream. Put the two together and you have a root beer float." He comprehended that much, but what really tripped him up was the cash register. It didn't have a root beer float button. He didn't know how he should charge me for it. Finally, when I saw that I was causing him so much stress, I made it easy for him. I ordered the root*

beer and ice cream separately and combined them at my table.
That made the clerk happy.

Values of Safe Zone Organizations

Safe zone companies, unlike rigid zone companies, are more likely
to live up to their ethical values. These companies are ethical, but not
very creative.

Philosophical/strategic and operational values in a safe company are
sacred and strictly enforced. The difference between the inflexibility of
the safe zone and the inflexibility of the rigid zone is that the safe
company is polite about it. Employees are more likely to be apologetic
and claim their hands are tied by management. In the rigid zone,
employees don't even realize an apology is appropriate. Of course,
courtesy doesn't reduce the anger of a sophisticated, demanding
customer, but it does smooth the feathers of a customer with lower
expectations.

Treatment of People

In a safe company, employees are treated with more respect than in
a rigid company, but management is still exerting control over everyone.
There is very little catering to individual needs. The archaic industrial
age mentality of employees as expendable tools prevails.

The company policy manual is a bible and to deviate is a sin. The
same attitude—that policies are sacrosanct—is held by front-line
employees dealing with customers. Courteous inflexibility is the
operating principle in the safe zone.

Businesses operate in the safe zone either when they think they don't
have to worry about competitors or when they're only trying to give the
appearance of catering to customers. Safe zone thinking takes a
defensive business posture. It's analogous to a coach telling his team,
"Let's play to avoid losing" rather than "Let's play to win." Imagine an
NBA coach saying, "Our strategy for winning is to keep the other team
from scoring. If we can hold them to 100 points or less and score our
usual 110 points, we'll win."

In business, instead of asking, "how do we do it better than our
competitors?" a safe zone manager might ask, "how can we do it *as
well as* our competitors?"

The safe zone attitude toward complaining or demanding customers
is, "Gee, I'm sorry, but there's nothing we can do about it." You've
heard all the cliches: "I can't do that. It would be against company

policy;" "If I do it for you, I'll have to do it for everyone," and so on. One of the differences between rigid service and safe service is that employees of safe companies are trained to listen to customers. It is the type of listening, however, in which they wait until the customer's lips stop moving before giving a response. That response, by the way, is the same for everyone, regardless of what the customer says.

Safe zone employees are not given the decision-making authority to resolve unusual problems on their own. When a customer pushes them to deviate from the company's standard operating procedure, it may take an inordinate amount of time to track down the rare person who can approve such an aberrant request. That authority lies with someone in the company, but they will be several levels up.

Management Style

Remember, the way employees treat customers is a reflection of how management treats employees. Safe zone companies treat their employees "by the book." They are as policy minded as managers in rigid zone companies. Safe companies are unlikely to sponsor such flexible programs as share-time, flex-time and other creative working arrangements.

Safe zone companies are generally structured as the traditional pyramid, with orders being barked from the top. Everyone works for someone directly above them, with only occasional thought given to the role of the customer.

The mind-set of managers in the safe zone is control. They see their jobs as ring leaders who crack the whip and make sure their employees adhere to the rules. There is little, if any, trust or creative license.

Marketing/Sales Focus

The attitude of companies in the safe zone is "Let's develop a product or service and find people who want to buy it." It's a "me first" attitude shaped by a myopic, internal focus rather than a "customer first," external focus.

Safe zone companies often take one of two approaches to business. They either sell an exclusive product or service or they sell a commodity. If they sell an exclusive product, they're convinced customers need them. If they sell a commodity, then they compete on price. Being price-focused, they figure they can always lower their prices to attract more customers. Few safe companies have any quality service consciousness at all. If they do, it is generally limited to the strategy of advertising their service rather than actually providing it. In fact, sales and service lack a team approach and may even be in conflict.

Differentiation

Companies in the safe zone can only differentiate themselves in terms of location, pricing, product or technology. Like rigid zone companies, those in the safe zone do not stand out in terms of service quality, so they must be competitive on other levels. Operating in the safe zone is neither a prescription for failure—as is rigid zone service—nor is it a secure modus operandi for success. Firms in the safe zone risk losing marketshare to competitors who provide better service.

A business can remain in the safe zone only as long as customers' expectations remain low or until a competitor comes along who provides quality service, a better product or a lower price. As soon as one variable changes, a safe company will lose marketshare quickly.

With a bit of luck, a company can survive, or even thrive, in the safe zone. Take Company A—it designs and publishes computer software. Customers buy its programs in stores, take them home and the programs work without a hitch. Customers have no further need for assistance from the company after the sale. Company A can afford to operate in the safe zone.

Now take Company B. It produces a more complex software program—one that requires technical support after the sale. Company B can also survive in the safe zone. For example, it might give mediocre service when people call its tech support number. Six months after Company B's program hits the market, however, Company C develops a similar program and begins to differentiate itself with excellent service. Company B will soon lose marketshare if it doesn't improve its service.

This gets back to our discussion of supply and demand. As long as you have an exclusive on the supply, you can get away with operating in the safe zone (or even the rigid zone). As soon as your exclusive disappears—and it will—you must compete on other levels, namely, quality service.

That's where the progressive zone company excels.

Chapter Six

The Progressive Zone of Service Quality

This is the level of service to which you and your company should aspire. Progressive zone service reflects an enlightened corporate vision and an understanding of how to provide exemplary customer service. It's the level of service that will truly differentiate your company from your competition.

To implement progressive customer service, a well-coordinated effort is required. You must commit your company to a long-term journey which, in effect, never ends. Additionally, you must have a vision of your destination, chart your course, and manage the journey. All this requires commitment, training, and teamwork at every level.

Progressive customer service is a market-focused philosophy (see figure 3.1) that makes the customer an obsession. That obsession, however, is a healthy one because the well-being of the company is also taken into account. The goal of progressive customer service is to delight customers by *managing their expectations* and then providing service that *meets and exceeds* those expectations.

Progressive customer service is rendered thoughtfully. Customers get what they want, not what the company wants them to have. It provides an immediate benefit to the customer, with short *and* long-term payoffs for the company. The amount of goodwill generated is tremendous and often has the effect of "golden handcuffs." That is, customers develop a sense of loyalty and feel cheerfully compelled to do business with you.

Service in the progressive zone is delivered with *sensible flexibility*. Employees are given a great deal of freedom and authority to use their judgement and problem-solving abilities. They're encouraged to go beyond the routine and stretch the normal operational parameters of their training. They are guided to do so, however, in a manner that doesn't cause the company unreasonable costs or risks.

SERVICE R$_X$:
In a progressive company, policies are flexible guide-lines, not hard-and-fast rules.

Herein lies the potential downside of the progressive zone. There is some risk in bestowing decision-making power on employees. Mistakes become a real possibility. It is necessary, therefore, to hire the right people, train them well, give them coaching, and reward performance so they won't misunderstand or misuse their power.

Bill: *I was vacationing in a mountain cabin and made an operator-assisted long distance phone call. The AT&T operator came on the line and said, "I'd be happy to put this call through, sir, but do you realize it is the most expensive call we offer? You can place this call more inexpensively by dialing direct." Of course, the operator didn't realize the cabin had a rotary phone, which precluded the option of dialing direct. I really appreciated, though, the fact that she cared enough to try to educate me. It made a lasting impression.*

Implicit in the AT&T example is the fact that the operator was thinking of her customer first and apparently putting AT&T second— as it should be. The cost means more to the customer than it does to AT&T. Looking at the bigger picture, however, the goodwill she created was worth far more than the difference in the rates of the two calls. AT&T's investment in a truly customer-oriented philosophy paid off. Now Bill not only uses AT&T for his long distance service, he also uses this example in his training seminars, so thousands of people each year hear the AT&T story.

Progressive customer service makes money in the long run. By keeping customers loyal, companies like Nordstrom and L.L. Bean have advertising costs that are half the averages for their industries. Word of mouth does the rest. So while other companies are struggling to maintain marketshares by chasing new customers to replace the ones they've lost, progressive companies are building their marketshares.

Destroy What You Create

One of your biggest customers walks into your office one day and sits down. He requests a new service—one that isn't unreasonable or expensive. What would you do? If you were smart, you would seize this opportunity to make him happy and build loyalty.

What does it mean when a customer comes to you with a unique request? Does it mean he has a creative imagination? It could be, but more likely it means he has experienced that level of service somewhere else and is now asking you to do the same. Your choice is simple— either give him what he wants or lose this customer to a competitor.

In progressive service, one means for staying ahead of the competition is through *creative destruction*. When you raise your customers' expectations by providing progressively higher levels of service, they will become dissatisfied with your competitors. With each successive step, you outdo yourself, create new quality service standards, and destroy the old ones. By the time your competitors catch up and meet the standards you set yesterday, you've already destroyed those and set new ones.

The key to creative destruction is never to rest on your laurels. If you do, the competition will not only catch up and meet your standards, they'll become more creative and surpass them. This means change is a constant in the delivery of progressive customer service. It is far better, however, to be the one creating the new quality service standards than to be forever playing catch-up.

SERVICE R$_x$:
In the race for quality service, there is no finish line.

With progressive customer service, it's not enough simply to comply with customers' special requests. You have to anticipate their needs and give them extra service *before they ask*. By doing so, you surprise and please them.

SERVICE R$_x$:
The difference between a good service company and a *great* service company is the great company *anticipates* its customers' needs.

SERVICE R$_x$:
Be innovative. Strive to set new standards of quality service in your industry.

Creative destruction has a golden handcuffs effect because it helps you spoil your customers. We like to think of it as creating demanding customers. The key is to introduce them to a level of quality service that they don't find elsewhere. And they notice!

SERVICE R$_x$:
Cater to your customers to the extent that they become so demanding that you are the only company willing to meet their needs.

Progressive customer service creates demanding customers and complaining ones. It manages expectations and exceeds them. By staying closely in touch with your customers and incorporating their feedback into your procedures, you will learn to give people exactly what they want . . . and more.

Progressive customer service is the way of the future. As the word progressive implies, it is an ever-changing form of service that picks up momentum and improves over time. *If* you operate in the progressive zone, your service will stay one step ahead as the standards of quality service in your industry change.

Values of Progressive Zone Organizations

Progressive service is possible only in a company that has made a 100% commitment to it. The first step is for the leadership of the company to examine their principles and decide what is important to them. They have to develop and articulate a set of ethical, philosophical/strategic, and operational values that results in a corporate culture reflecting those lofty ideals. Honesty, mutual respect, and maintaining people's dignity are basic ethical values held by enlightened companies. They make working for those companies, and being a customer, a rewarding experience.

A progressive company remains true to its philosophical/strategic values. There is, however, the possibility of flexibility. In rigid and safe companies, employees won't even go to management to see if a policy can be stretched or broken. In a progressive company, employees are more willing to go to bat for a customer who wants to break a philosophical value. Remember, philosophical values *can* be broken, but only by those who created them—top management.

Take the example of automobile repair facilities. Most of them have insurance rules that prohibit customers from standing around the work area of the garage. Let's say a highly valued customer—the owner of a fleet of taxicabs—sent an employee into the garage one day with his personal car, a new Porsche 928. Part of the employee's job is to make sure the car is being repaired correctly. So he asks the mechanic if he can stand around and watch. A mechanic in a rigid or safe company would refuse and cite company policy: A rule is a rule. A mechanic in a progressive company, however, would go to the owner and ask if an exception could be made. Considering the stature of the customer, the owner would probably take the insurance risk and break this philosophical value.

Operational values in a progressive company are flexible guidelines. Rules, procedures, and policies are not rigidly enforced, nor are they flagrantly broken. The key here is sensible flexibility. Employees have the authority to bend, stretch, reshape, or break the rules to accommodate their customers within reasonable parameters. This is what Burger King meant in their advertising campaign "Sometimes you gotta break the rules." Unfortunately, the marketplace had no idea what they meant. Burger King would have been better off saying, "We're going to give you exactly what you want, even if it means breaking the rules."

Treatment of People

Progressive customer service doesn't just happen. It reflects a company-wide culture in which the number one value is *people*—internally and externally. Everyone treats everyone with respect. The phrase sensible flexibility does not apply just to the enforcement of rules, it applies to the treatment of people as well. People are treated the way rational, mature people should treat other rational, mature people. Each situation is assessed on its own merits, so management is fair and reasonable. When standard operating procedures fail to offer a solution, creative problem-solving is used. In a progressive company, employees are trained to be self-managing and, in turn, take responsibility for being so. When mistakes occur, the mistakes are kept in perspective. After all, management is held accountable for the overall batting average, not each individual appearance at the plate. That same attitude is passed on to employees. An air of fairness pervades the working environment.

One of the values of the progressive corporate culture is optimum cooperation, treating each other (including people in other departments) as if they were customers. Each person realizes they are working for the same purpose—the acquisition and maintenance of customers. So each one is given the support they need.

It's easy for prospective customers to build a working relationship with a progressive company. Sales people and others involved in generating new business are open-minded and willing to go to great lengths to accommodate special needs. The progressive way of selling is to discover the needs of the prospect and put together packages to meet those needs. Progressive companies never promise more than they can deliver. The key is managing expectations.

When you buy goods or services from a progressive company, you have confidence that it is reliable, responsive, and committed to your business relationship.

Progressive firms treat their routine customers like members of the family. On a daily basis, they exemplify a level of service which generally costs nothing, but easily exceeds customers' expectations. This means employees are sincere, courteous, respectful, thoughtful, and pleasant. Excellent service is often as easy as being attentive and anticipating needs.

One of the basic principles of progressive customer service is the way the company views and handles its most important customers—complaining and demanding ones. Both groups are encouraged and welcomed. Feedback from complainers shows a company where its service is falling short of expectations and how it should be improved. Demanding customers show how to take service from just meeting expectations to the higher level of exceeding them. Both types of customers provide opportunities to build relationships and create loyalty.

Progressive companies give their front-line employees the authority to make decisions on the spot. By pushing the decision-making process down to the front lines, they allow employees to please customers without time-consuming searches for approval. If a situation arises that is too far out of their operational parameters, employees know how to turn the decision over quickly to someone who has more training or experience. Expediency is the name of the game.

Management Style

The management structure of the progressive company of the near future will be transformed from the traditional pyramid to a flattened model. Self-managed teams, cross-trained personnel, managers as coaches, and decision-making participation are some of the many features of the new high performance organization. These will be discussed in chapter thirteen, Creating the Vision-driven and Values-guided Organization.

Two of the most important values in a progressive company are trust and commitment. These values are at the very heart of providing quality service. Without them, an effective, company-wide service philosophy cannot exist.

Trust starts at the top. In a progressive company, top management has adopted a quality service philosophy. They have started the wheels of implementation turning, believing this will pay off in the near and distant future. Commitment to a quality service philosophy is long-term and full-time. It is championed by middle management, supervisors, and everyone else in the company, with no exceptions. Everyone's job is to understand, support, and exemplify the company's operational and philosophical values.

The Excuse"less" Culture

The second aspect of the trust cycle is faith in the company's employees. Since front-line people are the ambassadors of the company, they should receive the same high level of training, coaching, counseling, (and pay!) as everyone else. Once that is accomplished, employees are given the responsibility, authority, flexibility, freedom, and trust to use their discretion in making important decisions. It is essential to push as many decisions as far "down" as possible; that is, decisions should be made by those closest to the people affected by them. This could mean more decision-making authority for assembly line workers, customer service reps, and salespeople, among others.

It is absolutely essential that managers not only get out of employees' ways, but also make it easy for them to do the jobs they were hired and trained to do. When mistakes are made—and they are inevitable—don't regard them as breaches of trust. They are simply honest mistakes. When one aspect of a new program doesn't work the first time, it doesn't mean the program is a failure. It means it's time to evaluate the effort and fine-tune the implementation. No program works perfectly the first time through. Eliminating bugs takes trial and effort. The management of organizational change is an art, not a science. And even science recognizes the value of trial, error, and serendipity.

Most managers and supervisors give their employees a short leash. There's little trust—employees are considered incompetent until proven otherwise. Employees who are afraid of their supervisors because they're too closely watched have a built-in excuse for not providing quality service. They blame the manager or supervisor: "My supervisor may be watching me, I better not stretch the rules."

SERVICE R$_x$:
Managers teach their employees to give poor service by watching them too closely and failing to convey trust. Instead, provide training, trust your people, and give them the freedom and authority to make decisions and take risks without the fear of punishment for mistakes.

SERVICE R$_x$:
It is a manager's job to eliminate all excuses for poor service or poor job performance. Create an excuse"less" culture.

Being a manager is not unlike being a parent; the same principles apply to both.

Phil: *There was a time when, every morning and every night, my wife would ask our daughter, "Have you brushed your teeth yet?" We got the same answer every time—"I was just about to do that." I told my wife to stop asking the question. Instead, we made it clear to our daughter that it was her responsibility to brush her teeth. If, when we occasionally checked up on her, she hadn't brushed, there was some form of punishment. If she had brushed, there was a reward. By establishing positive and negative consequences, she was responsible and accountable for her behavior.*

Phil once met with a group of advertising sales representatives from the *Washington Post*. During the conversation, the salespeople complained that they were unable to spend more time in the field. Further discussion revealed that whenever they sold an ad, they had to walk it through the production department to make sure no mistakes were made. This constant babysitting had conditioned the production department to take a nonchalant attitude toward their work. After all, the sales reps were accepting responsibility for the ads.

This is a typical problem in American business. We over-manage people and condition them to not take responsibility for their work. A general supervisor in one of our client companies used to receive an average of 22 calls a day from his boss!

The way to create an excuseless culture is to hire the right people, train them well, give them responsibility, and make them accountable. Then let them do the jobs they were hired to do.

SERVICE R$_x$:
If *you* take responsibility for other people, they'll never take it for themselves.

Managers have to trust their people implicitly. At the same time, employees must realize that the consequences for breaching that trust can be severe. What the company is saying, in effect, is, "We're going to give you more freedom and authority than you've ever had. We trust you will not abuse it. If you breach that trust, there will be serious consequences."

SERVICE R$_x$:
People thrive on responsibility. Give it to them.

The third participant in the trust cycle is the customer. Progressive companies believe their customers' complaints and demands are opportunities for improvement. As such, customer feedback is solicited and heeded in an ongoing effort to raise the company's service standards—the practice of creative destruction. The trust loop is made whole when customer feedback has a direct impact on corporate philosophies, decision-making, and the design of policies, procedures, products, and services.

Marketing/Sales Focus

The attitude of companies in the progressive zone is, "We've combined our resources with the needs of the marketplace to meet or exceed our customers' expectations." It's the type of service quality that addresses a customer's specific needs. At the same time, at this level of service it may be appropriate to charge for certain services. In chapter eight we will discuss selling with service as a way to get paid for giving customers those extras.

In chapter four we referred to a restaurant in the rigid zone and said its attitude would be "If it's not on the menu, we ain't got it." By contrast, the attitude conveyed by a progressive restaurant would be, "If you can describe it, we can make it." Take Max's Deli in San Francisco. They have 20 rules their customers must abide by, but their rules are for the benefit of customers, not employees.

Differentiation

Everything we've discussed so far answers the question, "How does a progressive company differentiate itself?" In a word: quality service. In three words—*Responsive, Reliable,* and dedicated to the *Relationship.* All of these are illustrated by the following story of some young entrepreneurs with a lot of business savvy.

PDH Computers is a small sales, service, support, and training firm in San Diego, California. They specialize in computer systems for legal firms and other professional offices that need somewhat larger networks. A few years ago, one of their clients, a law firm, had a problem with a hard disk. Evidently a tremendous amount of important data had become

MAX'S LAWS

1. This restaurant is run for the enjoyment and pleasure of our customers, not the convenience of the staff or the owners.
2. You get a free round of drinks if anyone on our staff comes up and says, "Is everything all right?" When we ask questions, they'll be helpful ones.
3. You must get your mustard and ketchup before your burger, sandwich or fries.
4. We hate soggy fries. If yours aren't crisp, the way you like them—send them back—maybe the kitchen will get the message.
5. Corned beef and pastrami are good because they contain some fat. If you want something lean, how about our turkey?
6. Our turkey is always fresh. Period.
7. Our iced tea is table brewed. Just pour it over a big glass of ice.
8. Soft drinks come in bottles or cans. No bar guns here.
9. San Francisco bakers don't bake on Wednesday and Sunday. Our breads are fresh all other days. The pastry we make is fresh every day.
10. Our ice cream sauces are a point of pride. They're made in New York by a certified chocoholic who refuses therapy. They are simply the best in the country. And we don't boast idly.
11. We use only Kozlowski's jams—what else!
12. We bring pastrami and ice cream sauces from New York City, mustards from Oregon, hot sauce from Jersey. Eat here. Save the airfare.
13. This is a bad place for a diet and a good place for a diet.
14. Our desserts are excessive because nothing succeeds like excess. We encourage sharing if you're not super hungry.
15. Substitutions are okay by us, don't be bashful, you've got a mouth, use it.
16. We cook hamburgers 2 ways: medium rare or well done; anything else is at your own risk!
17. Please do not take the menus, they will cost you $10 cash (we've got miniatures for free).
18. We reserve the right to refuse service to anyone using the word, "nouvelle."
19. We use cholesterol free oil for frying and sauteing. Eat your heart out, Mr. Surgeon General.
20. Our to-go containers are Serco-Foam products and contain no CFCs, thus they will not harm the environment.

WHO IS MAX? Max is my father. If he were alive today he'd probably love our corned beef and maybe he'd be proud of his boy for running restaurants the best he knows how.

Max's Diner: San Francisco, San Ramon
Max's Opera Cafe: San Francisco, Walnut Creek, Burlingame, Palo Alto
Sweet Max's: San Francisco
Silver Max . . . The Eating Express: San Jose
Max's Deli: San Francisco
Cafe Tomatoes: San Francisco

Everything you always wanted to eat

Max's Laws are worded to encourage customers to be demanding.

scrambled and there was a good chance of losing it. Unfortunately, the only company with the technical ability to recover the lost data was the one that manufactured the hard drive. That company was located in

New Jersey. The law firm needed the data in a couple of days to do its billing. To make matters worse, the hard drive could not be shipped without risking further damage.

Harry Pfeffer, one of the three brothers who owns PDH, bought two plane tickets—one for himself and one for the defective unit—and flew back to New Jersey. The company recovered the scrambled data and fixed the hard drive and Harry returned to San Diego as a hero.

Was it worth the time, money, and effort for PDH or was Harry's trip really an example of indulgent customer service? You be the judge. The law firm's initial purchase was a computer system in the $100,000 range. There is no doubt that PDH lost money on their service contract for the first year, but during the next two years that firm upgraded its system to the tune of $600,000. Not a bad return for a couple of plane tickets! As you can imagine, the law firm was thrilled, so, undoubtedly, they told a lot of people about PDH. In the long run, PDH made out quite well.

What effect will progressive customer service have on your company's growth? There are no hard and fast formulas, but research by the Strategic Planning Group has shown that market-focused companies outperform operations-focused companies by at least ten to one.

	Market-Focused	**Operations-Focused**
Average Annual Growth	10%	0%
Average Annual Profit	12%	1%

The evidence is irrefutable that progressive customer service works. It is the most cost-effective way to differentiate your company and to generate profits significantly higher than the industry average.

The question remains, "How do you implement a progressive service program?" That question will be answered in the chapters to come, when we discuss all the necessary elements: creating complaining customers, creating demanding customers, selling with service, managing the market-focused organization, and controlling moments of truth, magic, and misery.

Progressive customer service is not an easy answer that can be implemented overnight. But it's the only answer to being competitive in the years approaching 2000 and beyond.

Chapter Seven

The Indulgent Zone of Service Quality

Progressive customer service taken to the extreme can become indulgent and irresponsible. Indulgent customer service caters solely to the customer's needs without regard for the company's financial well-being. In figure 3.1, you can see that indulgent service is 99.9% market-focused. It exceeds reasonable expectations of quality service and places a financial burden on the company.

The attitude of a company in the indulgent zone is not unlike the attitude in the progressive zone: "Let's give our customers what they want." In the indulgent zone, however, there is no consideration given to the company's needs in the transaction. So the customer is not only getting more than expected, but also not being charged for it.

Indulgent customer service stems from a corporate vision that seeks to improve service, but lacks a sound plan for doing so. It is exceptional service delivered by the seat of the pants. The sole consideration is the customer's happiness. The expectations created in the marketplace are so inflated they cannot be met, so employees try to compensate by overindulging customers. There is a short-term benefit to the indulgent zone company in the form of goodwill, but significant, long-term, financial harm is inevitable.

Indulgent service is provided by employees who are out of control. The reason may be that management is decentralized and out of touch. Another reason may be the company is in a start-up mode. This happens when a new company lacks a clear understanding of its market niche and what it needs to do to attract and keep customers. Instead of figuring out what to do to please customers, it is constantly trying to "win" customers.

Indulgent service can also be found in well-established companies that are losing marketshare. To compensate and win back customers, they give away the farm. Marketshare increases, but at a loss or with decreased profit margins.

The indulgent zone of service is a level of generosity that is difficult, if not impossible, to maintain. At some point, customers have to be weaned from this extravagant service. When that happens, they become disappointed and take their business elsewhere. The worst thing you can do as a new company is to jump out and try to be something you can't be in the long run.

Imagine a new beauty salon located on Rodeo Drive in Beverly Hills. A novel marketing idea would be to offer to pick clients up at their homes. To deliver this service with style, the salon would rent a Rolls Royce for a month. Now let's say at the end of the month they could no longer afford to provide this service. What have they done? They've created an expectation in the marketplace and then failed to find a way to pay for it. That would be indulgent service.

The right way to use the Rolls Royce as a promotional tool would be to make it an introductory special. Promote it as a way to show off the salon's quality services, but make sure everyone understands it's for a limited time. If used in this manner, the Rolls would be a good idea. However, if the promotion communicates a posh standard, the salon must be able to back it up with posh service.

Airphone, Inc. is a perfect example of a company that created a promotional campaign to show off its service and then fell flat because it disappointed its customers. Airphone was the first company to install cellular phones in airplanes. To make subscriptions take off, it launched a promotional campaign with a special offer. The target market was American Airline Advantage Gold frequent flyers—Phil being one of them. The offer was unlimited use of the airphones for 90 days for a flat fee of only $49.95. Furthermore, there was no extra charge for long distance calls. So you could literally call overseas for the same price as a call right beneath the plane.

As an incentive program, it was excellent. In fact, Phil and some of his associates signed up. Where Airphone failed, however, was in the delivery of service. The transmission quality was so poor that in a short time Phil and his associates were convinced they would not continue their subscriptions.

Indulgent service is not always company-wide. There may be departments or individuals within a company that operate in the indulgent zone. This being the case, it is important to differentiate between indulgent companies and indulgent behavior. Take the insurance adjuster who thinks he always has to be the nice guy. He overestimates the damage of wrecked cars solely for the benefit of the customer. There isn't a customer in the world who would object to such generous treatment. On the other hand, his supervisor would consider his altruistic behavior to be irresponsible. Despite the goodwill created, his behavior is financially and ethically dangerous.

Indulgent customer service is generally provided by employees who are either poorly trained, unhappy with their jobs, desperate to prove their worth, or anxious to improve customer service ratings. Their recklessness may or may not be conscious. In fact, at times there may be a fine line between progressive and indulgent service; hence the need for proper training and supervision. Both make this line clear to employees.

There's an old story that illustrates service in the indulgent zone.

> *A woman was flying from Los Angeles to Miami via Atlanta. She shipped her dog in a pet carrier. In Atlanta, the luggage handlers were transferring the dog from one plane to another when one of them noticed the dog was dead. They panicked. Here was this expensive dog and they figured the owner was going to have a fit. Suddenly, one of them remembered seeing a similar dog downtown at the Humane Society. So during the two hour layover they got the substitute dog and put it in the dog carrier. They took the dead dog, wrapped it up and threw it away. Later that day, when the woman arrived in Miami and got her dog carrier, she was hysterical. An airline employee came up and asked her if there was a problem. She said, "You bet there is. When this dog left Los Angeles it was dead!"*

Your first impression may be that this was progressive customer service. After all, the baggage handlers went above the call of duty to please their customer. Although they were well-intentioned, what they did was unethical. It severely upset the woman and could have gotten the airline in trouble.

Values of Indulgent Zone Organizations

Indulgent service is provided by a company that has good intentions, but no idea of how to wisely provide quality service. Core values have either been poorly conceived or have never been articulated. The lack of training and coaching creates a free-for-all in which everyone is shooting from the hip. Employees give customers virtually anything they ask for. Accountability is nonexistent, so it's easy to give away the store.

Treatment of People

Companies operating in the indulgent zone usually treat employees extremely well. They are generous, flexible, and accommodating. As a result, these companies can be great places to work—while they are in business!

Prospects, customers, complaining and demanding customers are all treated like royalty. They get whatever they want whenever they want it.

Management Style

Indulgent companies lack all the controls and guidelines that help healthy companies survive. Starting at the top, these companies either lack a vision or possess a misguided one. Without a vision and set of core values, they also lack behavioral guidelines. This free-for-all operational environment is made possible by loose supervision and a lack of financial controls. We could go on and on, but you get the point. It's beginning to sound like a company run by the Marx Brothers or the Three Stooges.

Marketing/Sales Focus

Like the progressive zone, the marketing and sales attitude of the indulgent zone is, "Let's find out what the marketplace wants and give it to them." Indulgent companies take it a step further. They build their customers' expectations to unrealistically high levels and then jump through all kinds of hoops to meet those expectations, even if it isn't cost-effective. This reflects a poorly developed marketing strategy and a lack of awareness of the marketplace.

Indulgent companies are more concerned with cash flow than with profits. Their focus is on good public relations, often at the expense of financial stability.

Differentiation

Indulgent zone companies do a fine job of differentiating themselves with service. They create a lot of goodwill, which stimulates word of mouth advertising. Business booms . . . until the bottom falls out. Then they are differentiated by another reputation: They've either disappointed their customers or they've gone out of business.

PART III

Achieving Service Excellence

Chapter Eight

Selling Quality With Service

Providing quality service means more than giving customers what they want; it means, if possible, getting paid for that service. Getting paid for the service you provide is vitally important. Few executives would champion a program to improve customer service if it didn't promise long-term payoffs.

Selling with service doesn't mean adding service to the sales process—a topic that would be of interest primarily to salespeople. It means adding the sales process to service. Most of the time that only requires a small, logical step, as the following example illustrates.

> Phil: *One night my wife and I went to dinner at a restaurant in which every course was a la carte. While giving our order to the waiter, I asked about the soup du jour, and he said, "It's cream of broccoli, but I would not recommend it tonight."*

What did the waiter do right and what did he do wrong? On the positive side, he should be commended for his honesty, assuming he wasn't using it as a technique for steering customers toward more expensive choices. On the negative side, the waiter failed to take the next logical step. He should have offered an alternative to the cream of broccoli soup. His recommendation would have served 1) his customer (by providing a more tasty choice), 2) the restaurant (by increasing the size of the check) and 3) himself (by increasing his tip).

The waiter had his customer's interest at heart, but he failed to see the big picture. The big picture is that he must strike a balance between altruism and greed. That balance is achieved by looking out for everyone involved, including the restaurant.

Imagine you're a customer service tech for a computer company. A customer calls and asks a procedural question about a software program. From the nature of the question, you discover this company has had a lot of turnover and could use some on-site training. You would be remiss if you didn't take that opportunity to sell your company's training services.

Selling with service is using service as a means to make more sales. It is combining the service function with the sales function in a marriage that's quite natural. Every customer encounter represents an opportunity to either sell, service, or reduce tension. (The service opportunity will be discussed in chapter nine, "Encouraging Demanding Customers." Opportunities to reduce tension will be covered in chapters ten and eleven, "Nurturing Complaining Customers" and "Managing the Recovery Process".)

SERVICE R$_x$:
Not trying to sell something to someone who needs it is just as bad as trying to sell something to someone who does not need it.

Selling with service addresses the issue of how service will pay for itself in the short-term. The nature of executive beasts is their preoccupation with the bottomline. They want to be assured their investment in service training will bring returns. Those returns, in the long-run, will be goodwill and a greater number of customers willing to spend more money. In the short-run, you get paid by selling things to people—and there is nothing wrong with that if you do it right.

SERVICE R$_x$:
The best sales presentation is quality service.

When you give excellent service, people trust you; and when they trust you, they're willing to take your advice and buy the things you recommend.

How Sales and Service Are Intimately Related

Figure 8.1 shows the functions of sales and service in any business. Before the sale, the functions are straight-forward; that is, salespeople sell and service people serve. It is interesting to note that salespeople, in their sales presentations, often tout their company's service as one of the features that differentiates them from the competition. Once the sale is made, however, the sales/service relationships change somewhat. Keep in mind that the acquisition and maintenance of customers is a company-wide responsibility. A rude receptionist can cost a company more customers than the best salesperson can bring in. Conversely, an excellent receptionist can attract customers like a magnet.

After the sale, quality service becomes even more important than sales in *maintaining* customers. It is the company's service that continues the "sales process" and salespeople are an important source of that service. In reality, both sales and service functions have a bearing on future sales. One thing you can be sure of: If a customer receives poor service after the sale, no matter how sharp the salesperson was, they will *never* get a second sale, a lead, or a referral from that customer.

The job of selling belongs to more than just the sales department. Even people in service can add value to a service call and dollars to the company's bottomline by asking questions to discover sales opportunities. Phil worked with Southern Bell Advanced Systems to teach new sales and customer service skills to over 300 service technicians. Before the training, additional sales by technicians were averaging a half-million dollars per month. The first month after the training, sales increased by 400% and hit $1.9 million. Sales hovered around that figure for several months until settling at $1.2 million per month.

The key to Southern Bell's increase was that, after the training, the technicians saw their jobs differently. Not only were they in the customer's home to repair or install a piece of equipment, they were there to help pay for the level of quality service they were providing. So when a need was uncovered, they either sold the customer small items right out of their trucks or, for larger sales, referred them to the sales department.

The Relationship of Sales to Service

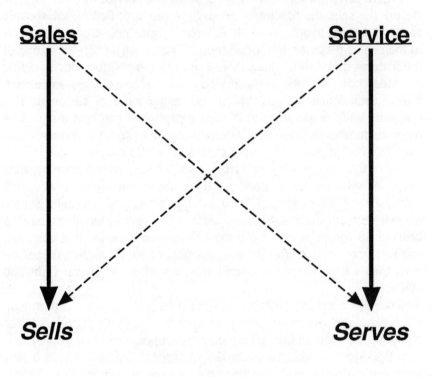

Figure 8.1: Both Sales and Service can create opportunities for increasing value to the customer if they each understand their secondary roles.

We're All Trying To Sell Something To Someone

All this leads us to the conclusion that everyone in the company, especially front-line people, are in sales. Surprised? Most people are taken aback by this news because, traditionally, salespeople have a negative image. That is about to change. You're about to learn an easy way to overcome an aversion to selling, a way to sell without feeling as if you are taking advantage of someone. When done properly, selling is *not* manipulative.

Rest assured, we're not asking you to try to make a sale every time you're with a customer, but you should be aware that sales opportunities arise all the time. If you regard them as opportunities to educate people, make them happy, and enhance the value of their transactions with you, you will not feel pushy.

Customers can make requests only if they have an awareness of what they need. Part of providing service is not just giving people what they ask for, but making them aware of additional needs. The Snowbird Ski Resort in Utah employs hosts and hostesses. These skiers take groups of 20 skiers up the mountain and show them around. The snow guides are trained to observe their guests and, if they see people with needs, view it as a selling opportunity. The host's attitude is one of helpfulness. "You know, you're not a bad skier, but you seem to become tense on the more difficult slopes. I think you would enjoy the mountain a lot more if you worked on your technique for an hour or so. Would you like me to introduce you to one of our instructors?"

Ski instructors also look for ways to enhance their students' enjoyment of the mountain. There are situations in which they might say, "You're a good skier and we've added some new skills today, but I think your equipment is giving you some problems. Why don't you come down to the pro shop and we'll get the bugs out of your bindings?"

The key to selling without guilt is to be a consultant. Simply ask questions that may uncover needs. Before delving into questioning and other sales techniques, however, let's put non-manipulative selling in perspective by comparing it to the type of sales most people have developed an aversion to.

Traditional vs. Non-manipulative Selling

Most people, when they think of sales, think of the hard-driving, fast-talking, used-car salesman who practically wrestles his customers into saying yes. Traditional sales techniques place an inordinate emphasis on the sales approach and the close. Traditional salespeople treat all prospects the same and gives a "canned" pitch to all of them. They spend relatively little time studying the prospect's needs; instead, they assume their product is the solution for everyone.

A Comparison of Traditional and Non-Manipulative Sales Techniques

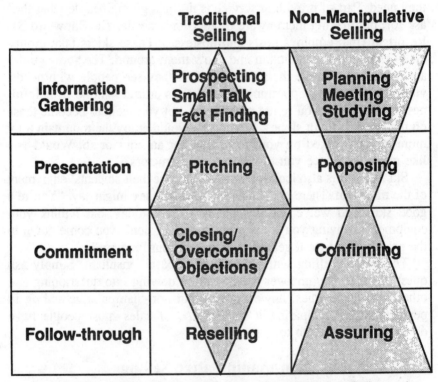

	Traditional Selling	Non-Manipulative Selling
Information Gathering	Prospecting Small Talk Fact Finding	Planning Meeting Studying
Presentation	Pitching	Proposing
Commitment	Closing/ Overcoming Objections	Confirming
Follow-through	Reselling	Assuring

Figure 8.2: In the non-manipulative sales process, the emphasis is on finding out the customers' expectations and then designing service to meet or exceed those expectations.

Non-manipulative salespeople are more like counselors. They spend more time asking questions to determine if their product will meet the needs of the customer. Their attitude is, "I don't know if I can help you. Let me ask some questions to see if we have a basis for doing business.

If we don't, I'll be the first to admit it. If we do, then it will be a win-win relationship."

Figure 8.2 shows a comparison of the two schools of selling. Note where the emphasis is placed in non-manipulative selling: before and after the sale. Non-manipulative salespeople spend time asking questions and diagnosing their prospects' needs. After the sale, non-manipulative salespeople make sure their customers are satisfied. This means, among other things, following up on the delivery of products or services. As you will see later, following-up is extremely important for customer service employees, especially after resolving a problem. It shows sincere interest, impresses the customer, and creates good will.

Assuring customer satisfaction after the sale also creates the opportunity to meet additional needs (and make additional sales) that may have come up. It is for this reason that non-manipulative salespeople see their customers in terms of ongoing relationships, not one-time sales. Put another way, customers are love affairs, not one-night stands.

The sales cycles depicted in figure 8.2 can be either long or short. The non-manipulative approach to selling works, whether you take a year to sell commercial real estate or five minutes to sell a hotel room upgrade. Both sales situations can be boiled down to discovering needs and providing solutions.

The Six Principles of Selling

No matter what your job is in your company, it is invaluable for you to know how people choose who they will do business with. If nothing else, remember these six principles and you will have learned more than most people learn in 25 years of business.

PRINCIPLE 1:
In selling, as in medicine, prescription without diagnosis is malpractice.

Solutions (and sales) can be made only after you understand your customers' needs.

PRINCIPLE 2:
People buy because they feel *understood*, not because they are made to *understand*.

You make someone feel understood by relating the product to the person's specific needs. When you try to make someone understand, you are simply giving an impersonal, generic presentation of a product's features and benefits.

PRINCIPLE 3:
If you solve problems for people, they resent the solutions. If you inflict the solutions on them, they resent you.

In non-manipulative selling, you make the customer a partner in the decision-making process. Solutions should never be imposed on a customer. People like to make their own choices, regardless of the wisdom of those choices.

PRINCIPLE 4:
Sales are made on the basis of trust.

A non-manipulative salesperson establishes credibility before recommending solutions. This is done through the art of questioning and building rapport.

PRINCIPLE 5:
If two people *want* to do business together, the details won't stop it from happening. If two people don't want to do business together, the details won't make it happen.

People do business with people they like. Focus on the business relationship, not on selling per se.

PRINCIPLE 6:
True professionals are known not by the business they
are in, but by the way they are in business.

Regardless of the position you hold now, if you are conscientious and take pride in what you do, you will be remembered for your professionalism. Professionalism and persistence will take you much farther than anything else you do.

The Elusive Art of Questioning

For the service provider who has little time to study his customer's needs, effective questioning techniques are indispensable. A well-phrased question can get to the heart of an issue and swiftly change a problem into a solution. In some situations, a simple question may open the door for upgrading, cross-selling, adding value, or exceeding a customer's expectations.

In the day-to-day routine of your job, questioning is, without a doubt, one of your most important communication skills. Combined with listening and observation, questioning enables you to tap into your customer's needs, wants, fears, and motivations. It also helps you build trust, determine behavioral style, and manage tension.

Open and Closed Questions

When you ask a question, you are inviting the other person to paint a picture of themselves. You provide a canvas on which they use either large or small brushes to express themselves. The size of that brush is determined by the type of questions you ask.

Open-ended questions require the other person to give a narrative answer. These questions get them involved in the conversation by asking for a description of the situation as they see it. Closed-ended questions, on the other hand, require a yes, no, or brief factual answer. They produce the small, fine brush strokes that fill in the details. When asking a customer questions, it is advisable to start with open-ended questions, then, if necessary, ask more pointed closed-ended questions.

Open-ended Questions

Open-ended questions have the following characteristics and uses:

- They require a narrative answer.

- They do not lead the other person in a direction, hence the name open-ended.

- They are asked only when the customer has the time for a relatively in-depth answer.

- They can be used to encourage the customer to think about your product or service.

- They create a situation in which the customer will quickly reveal their behavioral style.

Open-ended questions should be asked thoughtfully. If you are a hotel desk clerk, it is pleasant but almost meaningless to ask, "How was your stay?" People have pat answers for that question. A more sincere and thought-provoking question would be, "What did you find most satisfying about your stay with us?" The key is to ask questions that require thought and an honest answer. Some examples of open-ended questions are:

1. Can you tell me what happened?
2. What are your plans for dinner tonight?
3. How can we be of further assistance to you?
4. How would you like to see this problem resolved?
5. How do you see yourself using this product?
6. What problems do you foresee in the implementation of this system?
7. What other training needs do you see arising after you buy this product?

Closed-ended Questions

After your customer has painted an over-all picture, you can ask some specific questions to help determine how to be of service. These closed-ended questions have many uses:

- They ask for simple and specific information.

- They provide feedback to let the other person know you understand their situation.

- They can steer the conversation in a desired direction.

If you are short on time and have to get right to the point, use closed-ended rather than open-ended ones. Here are some examples of pointed, closed-ended questions:

1. How many people in your office will be using this computer?

2. May I make a reservation for you to dine in our restaurant tonight?

3. May I call our tailor to alter this suit for you?

No matter what questions you ask, ask them in a way that takes the pressure off. Use a relaxed, matter-of-fact tone of voice and give your customer as much time as needed to answer. If you work the telephone, don't rush to hang up and answer the next call. Invest whatever time you need to sell (if appropriate) to this customer. Worry about the next call later.

Your questioning skills get the ball rolling. To keep it rolling and take advantage of the momentum you have created, you must listen . . . and listen well.

Listening Skills

The flip side of questioning is listening. It, too, is an essential communication skill you *must* take the time to learn. Selling with service requires an exchange of information and that exchange is always two-way. Listening is as important a part of the process as questioning. In fact, you should spend more time listening than talking. Year after year, surveys reveal that the number one complaint corporate buyers have of salespeople is they talk too much! Buyers want salespeople to address the specific needs of their companies.

When you are a poor listener, you run two major risks: alienating your customers and prescribing the wrong solution to their needs. Both can get you in trouble. By contrast, when you are a good listener, you build trust, reduce tension, and become a problem-solver—something everyone appreciates.

Listening is not the same as hearing. Most people listen with about 50% accuracy. In other words, *half* of every message is being lost or distorted. That's a significant portion.

Where do you lose the message? During a conversation, a lot of people become preoccupied with their own thoughts. They think about what they just heard or contemplate what they're going to say next. You know how distracting it can be when someone says something you disagree with. Some people actually let it bother them to the extent that they interrupt to argue.

Clearly, it takes a concerted effort to be a good listener. When you give customers the opportunity to explain a situation and say how they feel, you help them release negative emotions. Listening to customers also makes them feel important. They see you—and therefore, your company—care about them and are committed to a long-term business relationship. This is how you make complaining customers your allies rather than your adversaries, smoothing the way for a mutually-beneficial resolution to any problem.

Listen with Your Eyes and Ears

The more time you have with a customer, the easier it is to practice active listening. Even short interactions, however, will benefit from your efforts to: 1) concentrate and be attentive, and 2) sense the *content* and *intent* of the message.

How can you do all of this at once? First, put everything else aside—mentally and physically. Give the person your undivided attention and look them in the eyes. Then pay attention to both the *words* and the *emotions* behind the words. Emotions are easily detected in the nuances of voice inflection, body language, and eye contact. Listen as well to what is not said, but implied. People rarely say things that are embarrassing, but they may beat around the bush hoping you'll get the message.

Another key to active listening is to let the customer say all that needs to be said. Don't interrupt. Resolving problems may be a routine part of your workday, but it is an emotional issue to your customers. Handle them with care! Interrupting can cause distress and be counterproductive.

SERVICE R$_x$:
Be sincere. Your attitude during the service process—not necessarily the outcome—affects your customers' loyalty.

The qualities that count in the service process are courtesy, empathy, active listening, and a commitment to resolution.

As listeners, there are a number of bad habits we all possess, some more than others. They are habits our family and friends have grown used to, but customers may find offensive. Look at the following list to see if you are guilty of any of these transgressions. Put a check mark by those you should work on to improve your listening habits.

1. You do all the talking.

2. You interrupt when people talk.

3. You rarely make good eye contact.

4. You nervously play with something while listening.

5. Your poker face keeps people guessing as to your attentiveness.

6. You come off as very serious because you never smile.

7. You phrase your questions in ways that make people defensive.

8. Everything reminds you of an experience you've had and you feel obligated to tell your story.

9. If a person pauses, you finish their sentence for them.

10. You constantly evaluate what is being said as either believable or unbelievable.

11. You make judgements about the speaker as they speak.

12. You keep thinking to yourself, "If I were a psychologist, I could be doing this and making big bucks."

Active listening is a skill that will serve you well in all facets of life. Some people need to develop the ability to slow down and listen to people. Others have to learn to concentrate. As a service provider, active listening is your pipeline to your customers' needs. With good listening skills you will be able to show more sincerity and empathy while you look for opportunities to reduce tension, make sales, or provide quality service. Active listening will show your customers what a valuable asset you are to them.

The Necessary Art of Feedback

Improving communication skills, is not limited to just asking questions and listening. You also have to give feedback. Feedback is a natural part of conversation you probably already practice. We just want you to realize some of the finer points.

Verbal Feedback

Feedback takes two forms—verbal and nonverbal. With verbal feedback you simply make a statement or ask a question that assures the speaker that you are listening. These include brief interjections such as, "I understand," "Uh huh," or "I see what you mean." Questions to enlist feedback may take the form of, "Would you be happy if we refunded your money or would you prefer a new toaster?" "I can understand why you're so upset."

Another way of giving feedback is to restate the customer's thoughts or feelings *in your own words*. This is far more preferable to repeating a statement verbatim. For example, "I understand you just want a bowl of lobster bisque . . . " Repeating a customer's words verbatim is acceptable if you are asking for clarification, as in, "I'm not sure what you mean by 'broadcast quality three-quarter inch tape.'" Otherwise, it can be insulting. You don't want to sound like a therapist. "You object to being treated like a number?"

Another form of vocal feedback is voice inflection. By controlling your voice, you can improve the quality of communication. You already know how to use your voice to convey empathy, confidence, determination, sincerity, and enthusiasm. Now make a conscious effort to use subtle vocal intonations to assure your customer that you are listening intently.

Nonverbal Feedback

Nonverbal feedback is given through body language. The subtle clues you give with your body say as much as your words, if not more. These physical clues are quickly observed by the person you are talking to. Research has shown that people can interpret a nonverbal gesture in the time it takes for one frame of a movie to be exposed—1/24th of a second.

The feedback you give while listening or speaking can enhance or undermine your relationship with a customer. It's essential that you be consistent; that is, your body language must match the attitude you are conveying verbally. There's nothing worse than a customer service employee acting (verbally) one way and looking (nonverbally) another way. It is an all-too-familiar scene on airplanes. While passengers are deplaning, the flight attendants stand at the door and, with forced smiles, repeat mechanically, "Goodbye."

As mentioned at the beginning of this chapter, a lot of customer service training focuses on smiling. A smile should be the sincere frosting on the cake, but don't mistake it for the cake itself. Interaction with a customer should always end in a smile. If you find it difficult to smile after an interaction, you may be in the wrong business. Or maybe you're just having a bad day. It's okay to not smile as long as the rest of you is pleasant. It is better to not smile and show genuine interest than to smile mechanically and feel indifferent.

The best nonverbal feedback is eye contact. It immediately and unmistakably shows the other person you are paying attention. Eye contact does not lie. It is as direct a measure of sincerity as you can get, second only to action. With eye contact, however, you have to strike a balance between too much and too little. Too much of a good thing will make people as uncomfortable as too little. If you have any doubt, it is better to err on the side of too much.

Your posture, arms, and hands send a subtle, nonverbal message as well. When you are interested in someone, you should lean toward them with your arms away from your body. Crossing your arms gives the impression that you are defensive or sitting in judgement. Putting your hands behind your head while leaning back in a chair implies a nonchalant or distant attitude. If you are sitting at a desk, it is better to sit with your hands above the desk so you look like you are ready to do something for your customer.

Employees—Know Your Customers

Employees have to understand who their customers are and what they expect. For example, in hotels, reservationists often don't try to sell the most expensive rooms because they make assumptions about the person making the inquiry. Put yourself in the following scenario:

You are a reservationist for the Plaza hotel in New York. The cheapest room is $275 per night and that room is tiny. It's so small

*you open the door and it hits the back wall of the room. You've
seen larger broom closets. The phone rings and a woman tells you
she is calling from Dubuque, Iowa. She's planning a trip to New
York with her husband. You can hear a baby crying on her
shoulder and kids screaming in the background. What's running
through your mind at this point? You're wondering if they can
afford to stay at the hotel. So you decide to quote the price of the
least expensive room—$275. The problem is that in Dubuque, $275
will buy the presidential suite at the nicest hotel in town. That's
exactly what this woman is expecting at the Plaza.*

*It just so happens that this woman is the wife of the wealthiest
doctor in Dubuque. (Even wealthy people have children.) They will
be going to New York for their 25th wedding anniversary. The
doctor has arranged for them to fly first-class. In New York, a
chauffeured limousine will pick them up at the airport. They have
tickets to all the top Broadway shows and reservations at the best
restaurants. They're expecting a big, fancy suite in the hotel. To top
it all off, the doctor is going to present his wife with a gift—a
$20,000 fur coat—and he plans to do it in their big, fancy suite.
What do you think their reactions are going to be when they go up
(if it's up) to their room and see their $275 broom closet? It's
going to be "#@$%&*#$+=#!!#$!!"*

Have you done them a favor by selling them the cheapest room in
the hotel? Actually, you've done a disservice. If they had wanted a
cheap room, they would have called elsewhere. The fact is, they called
the Plaza Hotel, knowing that it was the most expensive hotel in New
York.

The point is this: You have to assume that the kind of person who
calls your business is probably part of your marketplace and should be
treated as such. Don't single people out for special treatment. They
called you for a reason and should be told what your products or
services cost. If what you sell is too rich for their budgets, let them be
the judges of that and not buy. If a caller is not part of your clientele,
you should not treat them differently. It's not your problem. For all you
know, they may be splurging on a once-in-a-lifetime expenditure. If you
consistently get phone calls from people who aren't in your marketplace, that's a problem your marketing department or advertising agency
must deal with. It means they are creating ads attracting the wrong
people.

> **SERVICE R$_X$:**
> As much as it is nice to try to relate to your customers, you have to realize that their perspectives are often much different than yours.

You will be amazed and delighted when you learn *who your customers are and what they want.* You may have no idea because you only see things from your own perspective, not from your customer's point of view. When you fully appreciate the values of your company's clientele, you will be able to sell without feeling guilty because you will know your customers are not pinching pennies.

Getting Paid for Service

If you look at businesses today, the demand for quality service is high; however, the supply is low. Businesses that provide quality service are able to charge more for their products. Nordstrom, Neiman Marcus, Westin Hotels, and Ritz Carlton hotels are cases in point. They are successful, upscale businesses that charge a premium for giving people what they want—impeccable service. In these companies, "fees" for top notch service are included in their prices. You get what you pay for.

Situations arise in many businesses throughout the price spectrum in which customers ask for services above and beyond the call of duty. What are appropriate responses? Should service always be given for free or should service pay for itself? How does a company avoid operating in the indulgent zone?

It's not always appropriate for companies to give away service; and certainly customers don't expect the extraordinary for free. One of the keys to charging for service is the frequency of the demand. Nordstrom provides an interesting example.

An employee was approached by a customer who needed to catch a plane at the airport. Evidently she was frantic because her ride had not shown up. The Nordstrom employee could have called a cab, but instead he found someone to cover his department and drove his customer to the airport, which was only ten minutes away. This service was certainly beyond the call of duty. The goodwill created, as you can imagine, was tremendous.

There's nothing wrong with providing this service free-of-charge, if it's done once in a while. But what if people started to think of Nordstrom as a place to shop for clothes *and* catch a ride to the airport? If employees were being used as an airport shuttle service, there would be no one left on the floor to sell clothes. What should a company do?

There are a dozen different operational ways to solve a problem, but the key is to find the best solution for your business based on its philosophical and strategic values. Let's look at several ways to handle an unusual request.

If the request for a service is occasional, it makes sense to find a way to meet your customer's need in an efficient, cost-effective way. If a customer wants a ride to the airport, calling a cab may suffice in 90% of the cases. For the 10% of the times when it is urgent, drive the customer yourself or delegate the task.

If the unusual requests are more than occasional, your company has several options. If customers are asking you for something that is an extreme departure from the nature of your business, you are fully justified in politely refusing. After all, it is not the business you're in and every company has the right to define its business with its own parameters.

If, on the other hand, you want to accommodate your customers, you can figure out a way to provide this unusual service regularly and charge for it; or you can provide the service free-of-charge, but limit the circumstances under which you will provide it. Of course, these are only three of the many solutions possible. What's important here is not that we brainstorm all possible solutions to a hypothetical request, but that you understand a solution must be consistent with your company's core values.

SERVICE R$_x$:
Serve your customers in a manner that will:
1) conform to your core values
2) manage their expectations
3) exceed their expectations to keep them happy without creating a financial burden on the company or affecting other customers.

One of the biggest mistakes employees make when they receive a special request is to give the service away for free. Customers don't expect extraordinary service for free. What's more important to them is getting the service when they want it. If there are no guidelines for you regarding the service a customer is asking for, use your best judgement. Your company's core values provide the best guidelines. If an operational value is in question, then ask yourself if breaking it would also violate a philosophical value. If no philosophical value would be violated, you're justified in breaking the operational value to serve a customer. If a philosophical value would be broken by your decision, then you need to consult with a manager or supervisor.

It's important to realize that it is appropriate to charge for some services and inappropriate to charge for others. A meeting planner who is holding a seminar in a hotel has every right to expect a technician to be on the premises in case the rented audio/visual equipment malfunctions. The meeting planner cannot, however, expect the technician to run the equipment. If this service were requested, it would be reasonable to pay for it. And offering this service for a fee does not take it out of the progressive zone of service. What determines the zone of service is the effort to meet the customers' needs, not whether the service is free.

Providing extraordinary customer service—and repeatedly giving it away—can put a company in the indulgent zone and on a path to bankruptcy. Think back to the Nordstrom employee who drove the woman to the airport. That type of service can get out of hand. Granted, driving people to the airport is not common, but there are other subtle and more frequent ways of losing money with over-indulgent service.

Phil: *I know a custom home builder who did excellent work, but never really made much money at it. It's hard to believe, but this is what happened for years: When he calculated the bid for a job, he would figure in every little detail, including a reasonable profit for himself. Time after time he would lose bids to his competitors. He never could figure out how the other guys could stay in business when they were bidding at close to their cost. What he didn't realize was that he was bidding the right price, the one including the inevitable changes that would come up during construction. His competitors were bidding low-ball prices and then later adding on large fees every time the customer wanted something changed. The typical custom home goes through a lot of changes from blueprint to finished product, so the competition was making a bundle on all the changes.*

There are two messages in this story that pertain to the indulgent zone of service. If you give too much, you're going to end up losing money. By the same token—and this applies to the home builder—if you include the extras rather than charge for them later, you have to let your customers know what you have done. What good is quality service if people don't realize they're getting it? That's how you build perceived value in your customer's mind. The home builder should have met with his customers and explained exactly what his bids included. Failing to do that, he lost both the job and the goodwill that would have come with being honest and forthright.

People don't expect something for nothing. They just want service providers to be fair and reasonable, with no unpleasant surprises.

> Emil: *I bought a new Volvo from a dealer who promised he would give me a loaner car every time I brought my car in for service. When I brought my car in and was given the loaner, it had no gas in it. I confronted the lot attendant and he told me the company didn't think they should have to put gas in their loaner cars because they were giving them to people for free. They tried to make me feel like they were doing me a big favor, even though, according to our sales agreement, I was entitled to the car.*

What did the car dealer do wrong? He missed an opportunity to please Emil on two accounts. First, the attendant had no right to imply the dealer was doing Emil a favor. The fact was, the dealer was simply delivering on a promise. So, indirectly, Emil had paid for the use of that loaner car.

Second, the dealer should have given Emil the car with a full tank of gas. That wouldn't mean he was expecting a free tank of gas; it would mean he expected not to be inconvenienced by having to get gas as soon as he drove off the lot. The tactful way to handle the situation would have been for the dealer to give Emil a full tank of gas and have the lot attendant politely ask him if he would fill the tank before returning the car. The attendant could have said, "It's just like a rental car, Sir. We can fill it here when you return it, but they'll charge you our rates. I'm sure you can find cheaper gas elsewhere." Emil would have understood completely and complied. Even if customers didn't understand and actually expected a free tank of gas, the attendant could have been trained to present the situation politely. Instead, the lot attendant handled the gas issue unprofessionally, which made Emil angry and lowered his opinion of the dealership's service quality.

Selling Is Service, Service Is Selling

Being a customer or a salesperson is an everyday part of life. Ask yourself where you go that someone is not trying to sell you something. This isn't necessarily bad. When you go to a full-service gas station the attendant asks you if he can check your oil. What is he doing? He's asking questions to discover needs. No pressure, he's just providing a service that may or may not lead to the sale of a quart of oil.

Which jobs in your company are the most highly valued? (And, therefore, the most highly paid.) People who are directly responsible for sales or raising profits are the ones who are well compensated. They are the salespeople, marketing people, and decision makers who devise ways of creating growth. That's why Lee Iacocca is worth tens of millions of dollars a year to Chrysler. He increased the bottomline by hundreds of millions of dollars.

As a service provider, you're not in the position to make million-dollar sales, but you are in the position to make a significant contribution to the company. Every sale has an impact on profits. The more you sell with service, the more you will be recognized and seen as an asset by customers and management. Valuable assets have a way of appreciating, so before you know it, you will advance and teach others how to sell with service.

Chapter Nine

Encouraging Demanding Customers

There are two important freedoms that you must give your customers: the freedom to be demanding and the freedom to complain. The latter will be covered in the next chapter. To encourage these freedoms, you must create environments that make it acceptable for customers to make demands or lodge complaints.

By "demanding customers" we do not mean loud, aggressive complainers who make life miserable for service providers; we mean people who feel comfortable telling you what they want. You have to make your customers know you want them to be fussy and bring you their requests. When you create this environment, you attract customers with high expectations who are willing to pay for what they want. You create demanding customers by conveying the attitude, "If you ask for it, we'll give it to you."

It pays for a customer to be demanding. Take the case of a man from San Francisco—we'll call him Ralph—who decided at the last minute not to attend a company convention. On Saturday morning of the convention weekend he got a phone call from Houston. A co-worker told him, "Ralph, you're supposed to get a major award tonight and you're not even here!" So Ralph had to scramble to book a flight to Houston, buy a tuxedo, and get to the convention. He happened to be a member of a service called, Les Concierges, and asked them to arrange everything. (Les Concierges is a company in San Francisco that, for a monthly fee, acts as an agent between clients and various services in the community. They arrange anything legal, moral and ethical. People become members so Les Concierges can be demanding on their behalf.)

Les Concierges got on the phone and performed miracles. The level of service they received from a department store in Houston seemed to be without precedent. The department store sent its tailor to meet Ralph at the airport when he arrived. The tailor measured Ralph and quickly called the measurements into the store. The banquet was due to start at 7:00 P.M. At 6:15 the tailor brought the tuxedo to Ralph's hotel and made some final alterations. Ralph was dressed and dapper in time for the awards banquet.

All of these things were done for Ralph because he dared to ask, "What can you do for me?" He had an intense need for immediate service, which provided several businesses with opportunities to please him. In the process, they stretched the old standards with which Ralph evaluated a company's service.

SERVICE R$_X$:
Be a demanding customer. If you don't ask for it, you won't get it.

It never hurts to ask for what you want. In fact, you'd be surprised how often you'll be accommodated when you make unusual, yet reasonable, requests.

How Do You Measure Service Standards?

Life for a market-focused company would be easy if there were a fixed standard by which service could be measured. Unfortunately, there is no granite stone in the Bureau of Measures and Standards in Washington, D.C., on which is engraved the service standards that people expect. In reality, quality service is measured against expectations.

Expectations are relative. You don't expect the same level of service at McDonald's that you expect at The Tavern On The Green. Both do what they do well, but everyone knows you get what you pay for, so you expect a different type of *service* and more *services* at The Tavern.

The concept of getting what you pay for has its limits, especially when you look at the end of the scale. No matter where your business falls on the service continuum—from first class to bargain basement—there will always be a minimum level of acceptable service you must provide. At every level, there are customer expectations to be met. To grasp this fully, imagine a fast food restaurant that has slashed its prices by 50%. Would you eat there? Yes. Now imagine this restaurant is filthy, has incompetent help, and serves burgers that taste like old shoes. Would you still eat there? No, you wouldn't. What if they cut their prices even more? Now would you eat there? No! How far would their prices have to be lowered before you would eat there again? They couldn't lower their prices enough because, no matter how low they were, the restaurant still wouldn't meet the minimum standards you expect.

This concept of minimum acceptable standards is an important one. You can only differentiate your business with service after you've taken care of all the basics. In a nutshell, the quality of your product only qualifies you to compete; it enters you in the race. Quality service wins customers. If your product is no good, all the service in the world will not compensate for its shortcomings. As A.B. (Sky) Magary, Vice President of Marketing for Northwest Airlines said, "You can't serve caviar on a cancelled flight."

What Do Customers Expect?

The business transaction is a peculiar mix of logic and emotion. Different people look for different things in their business relationships. Fortunately, some patterns do appear to be common. In general, there are five qualities customers look for in their experiences with an organization.[2] These qualities are listed below in order of their importance to consumers.

Reliability. Customers expect consistency, timeliness, accuracy, and dependability. They expect that promises will be kept. To the customers, this is the most important aspect of a company. Unfortunately, reliability is perceived by customers to be the weakest link in most companies' performance and is the source of most service complaints. If a company wants to know where to begin pleasing customers, they should start here.

"We use the lowest paid employees in the airline industry and pass the savings on to you!"

Responsiveness. Customers want to deal with employees who are willing to help and eager to serve. Customers don't want to feel as though they're interruptions. It's the service provider's job to convey enthusiasm and a willingness to jump through as many hoops as necessary to satisfy a customer.

Confidence. Customers want to be assured the company and its employees are competent, knowledgeable, and courteous. Confidence in a company's expertise must be unshakable. When you're talking to a customer on the phone, a quick and easy way to make them feel confident is to give your name. Customers feel much better when they have the name of someone to ask for if there's a problem.

Caring. Most customers like to be treated as individuals. The more high tech our world becomes, the more personal service we want to soften its impersonal nature.

Physical Impression. This is the least important aspect of a company to customers; however, it tends to be the dimension in which companies perform best. It should come as no surprise that American businesses are more concerned with outward appearances than reliability.

All the physical details—your building, office, desk, and personnel—must make a good impression. Would you put your money in an S&L that had a stained rug or broken window? Many people have. And look at the mess we're in.

These five qualities are the building blocks of credibility. A new business must use all these elements to position itself in the marketplace.

Expectations Are Relative

To illustrate the effect expectations have on customer satisfaction, let's look at a situation in which expectations cause two different service experiences.

Imagine you and your spouse have heard about a restaurant from another couple. Your friend, Alan, described it to you as "nicely decorated, a good location, and good food." How anxious would you be to go to this restaurant? You'd be interested, but not motivated to drop everything to go that night.

Now imagine Alan's wife, Barbara, gave this description of the same restaurant to your spouse: "You approach the restaurant on a tree-lined road leading down to the water. On the edge of the lake is a beautifully restored Victorian mansion with a dramatic fountain in the middle of a circular driveway. A red carpet stretches out from the front door to the sidewalk. A doorman opens the front door and you walk into one of the most elegantly decorated foyers you've ever seen, with crystal chandeliers and rich Persian rugs. From your table, you glance out the window to see sailboats standing on their silhouettes, swans meandering aimlessly with their mates, and the moon reflected on a sheet of black marble. Your waiter appears and expertly describes an appetizing variety of gourmet entrees . . . " You get the picture. How anxious would your spouse be to go that very night? Very anxious!

So you go to the restaurant that night. After dinner, which one of you is *more likely* to be pleased? Which of you is more likely to be disappointed? You are more likely to be pleased. Your spouse is more likely to be disappointed.

Expectations Influence Satisfaction

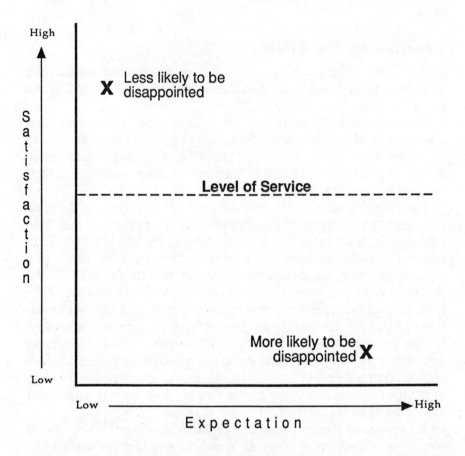

Figure 9.1: When expectations are effectively managed, it is much easier to meet or exceed those expectations. If expectations are not effectively managed, it is virtually impossible to satisfy the customer.

Look at Figure 9.1. The dotted line across the middle shows the level of service in the restaurant. It was the same for both of you. In your case, the service exceeded your expectations. In your spouse's case, however, the service fell below her expectations and, therefore, was disappointing. So it isn't always the service per se that satisfies or dissatisfies people. It's the degree to which that service meets, exceeds, or falls short of expectations.

SERVICE R$_x$:
People do not buy _things_, they buy _expectations_.

The key for any company is to create expectations high enough to attract its target market and reasonable enough to fulfill. This is done by managing expectations—not raising or lowering them, but _targeting_ them to the specific needs of your customers.

Managing Expectations

Years ago comedian Flip Wilson created a character, named Geraldine, who used to say, "What you see is what you get!" Geraldine was Flip Wilson dressed as a woman, so in retrospect, what you saw was not what you got. When it comes to customer expectations, however, what the customer sees better be what they get. Stated another way, what you promise customers should be what you deliver.

Managing expectations can done in many ways and it is always done one customer at a time. You can't manage the expectations of the marketplace. Even advertising, despite its broad coverage, reaches one customer at a time.

Managing expectations can be as subtle as the type style of printing on a menu or as obvious as extraordinary claims made in prime-time television commercials. Everything you do in business—and _how_ you do it—contributes to your customers' expectations. Expectations are formed by advertising, word of mouth, previous experience, the business's ambiance, and employees' behavior.

Advertising. Advertising plays a major role in how the public perceives a company and, therefore, what expectations are created. In designing ads, you must walk the fine line between building expectations that will attract new customers and promising things you can't deliver. There's nothing worse than promising the world and delivering a plastic globe. It's better to promise less, attract fewer customers, and make them happy.

In May 1990 Pan Am provided an excellent example of living up to the expectations created in advertising. They ran a newspaper ad in Orlando, Florida, that promoted a one-way flight to Nuremberg, West Germany, for only $109. Oops. The ad should have read $409. The printer made a mistake.

What would most companies do? They would deny any responsibility by saying, "We're sorry, but the printer made an error, the airfare is really $409." Lots of disappointed customers would curse under their breaths. What did Pan Am do? They stood behind the ad, which ran for two days, and gave 75 people the advertised price for the flights. The printer said they would pay the difference. There's no doubt that Pan Am would have honored the $109 fares even if the printer hadn't offered to pay the difference.

A poor example of managing expectations through advertising is the car rental industry. For years they have been under fire for deceiving customers. A glance through the yellow pages and a couple of phone calls reveal a lot. Most agencies advertise that their prices are low, low discount prices. When you call, however, you discover several things. They all charge about the same price for similar cars. Those cars rented for discount prices often lack automatic transmissions, air conditioning, or reasonable mileage allowances. To add insult to injury, when you get to the rental office, they use every trick in the book to try to rent you a more expensive car. A very common tactic is to pressure customers into buying damage waiver insurance, which is unnecessary if the renter has auto insurance. In 1989, these deceptive tactics and others prompted the National Association of Attorney Generals to issue advertising guidelines for the industry.

Advertising must also realistically respond to the needs and wants of your target market. C&R Clothiers had good intentions when they tried to appeal to the business traveler who needed to have his suit pressed. Their ads said, "Bring your suit in and we'll press it for free." Nice, but not very realistic. No busy executive is going to look up C&R in the phone book and then drive his rental car 20 miles to get his suit pressed. Any hotel will provide the same service. C&R changed their appeal to busy executives by offering overnight tailoring on suits.

In advertising, the choice of media you use implies a great deal about your credibility. The most credibility is derived from major newspapers, magazines, radio and television stations. Less credibility, and often skepticism, is associated with minor league newspapers and magazines and less popular cable TV channels. Compare your impression of a commercial on late night cable TV for a discount furniture business with a prime time, major network commercial for Levitz Furniture. There's no comparison.

The focus of your advertising directly influences expectations. Your company will give a much stronger impression if you emphasize service quality and customer satisfaction than if you try to capitalize on product features and benefits. As we mentioned in chapter two, this is a lesson that more than a few American businesses have yet to learn.

Ambiance. Expectations and credibility are directly tied to the way your business looks. Guests expect a higher level of service from a plush, upscale hotel than from a plain, unimpressive one. They may be wrong. Both may provide quality service, but first impressions do create expectations.

> Emil: *I flew into a city late one night and went to a car rental agency. The sign out front was in a state of disrepair—half of the letters and bulbs were missing. I couldn't help wondering if they maintain their cars as poorly as they maintain their sign. When I got my car, for the first time ever, I walked around the car to make sure the headlights and taillights were working.*

Ambiance is something that most American businesses do very well. In fact, surveys conducted by the Forum Corporation have shown that consumers perceive "appearance" as the strength of American businesses. Companies put a lot of money and effort into their facades, but they fall short on most of the other dimensions important to customers (i.e., reliability & responsiveness). Clearly, a balance has to be achieved between outward appearance and treating customers well.

Attitude. Attitude is the Achilles heel of American businesses. It's also at the root of all change that must take place for a company to become market-focused. Why do customers take their business elsewhere? Surveys have shown that 68% of customers leave because of an attitude of indifference by an employee. You've experienced it—the store clerk who treats you like an interruption rather than *the* reason they are working there, or the employee who is more concerned about following the rules than responding to your needs. There are 1001 stories that illustrate the importance of attitude. As you will see in the second story below, in some situations the right attitude is not just desirable, but essential.

What is the attitude of the typical hospital orderly? Indifference. He doesn't care about anything except getting through his eight-hour shift, but it doesn't have to be that way.

> Phil: *My father had an operation a couple of years ago. On the day of the surgery, my wife, my mother, and I were in my father's hospital room. An orderly walked in. He was short, overweight, and slightly balding, but had a smile that could charm a pit bull. He smiled at all of us, walked over to my father, and said quite boisterously, "You must be Ben Wexler! I can tell because you're the one in bed." He then looked at the rest of us, "You must be Mr. Wexler, Jr., you must be Mrs. Wexler. And who is this gorgeous creature?" I introduced him to my wife. He then said, "I'll tell you what we're going to do here. Everyone except Ben is going to get out of this room 'cause I gotta get Ben from this bed onto that gurney and there isn't enough room in here for me to do that if all of us are in here."*
>
> *He continued with an explanation of what would happen next. "We're going to wheel Ben down to the prep room. Actually, we're going to take the elevator because it's real hard to wheel one of these things down a flight of stairs. Once we're down there, you guys can go as far as the door, then you can't go any further. I'm going to take Ben into the prep room, clean him up real good . . . " When we got downstairs he said, "Okay, this is it for you guys. Ben gets to play and you don't. The waiting room is over there. They have magazines, coffee and donuts for you. You can wait there or you can go home, but you ain't gonna see Ben for about five hours. If it were me, I wouldn't wait here, but it's your choice. Before you go, let me go inside and get the doctor so he can come out here and tell you that everything I just told you is the truth."*

This orderly's behavior was exemplary. What do you think the chances are that anyone else in the hospital would have such a good attitude? Slim? Read on.

> Phil: *We walked into the waiting room and two ladies behind a reception desk said, "Hi there, you must be the Wexlers! We're going to be spending the day with you. If you'd like to visit our cafeteria, it's upstairs . . ." They had their whole routine to tell us.*

We went up to the cafeteria and again we were greeted like a part of the family. It was incredible—more like a resort than a hospital environment. After spending a day in that hospital, I couldn't wait to get sick.

For the sake of contrast, here is a situation that we hope you never experience.

Phil: *In September of 1989 my father had a mild heart attack. Fortunately, it happened in his doctor's office. I arrived at the doctor's just as the ambulance was getting ready to take my father to the hospital. I asked if I could ride along and was told yes. Our doctor told the ambulance driver not to take my father to the emergency room, but to go directly to intensive care. The driver said, "No, we can't do that. We have to take him into the emergency room first; they can take him to intensive care." The doctor insisted that the driver take my father to intensive care and told the driver that he would call the hospital to make the arrangements.*

We got to the hospital and there was an intensive care nurse standing at the entrance. She told the driver and paramedic to take my father directly to intensive care. The driver again refused, stating that his rules required that they take their patient into emergency first and admit him as an emergency patient; the hospital could do whatever they wanted after that. The nurse said, "Fine, go stand over there. We'll take him upstairs." The driver said, "Not on our gurney. We have to put him on one of your gurneys and then you can do whatever you want with him."

If you were to choose *just one* area to improve in your company, it should be attitude—both internally and externally. Internally, employees must be treated like family. Externally, customers must be treated like family. Without attitude changes all other facets of a service program will fail.

Bill: *One day in San Diego I had lunch in a modest Mexican restaurant. The owners were a family who barely spoke English, but they were very hospitable. As soon as I sat down I was given water, chips, and salsa. I glanced at the menu and what I read on the cover set the tone for the entire meal: "Welcome! We take great pride in the preparation of our food and use only quality ingredients to present authentic Mexican cuisine. Our food speaks for itself. Allow us the pleasure of providing you with a memorable dining experience. Relax and enjoy yourselves."* They created an expectation and lived up to it. The service was friendly and attentive; the food was freshly-prepared and tasty.

Customer Contact. Expectations are often created before a customer takes a step through your door. The impressions given by hotel reservationists, restaurant hostesses, receptionists, secretaries, and other front-line people speak volumes about the companies they work for. The difference can be as subtle as a courteous, "May I help you, Sir?" at McDonald's versus "What can I do you for?" at another fast food restaurant.

Salespeople play a major role in managing expectations—by the promises they make, style of selling, after-sale follow-up, and overall professionalism. Take the automobile industry. To make a sale, the stereotypical car salesman promises the world. For doing so, he has no credibility with the service department, which must operate under realistic parameters. So customers are often disappointed when the service department can't deliver on the salesman's promise.

Instead of promising everything under the sun, the salesman should take the time to find out what is important to his customers. Then he can customize his approach and manage expectations more realistically. For example, Phil travels an average of 130 days per year. When he brings his car in for service, he does so just before leaving town for three to five days. Sometimes he drops it off on his way to the airport. When he has a plane to catch, Phil can't wait around while the service manager fills out the paperwork and takes care of the people before him.

If Phil were shopping for a new car, an astute salesman would discover Phil's needs, likes and dislikes, and would come up with a promise that made sense for Phil.

Salesman: "Mr. Wexler, if you buy a car from me today I will make these arrangements with our service department. The day you want to bring in your car, simply call first, tell us what you need, drive up and leave the car. You won't have to wait. In return, we understand that we can have your car for three days."

That is how you add value to a sale—by creating realistic service expectations.

Promises. Managing expectations can be as simple as telling people what to expect! A couple of years ago American Express Travel Service solved a problem in this way. People would charge airline tickets on American Express, not take the flight and call to arrange for a credit to their accounts. For some reason, the credit from the airlines took longer than other credit transactions, so the credit didn't show up on the next statement as people had expected. After a lot of complaints, management simply had their customer service people tell the customers to expect the credit to show up two months later. Once they were told the reason, people didn't mind waiting.

When you promise a customer something, promise only what you can realistically deliver, and then work at delivering more. A friend of ours relates the following story.

> Garry: *I was in a car accident in which the other driver was at fault. I called a body shop and, among other things, asked how long they would need the car. The owner said they could fix the car in a week to ten days. The job ended up taking seven weeks! During that time I spoke to someone whose car was also repaired at that shop. Her car took seven weeks as well.*

There are three facets to managing expectations: the promises you make, your ability to keep those promises, and the degree to which you have matched your promises to your customers' needs. You need all three facets to realistically and effectively manage customers' service expectations.

Consistency. We know a man who traveled halfway around the world to Japan on business. It was late at night and he was hungry, so he looked for a McDonald's. Why? He knew what to expect from McDonald's. Their food is consistent and predictable. It was a safe bet for him to make late at night when he wasn't in the mood to experiment.

Doing business with your company shouldn't be hit or miss. Your products and services must be consistent. There is a time and place for being operations-focused, when you are smoothing out and perfecting what you do. But that focus is part-time and lasts only as long as it takes for you to put your systems in place. Once that's done, you need to focus primarily on the customer.

Pricing. Pricing plays a major role in how you manage expectations and what kind of customers you attract. The higher the price, the more demanding your customers will be; and your service must meet or exceed the standards your customers expect.

> Garry: *I went into a men's clothing store that carries very expensive Italian suits, slacks, and shirts. Although I had never done it before, I was ready to splurge and spend a lot of money if I found the right pair of pants. I found them—a pair of beautiful silk pants for $265. The fabric and colors were gorgeous. I tried them on and knew that, with a little tailoring, they'd look great. In the dressing room I figured all I needed was a little nudge from one of the salespeople and I would buy the pants.*
>
> *I went out to the three-way mirror, stood on the platform and waited for someone to come over and say, "They sure look good. How do they feel? Let me pin up the hems so you can really see how they look." What I got was nothing—and I was the only customer in the store! I must have stood there for five minutes. I was furious! There I was, ready to buy this very expensive pair of pants and no one had the sense to come over and be attentive. I wasn't about to close the sale myself!*
>
> *I was so annoyed I decided not to buy the pants, out of spite! That store didn't deserve my business. In my mind, if I'm going to pay $265 for a pair of pants, I want the clerks to treat me as if I were royalty. Or even to act as if they knew I was in the store!*
>
> *On my way out I said to the clerk, "Those were nice pants." She agreed. "You would have had a sale, too," I told her, "if you had given me some service." She looked at me as if I were from Mars.*

Price integrity is an important part of managing customer expectations. It also says a lot about your professionalism. It doesn't matter what criterion you use to set your prices, as long as you charge every customer the same price. (We're not talking about volume discount pricing here.) Either your price is a fair price or it isn't. If it isn't, then you should lower it for everyone. The only time you charge someone more is when there's an extenuating circumstance you can explain to the person.

Price integrity adds to your integrity and professional image. Playing with prices leads to distrust and a poor reputation. Ask the average person if they enjoy buying a new car. Why do you think most people are skeptical about a car salesman's integrity?

> **SERVICE R$_x$:**
> Carefully manage your customers' expectations; then exceed them.

Expectations and Perceived Value

Expectations are relative to the price you pay for a product or service. The number of services you expect at Marshall's is much fewer than the number of services you would expect at Georgio Armani. The same can be said of the services you expect in a hotel compared to the services you would expect in a motel. In essence, you get what you pay for.

When comparing two or more companies on the basis of service, you have to be careful not to compare apples with oranges. It isn't fair to compare a Westin hotel to a Super 8 motel. The question is not how they compare to each other, but how they compare to other hotels or motels in their class. Super 8 motels give you what they promise. They promise a clean room, a low price, and friendly service; and that's what you get. There are *fewer* services, but the things they do are done well.

An analogy from the yacht racing world is appropriate here. When a sailboat race is held, all kinds of boats participate. There are different classes of boats, from large, fast ones to short, slow ones. When the starting gun goes off, the race seems to be between all the boats on the water. In reality, however, it is between boats within each class. So if you are at the helm of a short, slow boat you would only have to worry about beating other short, slow boats. You could be the 15th boat to cross the finish line, but still be the first place winner in your class.

Perceived value is something we use to evaluate a business. Simply stated, do you get your money's worth? This judgement automatically takes into consideration price and services offered. You could even formulate a hypothetical mathematical equation for perceived value:

$$\text{PERCEIVED VALUE} = \frac{\text{SERVICES} \times \text{SERVICE}}{\text{PRICE}}$$

When you've paid more than the services were worth, you come out with a number less than one. When the services are greater than the price, the number for perceived value is greater than one. Whenever you ask yourself if you got your money's worth, you're unconsciously calculating the relationship between price, services, and service—perceived value.

There is an important lesson here for people in a position to affect the perceived value of their products or services. When competition is stiff, most businesses immediately think they have to lower their prices. Lowering prices is not always the answer and can, in fact, lead to financial trouble.

In the '90s, many industries are facing the curse of being positioned in the "middle of the road." Companies such as Holiday Inn, Sears, and J.C. Penney are struggling against a slew of competitors attacking from above and below. Rivals are offering either more luxurious goods or just plain less expensive ones. Companies positioned in the mid-price range are finding their marketshares shrinking. They need ways to break out of being lost in a morass of mediocrity.

The problem is due to increased competition and changing demographics. The middle class is slowly disappearing. People want to shop either at the discount stores or the glitzy, exclusive stores. Low-priced Wal-Mart is prospering, as is swanky Neiman-Marcus.

Restaurants have been affected as well. Marriott Corporation quit the restaurant business because its middle of the road chains—Allies, Bob's Big Boy, and Wag's coffee shops—were stuck in a nebulous niche that few customers wanted. They were not as cheap or appealing to children as fast-food chains; nor could they please adults who wanted a more upscale dining experience.

For some companies, the answer is to add value by improving service and adding services that cost little or nothing, but are greatly appreciated by customers. For other companies, the answer is to target their markets more carefully. For everyone, the answer is to find out—in exacting detail—what customers want, and give it to them.

Invite Creative Demands

Companies with excellent service also create an environment in which customers can be creative with their needs and wants. This is done in two ways: by encouraging customers to verbalize their requests and by giving customers ideas for new services.

Why aren't people more demanding? Why don't people ask for better service—whether it's in a restaurant, hotel or a retail store? The reason is they are afraid of being turned down—or worse, laughed at. How do you feel when you read a menu and it says, "No substitutions." Does the restaurant's inflexibility inspire you to come back? Conversely, imagine how you would feel if the bottom of the menu said, "If you don't see it, please ask for it. If we can make it, we will."

In a market-focused organization, one of the goals is to encourage requests. The request that someone makes one day may be a service that 100 other customers need, but have not verbalized. Before you implement the change or introduce the new service, however, you should ask 100 other customers if that is what they want. Don't assume the vocal minority reflects the needs of the silent majority.

By creating an environment that encourages demanding customers, you will:

- Gain a more accurate picture of your target market's wants and needs.

- Learn what your competition may be doing for your customers.

- Get the jump on your competition by providing a level of service they're not providing. This is what progressive customer service is all about—getting ahead and staying ahead.

- Create opportunities to exceed customers' expectations, which lead to loyalty and word of mouth advertising.

- Make the extraordinary the ordinary. With progressive customer service, every routine service you provide today was, at one time, a special request. Creative destruction is making yesterday's exception today's standard practice.

Your customers must not be afraid to speak up and ask for what they want. The way to rid them of their fear is to make it obvious that the lines of communication are open. Let customers know you care. When someone makes a request, the attitude of the person taking the request should be genuine appreciation for the request and an automatic attempt to comply. Too many employees get into the habit of reacting with an automatic, "No, we don't do things that way around here." If a request is outside the parameters of the authority a service provider has been given, the answer should be, "Let me check into that and get back to you," or "Let me ask my manager how we can do that for you."

We've all had experiences in which a request was met by a blank stare, folded arms, or some other indication that a tremendous burden was being placed on the service provider. Reactions like this are the business equivalent of cyanide. This type of resistance to service is one of the major problems that must be solved in American businesses. Far too many employees have the attitude that their jobs would be great if it weren't for the intrusion of customers.

Sincerity is essential in providing quality service. You have to want to help your customers. If you don't like people, find a job where you work with machines or animals. False sincerity in a service culture will not work. Note the difference between a waitress asking, "Is everything all right?" and "Is your steak cooked the way you like it?" The former is perfunctory, the latter is specific, sincere, and more likely to evoke an honest answer and a better tip.

Compare the sincere desire to serve people demonstrated by the people in the next two stories.

> Phil: *I took a flight recently that was a through-flight. When it landed, everyone got off the plane except me. The plane was empty except for the crew. I was sitting in first class reading. When it was time to board the new passengers, one of the flight attendants, not knowing I could hear her, said, "Here come the cattle."*
>
> *Another time I was having dinner with my family at La Pomplamousse in Las Vegas. Toward the middle of our meal, my daughter said to the waiter, "I noticed there wasn't any ice cream on the menu. I would really love some ice cream. Could you check the freezer and see if there is any to be had?"*
> *The waiter disappeared and returned with good news and bad news. The bad news was that the restaurant had no ice cream. The good news was that the chef offered to make some. He then asked what her favorite flavor was and she said chocolate.*

The chef may have made the ice cream or he may have sent a bus boy to the local store. Does it matter? No. Even if he sent a bus boy, that's okay. The important thing was that the waiter made Phil's daughter happy. The waiter's commitment to excellence and his sincere desire to accommodate his customer's wants created an immeasurable amount of goodwill and, no doubt, a generous tip.

Saying yes will train your customers to speak up with their requests rather than remaining silent. Every time they get creative and ask for something unique, your service will give them a new standard by which to judge you and your competitors. When customers ask for what they want and discover, from disappointing experiences elsewhere, that you are the only one willing to give it to them, they will be your customers forever.

Give Customers New Ideas

Another way to create demanding customers is to give them ideas they haven't had before. Trigger their imaginations so they will ask for services and give you ideas for serving them in ways your competition hasn't thought of. That is how you continue to differentiate yourself in the marketplace—with progressive customer service.

Giving your customers ideas that allow you to exceed their expectations is, in effect, showing them how to increase the perceived value of their business with you. The ideas can be presented with the glitz and splash of an ad campaign or with subtlety.

> Phil: *I checked into a hotel, got up to my room and was famished. On the dresser was a room service card and a miniature menu from the hotel's restaurant. There was nothing on the room service menu that looked attractive. Now normally I wouldn't have thought to order a meal from the restaurant and have them deliver it to my room, but the association of the two menus there on the dresser gave me the idea. I called room service and gave them my order. The woman on the other end said they didn't serve the restaurant items in rooms, only in the restaurant. I asked her why they had put the menu in the room and her response was, "We were hoping you would see something on the menu that you liked and it would entice you to come down to our restaurant for dinner." I told her that it half-worked.*

There are two endings to this story. The best ending goes like this:

> *The room service woman said, "Rather than disappoint you, I'll have one of the waiters get the meal from the restaurant and bring it up to your room. You can plan to have it in about twenty minutes. By the way, you've just given us the type of feedback that allows us to keep in touch with our guests' needs, so as a token of our appreciation, I'd like to send up a glass of wine with your meal. Would you care for a glass of Cabernet or White Zinfandel?"*

What has happened in this case? The hotel management created an expectation and not only met it, but exceeded it. At the same time, they turned Phil into a more demanding customer. The next time he goes to a hotel, he's going to expect to be able to order the restaurant's menu items from room service. In fact, since that incident, every time Phil goes into a hotel, before going up to his room, he gets a copy of the menu from the restaurant. He now has a new level of service to expect. So not only did he judge the first hotel by the new standard of service it provided, he also judges every other hotel by this new standard. That is how businesses create demanding customers who will not be satisfied elsewhere.

SERVICE R$_x$:
Set the quality service standards in your industry. That is where the competitive advantage lies. Avoid being the one playing catch-up to your competitors.

Now the second ending to the story, which, unfortunately, is what really happened.

The woman on the phone said, "I'm sorry the restaurant items are not available through room service," and that was the end of it. I didn't get my meal.

Certainly not an outcome that would make you rush back to that hotel. What the hotel was doing was creating demanding customers and failing to live up to the expectations. They would have been better off not creating demanding customers in the first place than building their expectations and disappointing them.

Employees play a major role in creating demanding customers. They are in the perfect position to constantly look for ways to anticipate customers' needs and fulfill them. That is how to add value to every interaction.

A man walks into your sporting goods store and says, "I've been shopping in this store for a long time. I'd like to buy a pair of ski boots, but I've got a narrow foot and am concerned about getting a pair that fits well. I was wondering if, after you take the time to fit the boots, you would guarantee the fit. If you will, I'll buy a pair today."

Where do you think this customer got the idea for a guaranteed fit on ski boots? Did he imagine it? In all likelihood, he heard about it at another sporting goods store and is now asking you to do the same. He is being precisely what you want him to be, a demanding customer.

It's important to give customers the opportunity to ask for the unusual. Realize that customers are doing you a favor when they make requests. In effect, they are giving you, out of loyalty, the chance to catch up to your competitors.

What if the scenario were slightly different. What if he were not a loyal customer? Instead of bringing his request to you, he'd simply buy his boots elsewhere. What if he were not a customer at all, but a prospect interviewing a handful of companies for his business? If you didn't comply with his request, you'd lose the sale. It is important to realize that the only scenario in which you get a chance to catch up or exceed your competitors is when a loyal customer gives you the opportunity by being demanding.

The Service Standards Meetings

It's a good idea to have one or two members from each department get together periodically to discuss service standards. "Where are we today?" and "Where do we want to be in the future?" are just two of the many questions that should be addressed. Evaluate how interdepartmental cooperation has fared and what can be done to improve it. When you think of how service standards are set, however, you will see why they often fall short.

One element often missing in service standards meetings is the most important of all . . . the customer.

SERVICE R$_x$:
Your company does not set service standards. *Your customers set service standards.* Your company only determines how well it will respond to customers' requirements.

By inviting customers to service standards meetings, you may discover that some of your services are unnecessary and a waste of money. Take that money and spend it on services your customers want. This is one way to ask customers, "What should we be doing to serve you better?"

SERVICE R$_x$:
Create an environment in which your customers are
continually guiding your service efforts.

Keep In Touch

Keeping in touch with customers is the only way to gather valuable
input. Your company has to evaluate its service and make the necessary
changes based on customer feedback. Ask a lot of questions, including
the most simple:

"How satisfied are our customers?"

"What percentage of the market buys from us again?"

"What elements are most important in maintaining customer
satisfaction?"

"How well do our sales and service people compare to the competition's?"

There are many ways to systematically keep track of your customer's
satisfaction. Surveys work well and can be conducted either formally or
informally. A formal survey would be a relatively lengthy, structured
questionnaire that people either fill out and return or answer with an
interviewer. An informal survey would be a couple of brief questions used
as an exit poll. For example, a new video store might ask, "How did you
hear of us?" as customers are checking out. A grocery store cashier might
ask customers, "Do you cut coupons out of the newspaper?"

Direct Mail

Some companies send their customers pre-paid postcards that ask for
feedback. One of the authors received a postcard from the May
Company. The card said:

Dear Customer,

All of us at May Company want you to be served properly. Our records show you recently shopped in our Mission Valley store. As a part of our continuing efforts to see how we are doing, would you please tell us if the service you received at Mission Valley (location of store) was:

[ ]　　　[ ]　　　[ ]　　　[ ]
1　　　　2　　　　3　　　　4
Below　　　　　　　　　　　　Above
Expectations　　　　　　　　Expectations

We would also be pleased to have any comments you wish to make: _____
_____
_____

This postcard is a good idea. There are several ways to make it even better; give the customer an incentive to fill it out. Tell them that their opinion is highly valued and if they fill out the card and return it, the company will give them a $5.00 credit on their account. Another way to do it would be to try to get the person to come into the store again. So the offer would be a gift for those who bring the card back to the store. A sentence on the card or in the cover letter should also encourage people to be honest. You do not want the $5.00 credit or gift to buy compliments, you want it to buy honest feedback.

In 1990 the Ford Motor Company implemented a direct mail customer feedback program. Ninety days after someone buys a new car they receive a feedback form in the mail. When Ford gets those cards back, it quantifies the responses and give each card a score. Any customer whose card falls below a certain score automatically gets a phone call from Ford to see what the problem is. Phone calls are also made to customers who report specific problems with their cars or dealers. If a problem can't be resolved over the phone, the customer's case is passed on to the dealer.

Ford's program is unlike any other in the American auto industry and represents a multi-million dollar commitment to stay close to the customers.

Surveys

The Red Lobster restaurant chain is a good example of a market-focused organization. It conducts numerous surveys to find out exactly what their customers want. The surveys are conducted by outside polling agencies and by Red Lobster. One is a bimonthly poll of nearly 35,000 people at different restaurants asking about their dining experience. Another method is a monthly mailing to 40,000 customers to ask them to rate Red Lobster against 15 competitors. They also conduct surveys to determine the success of new products.

Surveys can be conducted in person, over the phone, or through the mail. The method used depends on the quantity and nature of the data you are seeking. If you want a lot of quantifiable data about existing products or services, then a direct mail survey is the answer. Direct mail surveys tend to paint broad pictures. People are either satisfied or dissatisfied to a greater or lesser extent. What you don't find out are the details of their emotions—exactly what caused them to feel that way.

When you want to find out details, give people the opportunity to answer open-ended questions and provide qualitative information. The only way to do that is by using telephone or personal interviews. Obviously, the number of people you can interview is significantly less than the number you can reach via direct mail. The quality of the data, however, is far more useful.

A survey based on interviews is labor intensive, expensive, complex, and difficult to analyze. The analysis is qualitative, so the people best suited to do the analysis are the interviewers. Since customers were responding narratively, the interviewers may come away with little more than an overall impression or intuitive sense. For this reason, it is wise to develop an interview questionnaire that seeks both qualitative and quantitative answers.

Customer Comment Cards

Customer comment cards are one of the easiest, least expensive, and most common methods of collecting customer feedback. Like surveys and direct mail cards, comment cards are helpful as broad gauges of customer sentiment. They fail, however, to elicit the specific complaints a company needs to become aware of. Customer comment cards are usually short—to maximize response rate—and can be construed as impersonal. Most people with bad experiences won't bother to cram the details of their dissatisfaction onto a small card, especially when they don't believe it will help to resolve their problem or change the company's service. It could be argued, therefore, that only a few customers, the most happy and the most unhappy, will take the time to respond to comment cards. Comment cards will be discussed in more detail in chapter ten.

SERVICE R$_x$:
The best market research measures perceptions, not choices. Whenever possible, give customers a blank canvas on which to paint a picture. Avoid closed-ended, multiple-choice questions.

Focus Groups

Focus groups are opportunities for you to interview your customers directly. Invite some of your best customers into the office, feed them to keep them happy, and ask how the company is doing. Representatives from each department should not be present. The focus is on customers.

Focus groups work very well despite the artificial setting. You might think a group of customers who have been well-fed and invited to participate in a discussion would be hesitant to air their grievances about their hosts. On the contrary, even in focus groups that are video-taped, participants waste little time in getting down to what's on their minds. For this reason, focus groups are a powerful market research tool.

When conducting the focus group, it's important to manage your customer's expectations. Avoid giving the impression that you will implement all their suggestions. The meeting is simply a fact-finding mission. Later, follow-up by letting everyone know what you did with their recommendations. If you plan to implement a suggestion, tell them. If you are not going to use some of their suggestions, let them know why.

Not So Simple Observation

Japanese auto makers can be very creative with their market research. Creative? How about meticulous and obsessive! In the 1980s the entire automobile industry became almost consumed with market research. Designers no longer isolated themselves in their Detroit offices. American and Japanese auto makers opened satellite design studios in Southern California, an area considered to be the real world laboratory for the auto industry.

The Japanese took their market research, which they call "observational research," to the nth degree. Their ways of digging deep into the motives, tics, and desires of consumers was nothing short of obsessive. In the summer of 1988, Nissan sent Takashi Morinoto, a design intern from Tokyo, to Costa Mesa, California, to live with an American family for six weeks. During that time, he accompanied the family everywhere, photographed their house from every conceivable angle and tenaciously studied the neighborhood. This last activity was noticed by a policeman, who stopped Morinoto on suspicion of casing the neighborhood.

"The important thing is to get inside people's minds," said Makato Tachikawa, Nissan's director of product strategy. "Sometimes they cannot say for themselves. So we are judges, carefully watching."

And they watch everyone, everywhere. They question school teachers about the cars their students' parents drive. They camp out at Big Bear Lake to watch families on vacation. They drive through UCLA's parking lots to see how students use cars to make personal statements. They follow wealthy Mercedes drivers through Beverly Hills and take notes of their stops and shopping habits.

All this in an attempt to design the types of cars their customers want. That's being market-focused. It's what you do if you want to be the best.

The Nuances of Market Research

Market research is a tool that some swear by and others denounce as meaningless. Those who denounce it often subscribe to the theory, "If it ain't broke, don't fix it." Those who believe in market research would say, "It's not broken, but let's break it and fix it anyway so we can strive for perfection." There is no doubt, however, that market research is here to stay. Each year companies spend millions of dollars to try to determine what people want and how to give it to them.

There are two ways to ask a marketing question, only one of which will yield a usable answer. You can ask, "Would you buy this product?" That is an operations-focused way of looking at the marketplace. In effect it asks the consumer, "Would you take it or leave it?" The market-focused form of the question would be, "What do you want this product to be like?" In other words, "Tell us what you want. How can we best serve you?"

The operations-focused question, "Would you buy this product?" is unrealistic and misleading. It's asked in a vacuum. No price is attached and you don't have to reach into your wallet for money. So you are not asked to make a value judgement. You would buy a lot of things under those circumstances, but would you buy them in real life? The best market research attaches a price to the product or service to determine what the market is willing to pay.

SERVICE R$_x$:
The best market research is a real salesperson asking a real prospect to buy. If there is a sale, what made it possible? If there was no sale, why not?

The way you phrase your research questions is important. Phrasing can be as simple as asking your customers, "How are we doing?" "Where is there room for improvement?" "How would you like to see things done differently?" By asking these questions, you not only get information, you also encourage loyalty. Customers like the fact that you care enough about them to ask for feedback.

It's not enough to ask customers, "What's broken and how can we fix it?" Ask them to create an entirely new model for you. Have them paint a picture of their ideal supplier.

SERVICE R$_x$:
Market research is not something you do once in a while. It is something you do continually. The company that takes its finger off the pulse of the marketplace risks losing marketshare.

What is the most effective way to win customers from your competitors? The common answer is to provide excellent service. That's one correct answer, but it is the "B" answer. The "A" answer is to find out what your customers want but are not getting from your competitors. Then give your customers what they're missing elsewhere. That's finding a need gap and filling it. That's managing your customer's expectations and then exceeding them. That's selling with quality service.

As a company, how do you prevent your competitor's from stealing customers away? Start talking to your customers. You've heard it before. Keep in touch with your customers. Find out what they want.

SERVICE R$_x$:
When doing market research, it is not enough to find
out what *you* are *not* doing for your customers. The
most effective sales strategy is to find out what *your
competitors* are not doing for their customers.

Consistency Is the Backbone of Reliability

Maintaining consistency can be a problem for some businesses when
their market gets soft. The common mistake is to cut back on services
in order to save money. By doing so, however, you turn yourself into
a commodity rather than remaining differentiated by virtue of your
service.

A good example is an experience that Phil had in Houston after the
decline in the oil industry affected the hotel business.

Phil: *I pulled up to a Hyatt Hotel late one night in a cab and was waiting for the bellman to come out for my bags. When no one showed up, I went inside and was told by the desk clerk that they had sent him home early because business had been so slow that day. I asked if they had lowered the price of a room because they'd sent the bellman home. The desk clerk thought I was joking and laughed.*

It's obvious that Hyatt missed the relationship between price, service, reputation, and expectations. Their reputation in the marketplace has created certain expectations in their guests. People expect a bellman. People expect 24-hour room service. People expect first-class service, regardless of price. Once that expectation has been created, the hotel service must live up to it. They can raise their prices if necessary—customers will decide if they still want to stay there—but they cannot disappoint guests by eliminating expected services.

The Houston Hyatt made two mistakes. First, they should not have sent their bellman home because business was slow that day. By doing so, they cheated their guests out of a service that was expected. Second, after they sent him home, they should have compensated their guests by lowering their prices. This, however, wouldn't have made Phil happy. Most business travelers don't care about price (within reasonable limits). They want the Hyatt's services, not a cheaper room. If they want to save money at a limited-services hotel, they choose a different hotel.

The key is consistency. You can raise or lower your prices as long as you simultaneously raise or lower customers' expectations in advance (through advertising, public relations, and customer contact). Remember, it would not have been sufficient for the Hyatt to tell Phil, "Mr. Wexler, business has been very slow lately so we don't have a bellman or room service tonight; however, we will charge you only $30 for your room."

In a soft market, the solution is not to lower your prices. Instead, market yourself better! While consulting for a Westin Hotel in the soft market of Houston, Phil was asked, "How do we avoid lowering our prices to meet our competition when they are lowering their prices because the market is so soft?" The answer was, you don't lower your prices, you remind your customers that they're buying more than a room. They are buying the Westin name and all the quality service that comes with it. Point out that the competition may have slashed their prices, but chances are very good that they have also slashed their services. Regarding the Westin's concern about losing business, short-term, they had to realize that in the long run they were better off with fewer guests in the hotel at higher room rates than more guests at lower rates.

From the company's point of view, it comes down to short-term versus long-term thinking. Long-term thinking dictates that you maintain your market differentiation with consistent service. Brian Palmer of the National Speakers Bureau has said the most important thing he looks for in a professional speaker is consistency. "I don't care what level of speaker you are compared to your colleagues. Whatever level that is, I want to be able to know that I can rely on that ability *every time* you do a speech for one of our clients. I don't care if you never get better as long as you never get worse."

The NBD Phenomenon

The NBD phenomenon occurs when a company touts their service as something special, when, in fact, it's quite ordinary. The customer's response to the special service is No Big Deal! (NBD)

There are always minimum standards that a company must meet to remain acceptable. When they make the mistake of trying to fool the public by touting those minimum standards as special, they insult customers' intelligence. And when the standards of an industry—such as the airline industry—fall to the point where people cheer the minimums, then the industry is in trouble.

Several years ago American Airlines sent an expensive brochure to their frequent flyers. The brochure reminded customers that American Airlines is committed to taking off and landing on time, handling baggage properly, and so on. At the time, the airline industry was a mess, so this reminder of a commitment to basic services was thought by American to be a big deal. In reality, once they started providing that basic service, it was no longer perceived by the customer as a big deal. The customer's attitude was, "NBD! That's what I'm paying for. That's the least they can do." When you pay hundreds of dollars for a plane ticket, you aren't just paying for a seat on a plane; you are paying to be fed edible food, to take off and land on time, and to receive courteous service and proper baggage handling.

Once you are given the basics, which are the minimum acceptable standards, you expect more if you've paid more and have been promised more. For example, Americans who fly first class receive less service than overseas first-class travelers. Foreign airlines (and U.S. based airlines that fly outside the U.S.) give first-class baggage a higher priority than baggage from other classes. If you fly first class, your baggage is tagged as such and is unloaded first.

Why haven't American airlines tried to think of new ways to increase the value of a first class ticket? The answer is simple: Before deregulation they got into the habit of being operations-focused. Now airlines are beginning to rethink their strategies, which means putting service at the top of their priority list.

At one point during 1988-89, Holiday Inn's advertising slogan was, "No Surprises!" The headline was, in fact, a little misleading. After reading the fine print, you realized they didn't mean there would be no surprises; it meant if there were surprises, they would fix them. If they couldn't fix them, they would refund your money and move you to another hotel.

If you go to virtually any decent hotel in the country and have a problem they can't resolve, they will give you your money back or give you the room for free. This policy is neither new to the hospitality industry nor is it new to Holiday Inn.

What made it special was that Holiday Inn decided to capitalize on it. They found out what was important to their guests and promoted it, thereby turning the ordinary into the extraordinary. Not only did they offer a money-back guarantee, but more importantly, they improved the environment for complaints, which is an important facet of service that we will discuss in the next chapter.

Is There Such Thing As Too Much Service?

From the customer's point of view, there is never too much service, *if* the service is relevant. People don't mind paying for the services they want, but nobody wants to pay for services they don't need. A customer can always ask for less service. For example, if you're in a clothing store and a salesperson is being too attentive, you can simply say you are just browsing. There is such a thing as too much service, if that service is not what the customer wants.

When targeting customers' needs, you must avoid giving them "extras" that only *you* think they want.

A fun story illustrates this well. In the play, Sugar Babes, Mickey Rooney reenacted an old vaudeville routine:

A man checks into a hotel, goes up to his room, and tries to go to sleep. There is construction going on in the middle of the night, so this guy can't catch a wink. At four in the morning he goes down to the front desk to check out.

"I'm checking out," the man says, "this place is noisy as hell!" The desk clerk hands him his bill. The bill is for $450.

"Four hundred and fifty dollars," the man screams, "I only had a lousy $100 room!"

"Yes, but what about our restaurants?" the clerk asks.

"I didn't eat in any of your restaurants," the guest replies.

"Yes, but they were available," the clerk says with a smile.

"How much was that?" the man questions.

"That was $100."

"What about the other $250?" the man asks again.

"That's for our health club," the clerk answers.

"I never used your health club!" the man screams.

"Yes, but it was available," the clerk repeats. This goes on and on for a while. Finally, Mickey Rooney hands the clerk $450.

"If that's how you're going to be, here's your money," he says, "and, by the way, I'm in New York to go to divorce court and I'm going to subpoena you as a co-respondent in my divorce case."

"I never even met your wife," the clerk said.

"Yes, but she was available!"

Make your "extras" relevant. Keep in touch and find out what your customers want. Jan Carlzon, Chairman of Scandinavian Airline System and author of *Moments of Truth*, proposed that you are better off doing a 3% better job at things your customers want than doing a 100% better job at things they don't care about.

> **SERVICE R$_x$:**
> **Create services that your customers *notice* when you deliver those services to them and *miss* when they go elsewhere.**

If you give your customers excellent service in an area they don't care about, they won't notice it and, therefore, won't miss it when they go somewhere else.

Attitude is Everything

How do you create an environment in which your customers feel comfortable being demanding? It requires open lines of communication and friendly, receptive people. Service is a people business in which attitude is everything.

Part of an attitude of excellence is the elimination of the words "I can't" from your vocabulary. In fact, "We can" should be a company-wide policy. Every service provider should get in the habit of thinking "I can."

When you tell a customer, "I can't," in essence, you are saying, "I don't want to," which is your customer's cue to take his or her business elsewhere.

Creating demanding customers provides you with ongoing opportunities to be creative in taking your customers from a state of contentment to a state of bliss. Sometimes customers need to be nudged a bit, that is, shown how they can get more if they want it. How do you encourage customers to be demanding?

- Ask. Form focus groups and conduct market research.

- Educate your customers. Tell them you want them to voice their opinions and make their needs and wants known. This can be done in your advertising and in person. (See Max's Laws.)

- Recognize and reward customers for their input. If you make a change based on a customer's suggestion, call and say so.

- Train management to support all employee efforts to serve customers. Provide ongoing training and coaching.

- Give employees the authority they need to say yes.

- Avoid having a "Black Hole" culture, a company in which information goes in and disappears forever. Establish an internal feedback system for following up on customer requests so they don't get lost in layers of management.

The marketplace is the most powerful entity in our society. In fact, the marketplace may prove to be the most powerful force in the world. The political upheavals taking place in the former Soviet Union and other Eastern European countries can be attributed to the push and pull of economic forces. Economic pressures are proving to be much greater than political forces. The marketplace has proven itself to be the great equalizer, the force that has removed the threat of communism and reduced the military tensions between the world's super-powers.

All this is a way of saying that you have to give customers what they want. And you can't give them what they want if you don't know what that is.

SERVICE R$_X$:
Encourage demanding customers.

Chapter Ten

Nurturing Complaining Customers

What would you do? Your airline flight is canceled, causing you significant inconvenience. Would you grumble to yourself and quietly wait for the next flight or would you complain? You should complain and demand to be put on another airline, a service that was mandatory before deregulation, but is provided now only when requested.

What would you do if you ate in a restaurant, got sick a couple of hours later, and were told by a doctor that you had a mild case of food poisoning? Would you suffer through and then swear never to eat at that restaurant again or would you call and tell the owner or manager about your illness and demand some form of restitution. You should call and demand restitution. You may not want to accept an offer of a free meal, but you would accept being reimbursed for the tainted dinner. Then you would swear never to eat there again.

In chapter one, we mentioned that service is bad because customers let businesses get away with murder. The sad fact is—most people do not complain. It could be a result of upbringing, experience, education, or socioeconomic status. Whatever the reason, there will always be people who are too timid to speak up or don't believe complaining will make a difference.

SERVICE R$_x$:
As a customer, there are two things you should do if you want to receive good service. Complain when you don't get it and reward it when you do. People can only meet your expectations when they know what your expectations are.

As a company, there are ways to help the timid become less inhibited and the skeptics become believers. The first step is to *create a positive complaint environment.*

SERVICE R$_x$:
One out of 27 people will complain when there is a problem. That's less than 4%! The other 96% will not complain to you, they will complain to their friends and family. In fact, they will tell between 8 and 20 people of their dissatisfaction. The 95% of those who were dissatisfied will not do business with you again.

The statistics on complaining customers and customer loyalty hold grave implications for those companies that don't welcome complaints. To appreciate the business lost to noncomplainers, consider the following hypothetical situation. The numbers are based on statistical averages.

For each person who comes to you with a complaint, there have been 26 others with similar problems who haven't come. They've taken their business elsewhere. What does it mean if you've had six customers tell you something is wrong? It means you have had that problem 162 times (27 X 6) and 156 of those times the customers chose not to complain. So you've already lost more customers than you've kept.

Now you have six people who are going to give you the opportunity to correct the problem. Five out of six of them (83%) will continue to do business with you *even if you do not fix the problem, if they perceive the person who took the complaint as friendly, caring, nondefensive, enthusiastic and committed to the relationship.*

Six more people walk in the door with complaints, which means you've had another 162 problems that caused 156 people to take their business to your competitors. Of the six people who were nice enough to complain, three (50%) will stop doing business with you *even if they get what they want, if they perceived the person who took the complaint as being unfriendly, defensive, and not committed to the relationship.*

SERVICE R$_x$:
There is a 33% swing between losing customers and keeping them, depending on how you treat them in a complaint situation.

Clearly, it isn't *what* you give someone in a complaint situation (within practical limits), it is *how* you treat them in the service process; that is, how customers feel when problems are resolved determines whether they will continue to be customers. People want recognition, validation, respect, empathy and assurance that someone cares about them as customers. The most loyal customers are those who have had a complaint and had it successfully resolved. They walk away feeling that they have an ongoing relationship with your business.

The statistics are powerful and carry a frightening warning worth heeding. They also beg the question, "Why?" Why do so many people remain silent when they should be speaking out? What determines the ratio of complainers to "silent grumblers?" Looking at the statistics above, the number of complainers is one out of twenty-seven.[3] If that's the average, then one could reasonably assume that there are extremes between the high and low ends of the scale. So, theoretically, there are companies that communicate so poorly that they hear only one out of 100 complaints. Conversely, there must be companies that communicate so well they hear every complaint. What's the difference? Why would one company hear more complaints than another?

Create a Positive Complaint Environment

A company hears more complaints when it creates an environment of receptiveness (versus hostility) towards complaining customers. Simply stated, some companies actively encourage complaints; others discourage them.

The airline industry has created a hostile environment for complainers. It's impossible to call them; they don't take phone complaints. If you have a complaint after a flight, you are directed to a customer service desk or a ticket counter. When you request to speak to the manager, you are bluntly asked, "Why?" They know why, but this is their way of running interference. When you tell the person you have a complaint, they hand you a form and say, "There's nothing we can do about it here. You'll have to write a letter."

"I'd like this bag to go to Chicago, this bag to New York, and this bag to go to Rome"
"We can't do that."
"Of course you can do it, you did it last month."

When you complain to the airlines and they ask you to write a letter, who should write it? They should. You should be able to stand there and speak your mind. Let *them* jump through the hoops and do the paperwork. If you wanted to write a letter in the first place, you would have. Most passengers don't bother.

SERVICE R$_x$:
Your company must always be interested in what customers think. Do more than listen to complaints. Solicit them. See them as opportunities for improvement. Resolve them with enthusiasm. The importance of a positive complaining environment cannot be overemphasized.

Given the fact that so few customers actually complain, what can be said about those who do? The good news is that complaining customers are doing you a favor. They care. They have made a choice of speaking up rather than quietly taking their business elsewhere.

The bad news is that most companies do not make it easy for customers to complain. When the complaint environment is hostile, only the most aggressive customers will speak up. The front-line people who handle the complaints end up resenting them, even though the front-line people were responsible for creating the environment that forced them to complain so aggressively.

This is where the downward spiral begins. Your front-line people who resent aggressive complainers make it even more difficult for them to complain. As the complaint environment becomes increasingly hostile, only the most hard-core of aggressive complainers will have the nerve to speak up. The cycle gets worse and worse until your customers stop doing business with you.

When you make it easy for people to complain, only a small fraction of the complainers will be the aggressive ones.

Tension Management

Questioning, listening, and feedback skills are all geared toward achieving one thing: reducing negative tension. Notice we said *negative* tension. Is there such a thing as positive tension?

The relationship between tension and productivity has been the focus of many studies, the most notable being that of Yerkese and Dodson. They found people function best within a range of tension that has become known as one's "comfort zone." As tension increases, so does performance, to a point. Beyond that point, if tension continues to increase, productivity decreases. In other words, either a lack of stimulation or too much stimulation is bad for performance. Between the two extremes is one's comfort zone or area of optimal productivity, which is different for everyone.

There are many types of tension, but they all come from three distinct sources: internal, relationship, and need tension.

Yerkese-Dodson Law

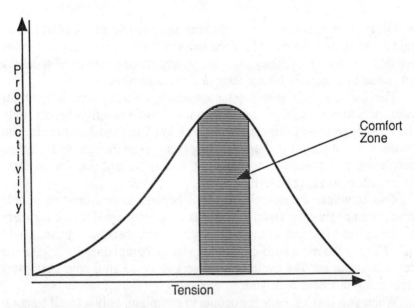

Figure 10.1: The Yerkese-Dodson Law suggests that some tension is desirable in keeping productivity high. However, productivity decreases when there is too much or too little tension.

Internal Tension

Internal or personal tension is an agitation due to negative thoughts or emotions. It could be something as simple as just having a bad day. As a service provider, and in your new role as a non-manipulative salesperson, you must be aware of *your* internal tension and *your* *customer's*. Part of your job is to be a tension manager; that is, reduce or increase tension as necessary. To do so, you have to operate on a tension level optimum for you.

If, in the course of working with customers, your tension level is high, you are going to upset people. Why would your tension level be higher than desired? There are several reasons, all of which can be eliminated:

Lack of preparation. If you come late to work or return late from lunch and have to hurry to get back to work, you may find yourself disorganized. Your frazzled state could be contagious and interactions with customers may suffer.

Lack of confidence. When you're new to a job, there are times when you feel inadequate. You may need more training or more time to sharpen your skills. At times like this, your internal tension will increase because you believe you should know all the answers. The solution is simple. Realize that you are working with a net! If you don't know the answers to every question, you can find out. Customers don't mind waiting for answers if the wait is reasonably short. So let yourself off the hook. No one said you have to be perfect.

Pressure to sell. Often a supervisor will implement a new program or introduce a goal or quota to be met. Perhaps you are a waiter being asked to sell more filet mignon. Whatever the case may be, you will naturally feel pressured. The key is to continue to serve your customers the way they want to be served. If the opportunity arises to increase your sales of filet mignon, then do it. If not, don't worry about it. Imagine two people going into a restaurant late one night and saying to their waiter, "We're just having coffee and dessert," and the waiter responding, "The dessert is lousy. May I recommend our filet mignon?"

Relationship Tension

Relationship tension is the normal tension that exists when two people interact. That tension can be either positive or negative, but it's always present. It is caused by the differences in the ways that people behave, handle stress, make jokes, prefer closeness, express emotions, disclose personal information, and other nuances of personal interactions.

Everything you do to help your customer remain in their comfort zone enhances the business relationship. Everything you do to take them out of their comfort zone will hurt the relationship. Non-manipulative salespeople are always observing customers, being sensitive to their tension level, and acting appropriately. Let's look at a common example.

Imagine you are a hotel desk clerk. One of your guests has just arrived from a cross-country flight. His day went something like this: His taxi to the airport got stuck in traffic, making him late for his flight. He ran to his gate only to find out a mechanical problem had caused a two-hour delay. He didn't sit in the waiting area, he *paced* for two hours while babies cried and mothers screamed at their rambunctious children. He finally arrived in your city and, due to poor air quality, his asthma kicked in. This exacerbated his fatigue as he made his way to an important meeting. He sat through a long, boring meeting that turned out to be a waste of time. After the meeting, he headed to your hotel during rush-hour traffic in a cab with no air conditioning. He walked into your lobby and up to the front desk looking like a man who had crawled across the Sahara pursuing one mirage after another.

Can you imagine how sensitive that customer would be to your disposition! One wrong word and he'd crack. Actually, one wrong word and you'd lose a customer. You see now why it is absolutely essential that you reduce your internal tension so you can deal with people objectively and pleasantly. A customer like this is someone with whom you must be flexible and willing to bend over backwards to accommodate.

How would you reduce this customer's tension? There are two ways to handle this gentleman. One way would be to politely say, "Gee, Mr. Schwartz, it looks like the world hasn't been too kind to you today." This observation does two things. It shows sensitivity, which Mr. Schwartz will appreciate, and it puts the blame for his condition on the world, not on him. The last thing a customer wants to hear is, "Gee, you look like you're in a terrible mood." That's a sure-fire way to annoy someone and make him defensive. Always put the blame on the environment. Better to show sympathy for Mr. Schwartz being a victim than to imply that he is to blame for his misery.

As soon as you acknowledge Mr. Schwartz's predicament, he will begin to relax. He will be less likely to look for imperfections in your service and may tell you ways to help make his stay more pleasant. He may, in essence, provide service opportunities that will help you exceed his expectations—service in the progressive zone!

Another way to handle Mr. Schwartz would be to say, "Gee, it looks like the world hasn't been too kind to you today. What happened?" Not only are you showing the sensitivity to acknowledge his physical and mental state, you are also showing him that you care enough to listen to his story. If he is inclined to open up, you have provided an invaluable service. His story-telling will reduce his tension and, again, he will give you hints as to ways to make his stay more pleasant. For example, you could ask him if he would like to have his calls held so he can sleep. If he's famished, you could immediately arrange for room service. You could recommend a masseuse or a soak in the hotel's jacuzzi. When you're creative, there are innumerable ways to add value to his purchase of a room.

Need Tension

At this moment, Mr. Schwartz has a lot of need tension. Need tension is the stress you feel when reality does not match what you desire. The discrepancy between real and ideal creates a "need gap."

As figure 10.2 illustrates, the larger the discrepancy between what you want and what you have, the greater your need gap. The more closely aligned the ideal and the actual, the smaller your need gap. This source of tension is based on expectations, wishes, and attitudes. If you had two customers with the need gaps shown in figure 10.2, which do you think would present more opportunities for sales, service and/or tension reduction?

As a non-manipulative salesperson and a service provider, part of your job is to size up a person's need gap and then find ways to reduce it. People often don't see the forest for the trees, so it is often necessary to make customers aware of their needs. That is where the gentle and tactful art of questioning comes into play.

With Mr. Schwartz, your questions could go like this: Mr. Schwartz, would you like to rest or eat first? If you like, I could take your room service order here and rush it through. If you want, I'll hold all your calls.

When a need is recognized by you and your customer, you can then propose a solution that will close the gap and eliminate that source of tension. After the solution has been implemented, you should follow-up to see if it did the job. With Mr. Schwartz, however, you might first let him sleep for a while.

Tension management, like relationship strategies, is a master skill; that is, it's a skill that affects virtually everything you do. It affects every aspect of your relationships with customers, co-workers, family, and friends.

One major benefit of non-manipulative selling is it eliminates the causes of tension for both the salesperson and the customer—the hard sell. The customer is an equal partner in the sales process, so he never

The Need Gap

The Difference between the Actual and the Ideal

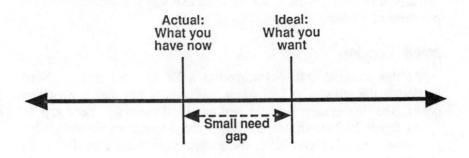

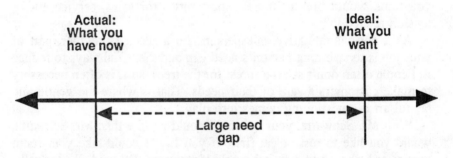

Figure 10.2: When the difference between what you have and what you want is small, the gap is easy to close. When the difference is great, the reverse is true.

feels manipulated or pressured. The salesperson is motivated by a sincere interest in the customer, so they sell only those things that are truly needed. It's a winning situation for everyone.

In a positive complaint environment, customers don't perceive their input as complaining. Front-line employees don't feel harassed and regard customers as allies rather than adversaries. Helpful suggestions are offered pleasantly. And let's face it, customers are doing you a favor when they complain—they're helping you improve your business.

Emil: *We were consulting for a newspaper group. They were evaluating their customer service by the number of complaint calls per 1000. They wanted to know how to reduce the number of calls. I told them, "Disconnect the phones." What they really wanted to do was reduce the problems that triggered the complaint calls, but they were only focusing on the ringing telephones.*

When you begin to make the transition from an operations-focused company to a market-focused company, the last thing you want to do is reduce the number of complaint calls. You want to encourage people to complain! They are trying to tell you how to improve your business. Complaints are only reduced over time as you provide a comfortable complaint environment, heed the feedback you receive, provide better service and, ultimately, give people fewer reasons to complain.

Communicate Openness

There are many ways to communicate to your customers the fact that your company is open to their suggestions and complaints. The most common way, one that works fairly well for small companies, is to have a suggestion box by the door. Many restaurants use variations of the suggestion box. They place customer comment cards on the tables.

The jury is still out on customer comment cards. Most marketing and customer service consultants believe they are, at best, a fair way to solicit suggestions. They're better than nothing. The problem with comment cards is that they start out being aimed toward everyone—demanding and complaining customers—but end up being used primarily by people with complaints. People who are satisfied or indifferent won't bother to fill them out; their comments are rarely heard.

A better way to solicit positive and negative feedback would be to have someone go right up and ask people about their dining experience. In other businesses, a survey and cover letter should be mailed periodically to every customer. Brief, nonthreatening surveys can gather a wide range of useful data from satisfied and dissatisfied customers.

When designing a customer comment card, don't fill it up with rating scales and questions that you want answered. A few closed-ended questions are okay, but leave most of the space blank as an invitation for customers to elaborate on their thoughts.

There are good and bad ways to handle customer comments. The bad way is to collect them and never thank customers for their feedback.

This is all too common. Granted, your ability to respond to each customer may be limited by manpower and the number of suggestions you receive. But most companies don't even think about responding, much less make an attempt.

The proper way to handle customer comments is to show your appreciation. Write a letter (a form letter will suffice) or call your customer to thank them. Then reward them by sending a coupon for a free dessert. Your response to the free dessert cannot be, " . . . but I'll be giving away hundreds of desserts every week!" If you were to give away hundreds of desserts for customer suggestions, imagine how much you would learn about your customers. That information alone would be worth hundreds of desserts! You have to spend money to make money. If you're going to improve your service, there's a price to be paid and hundreds of desserts is a very reasonable investment.

Another way to improve your company's complaint environment is to follow up after a sale. Too many salespeople are guilty of closing a sale, moving on to the next prospect, and forgetting about current customers. By following up at regular intervals after a sale, you not only create an opportunity to hear complaints, you also create opportunities to uncover additional needs and sell more.

There is overwhelming evidence to support the idea that customer satisfaction translates into bottomline dollars. To improve customer satisfaction, thousands of companies are using toll-free 800 numbers to help them keep in touch with their customers.

The Technical Assistance Research Program conducted a survey for Coca-Cola in which they found significant benefits of toll-free phone systems. They were able to show that a complaining customer who was denied a request over the phone was 30% more likely to remain loyal than a customer who was denied the same request by letter. Phone conversations are more personal. They give a service representative the opportunity to explain the company's position in a way that sounds fair and reasonable.

Toll-free numbers are faster and less expensive for the company handling a large volume of complaints. American Express saves five to ten times as much by answering their 800 number than by replying via the mail.

The key to an effective toll-free number is to properly train, manage, and empower the people who field the calls. Proctor and Gamble puts its new customer service representatives through a five-week training course that teaches them how to calm angry customers and solve problems. One of the traps to avoid in measuring the performance of service representatives is the "more is better" syndrome. Instead of rating service reps on the basis of the number of calls they handle in a given time period, rate them on how well they talk with customers. It's also important to give service representatives the authority they need to handle common problems. That authority should include the ability to refund money. Every business is different, but the upper limit for refunds should be high enough that reps will not constantly be seeking the supervisor's approval.

The working environment of the telephone room is important as well. A service representative who feels like they are working in a sweat shop will not have a very pleasant outlook. Digital Equipment Corporation realized this factor when they designed their customer support center in Colorado Springs. They placed service reps next to the windows where they can look out at beautiful Pike's Peak. Managers, on the other hand, sit in windowless offices.

In 1983 General Electric established their Answer Center in Louisville, Kentucky. This 800-number operation fields calls on everything from complaints and compliments to product information and repairs. The center handles over three million calls per year, costs more than $8 million to operate and has a giant computer with over 750,000 answers to questions on 8,500 models in 120 product lines. Quite an undertaking. It literally makes every service rep an expert and, in fact, GE claims it can solve 90% of the complaints or questions on the first call.

In fact, a homeowner can call up, speak to a technician, describe what's wrong with his dishwasher, and receive explicit directions on how to fix it. Is GE taking business away from independent service technicians? You bet it is. But most customers are not inclined to try to fix major appliances themselves. For those who are, however, GE creates a tremendous amount of goodwill by helping them out.

SERVICE R$_x$:
Create a comfortable environment for satisfied and dissatisfied customers to voice their opinions. Every suggestion is an opportunity for your company to learn and grow.

Creating a positive complaint environment is a major step in becoming a market-focused company. Welcoming complaints reflects the attitude that the company can always learn from its customers. This is modeled internally in the way management treats people. If a company creates a learning culture in which employees are encouraged to offer suggestions, then employees will turn around and treat customers the same way. If employees are abused for making suggestions ("That's not your department,") their behavior toward customers will mirror that treatment.

It is impossible to just keep customers. Like the tide, your customer base never stands still. It is fluid and dynamic, rising or falling as people are won or lost. When you run your business in a market-focused fashion, you win more customers than you lose, so your marketshare slowly increases. Remember, every satisfied customer tells an average of five friends.

When you give poor service, you not only lose current customers, you also lose prospects. Every dissatisfied customer tells 20 others. It is a dangerous and foolish delusion to think that new customers can compensate for those you are losing.

One of Buick's top dealers, speaking at an annual Buick dealer's meeting, said, "We cannot expect to grow or hold on to our marketshare if we are constantly trying to replace customers we lose."

The Customer Is Not Always Right

We want to set the record straight. The customer is not always right, but the customer doesn't have to be right. It's okay for customers to be wrong, because the customer is always the customer. Right or wrong is not the issue. It isn't a service provider's job to stand in judgement. Your job is to resolve problems, not play Judge Wopner.

SERVICE R$_x$:
The customer is not always right, but the customer is always the customer, even when they are wrong.

SERVICE R$_x$:
The primary function of every employee of every business is the acquisition and maintenance of customers, even when they're wrong.

Managers take note—it is important to teach this concept clearly to your people. If you simply tell them the customer is always right, most people will interpret that literally. When they encounter a customer who is obviously wrong, they will think, perhaps unconsciously, "this customer is wrong, but if customers are always right, then this person must not be a customer." This cognitive dissonance often results in poor service.

Let's take the case of a hotel guest who is checking out and believes he was quoted a different rate on his room. He claims there is a $100 overcharge on his bill. Assume the total bill is $500 and he's asking for $100 to be deducted. The initial reaction of most front desk clerks would be resistance; after all, $100 is a lot of money. The common mistake is to think of the $100 without putting it in perspective. And there are many perspectives.

As the front desk clerk, if you focus on the $100 without seeing the big picture, you will refuse to deduct it, especially if you think the customer is wrong. A hundred dollars is a hundred dollars! If, however, you look at the $100 relative to the cost of acquiring a new customer or relative to the amount of money that customer is going to spend at the hotel in the future, the $100 is put in its proper perspective—it's insignificant! So give the customer his $100. He's going to come back and spend thousands more, especially if he's a business traveler.

Another realistic way to look at the $100 adjustment is in terms of what the hotel is really losing. It is not losing $100. If the disputed charge is for one night's stay in a room, the hotel is only losing the cost of that room for one night. So now you can be more flexible because you're dealing with less of a loss. Sensible flexibility.

The bottomline is that the hotel should be willing to give the customer back $100, but that's the least creative way to resolve this situation. Why not think of alternatives that will allow you to keep the $100, make the customer happy, and guarantee that he will return. One possibility would be instead of giving back the money, to offer the following: "Mr. Jones, here's what I'd like to do to compensate you for this discrepancy. The next time you're coming to town, call me a week in advance and I will be happy to give you the presidential suite at no extra charge, if it's available. And if you tell me when your flight arrives, I'll send our limousine to the airport to pick you up. Does that sound fair?"

As we said before, the most important aspect of this situation is the way it is handled. We will discuss the recovery process in the next chapter. For now, suffice it to say you must resolve problems quickly, sincerely, enthusiastically, and generously.

Is Preferential Treatment Fair?

One of our clients brought up an interesting issue regarding preferential treatment. He wanted to know if a truly market-focused company would provide more services to one customer than to another. Here's the situation:

The client was a bank. The loan officer was willing to go to people's homes to discuss home loans. She would not, however, do it for everyone. She accommodates a $200,000+ loan customer, but a $10,000 home equity loan customer would have to come into the office. Is the bank's practice fair and wise from a customer service point of view?

The answer is yes to both questions. The bank has every right to determine who they can afford to provide any given level of service to. After all, they make less money on smaller loans. Customers, on the other hand, should expect to get what they pay for. When you fly coach you don't expect champagne. When you take out a small loan from a bank, you can't expect to be courted like a jumbo loan customer.

There is a qualification to the axiom, "You get what you pay for." No company should be so rigid as to turn down repeated requests. There are times when a loan officer should visit a borrower's home for a small loan. And there are times when a flight attendant should give a coach passenger a glass of champagne. This is where sensible flexibility in decision-making becomes important and why you hire people who can think for themselves and evaluate the merits of each situation.

Good Customers, Noncustomers

The reason you provide more services to some customers is because they pay for them, not because they are better customers. There is no such thing as a bad customer. There are only good customers and noncustomers. Referring to people as good customers and bad customers is a short-term way of thinking. It is looking for the payoff from every transaction. A bad customer, therefore, is one who does not give you an immediate return. If you are truly going to differentiate your business with service, you have to make an attitude change and regard every customer as a good customer.

Noncustomers are another story. These are people with whom you do not do business, including people with whom you refuse to do business. The airlines' computer system has the ability to flag the names of passengers to whom they do not want to sell tickets. When one of these noncustomers calls for a reservation, they are told there are no seats available. The company may have a dozen reasons for categorizing someone as a noncustomer, not the least of which is that the person has a history of causing problems on flights.

The Collections Dilemma

The typical reaction to customers who don't pay their bills is to use strong-arm collection techniques that not only fail to get money, but drive the customers away. This is a short-term solution to the problem and, as such, *not always* a good idea. An example will illustrate why bad debts do not necessarily make bad customers.

Phil: *I set out to prove to the head of the collections department at Cox Cable in San Diego (one of the largest cable TV companies in the U.S.) that there is no such thing as a bad customer. She replied, "You've obviously never worked in a collection office." I told her she was right, so I hung around her office to see what I could learn. After some time, I told her I was sticking to my point. "There are no bad customers, and I can prove it."*

She said, "Okay, prove it." I asked her, "What happens when customers don't pay their bills?" She answered, "We send threatening letters." "If they still haven't paid?" "We phone them," she said. "If they still do not pay?" "We phone them again and give them an ultimatum: Either pay us with cash or a certified check within 48 hours or we will discontinue service." "What happens if they still don't pay?"

For the first time in our conversation the head of the collections department smiled, then snarled, "We cut them off!"

I continued questioning her, "Then what?" She asserted, "People will do without a lot of things in life, but TV isn't one of them. When we cut off their service, within 36 hours they usually pay their bill." "What do you do then?" I asked. "We reconnect their service."

After paying his bill, what has that person become? A good customer. If he were a bad customer, the cable company would not have reconnected him; they would have made him a noncustomer. So it's not that he's a bad customer; he's a good customer that has a problem paying on time.

There's no denying that collections is one of the most difficult aspects of business. If done improperly, it makes everyone look bad and can even culminate in a lawsuit. Your company has to achieve a balance between aggressively collecting money and alienating customers. Aggressive collections techniques make everyone angry, including those who you can't afford to alienate, those who intend to pay you.

How does a collector track his success? He measures the percentage of outstanding debts that are collected. It's a one-dimensional measure. The fundamental problem, however, isn't the ability to measure money collected, it is *the inability to measure the percentage of customers who were lost in the collection process.* With each account, you have to ask yourself what the debt is worth. Are you willing to lose this customer and the future business they represent for the amount owed? It is often wiser to write off some debt and tone down the collections techniques than to alienate everyone who owes money.

How you try to collect your money is the issue here. Whether you do the phone calling or an agency does it, collections should be conducted with the attitude that all your customers are good customers and deserve to be treated as such. Most people doing collections automatically treat everyone like deadbeats. There are all kinds of reasons why people owe money. Until you are 100% certain that someone is trying to cheat you, don't get nasty. Your customers don't deserve to be antagonized just because they owe money, yet that is exactly what many collection agencies do. They use the strong-arm approach. After all, it's not their customers they're losing.

When collection agencies slap customers in the face with threatening letters or phone calls, people don't roll over and write checks. They fight back.

SERVICE R$_X$:
People should never spend their entire careers in collections; they'll end up hating customers! People should be rotated through collections, not deposited there. When employees hate customers, they treat them like they hate them.

It is important to recognize and counteract the stress that comes with collections. At the very least, companies should provide ongoing training, coaching, and counseling for the collections department.

SERVICE R$_X$:
Include the collections department in all sales and customer service training. Give them a sense of participation in the acquisition and maintenance of customers.

Problem Customers

The customer who takes forever to pay bills is not one anyone is thrilled with. There's nothing wrong with designating this customer as a problem customer. Should you drop this customer? Instead of terminating the relationship, a better solution is to determine what conditions must be met for you to continue doing business. If your problem customer will play by your rules, then why not continue the business relationship? You might stipulate that all shipments must be prepaid or COD. You might ask for a deposit on services before those services are rendered. You might accept credit cards or cash only from that account. There are any number of options; the point is, if you specify the conditions and they are met, you have turned a problem customer into a good customer.

Keep in mind that we are not dogmatically saying you have to do business with everyone who walks in your door. You have every right to deem someone a noncustomer. The habitual problem customer can, at your discretion, be banished. In fact, if you want, you can even be flip about it and send him an official-looking certificate that says, "Congratulations! You have recently been inducted into the ranks of the select few who hold the distinction of being NONCUSTOMERS OF ACME PLUMBING. We look forward to your continued business with our competitors."

Differentiation Strategy: The Service Guarantees[4]

Everyone knows that the service sector is now the largest sector of the American economy. It can be argued, however, that every business is a service business. Even if your product is steel girders, you must differentiate your company with service quality if you hope to be competitive.

The more obvious service businesses are those that sell intangibles. Management consultants, lawyers, psychologists and financial planners are some of the many professionals who sell advice. A hair stylist sells haircuts and perms. The telephone company sells phone calls. A massage therapist sells torture, which some people find heavenly.

Selling an intangible presents an unusual problem. How do you know when your customers are dissatisfied? Certainly repeat business is an indicator. When customers never come back, however, you haven't got a clue as to the reason why.

SERVICE R$_X$:
Use a service guarantee as one of the ways to nurture complaining customers.

A service guarantee assures customers that they must be satisfied, otherwise they are entitled to a discount, credit or refund. Simple, but profoundly useful.

"Of course we can't guarantee success every time,
but here's our 800 number if any problems arise."

Service guarantees have been around for a long time. You've heard them on TV and radio. Federal Express is the classic example; they are the ones to use when your package absolutely, positively must be there the next day. In fact, they guarantee their overnight deliveries will arrive by a specific time—depending on the destination—or the delivery is free. Domino's pizza is another familiar story.

A package or pizza arriving on time is an easy performance criterion to measure, but what about something as subjective as a good haircut or a bank teller's attitude? In the absence of an objective measure, J.C.

Penney strives to keep its customers satisfied by offering a service guarantee on its beauty salon services. If you don't like your new coif, tell them at any time and you'll get a full refund. You can even live with your hairdo for a week and still come back to complain.

Waiting in line is one of the most prevalent irritations of modern times. Knowing this, a few New York banks began giving customers money if they either waited in line for more than seven minutes or received discourteous service from a teller. That's a progressive guarantee.

SERVICE R$_x$:
Service guarantees force your company to gain control of its service quality, nurture a positive complaint environment, increase marketshare, and boost profits.

How To Recognize a Good Guarantee When You See It

If the thought of offering a 100% guarantee frightens you, you're not willing to commit your company to service in the progressive zone. If, however, you would like to develop a stellar reputation, a service guarantee will work wonders for you.

Unfortunately, most service guarantees fall short of proving the company's commitment to its customers. Have you ever heard of an airline that guaranteed your luggage would arrive at the same airport as you, every time? Imagine how impressed you would be with an airline that did guarantee that or they would give you a free ticket to visit your luggage in whatever city it landed.

The more conditions and contingencies placed on a guarantee, the more impotent it becomes, especially if those conditions are factors the company can control. For example, customers would laugh if Domino's Pizza guaranteed their pizza would be delivered within a half-hour except when their ovens were broken or when they were unusually busy. That would be absurd! They're in the restaurant business—they have to guarantee their ovens and their capacity to bake a lot of pizzas.

Strings and conditions attached to a service guarantee also undermine employees' attitudes. The less teeth the guarantee has, the less likely employees are to be committed to it. A tough guarantee forces employees to eliminate all excuses and deliver the promised service.

A commercial airline, on the other hand, can't control factors such as the weather or air traffic congestion. As a result, they would be foolish to give you a money-back guarantee that you will arrive on time. Most passengers are willing to be fair and reasonable. They understand there are limitations imposed on any business, so airlines are usually forgiven for factors beyond their control. What passengers object to are poorly delivered services *within* the airline's control: things such as perfunctory service, unappetizing food, mechanical problems, the crew showing up late, or luggage having its own itinerary.

SERVICE R$_x$:
A service guarantee assures customers that their reasonable expectations will be met or exceeded.

All good service guarantees have several elements in common. They are:

- liberal
- straightforward
- relevant
- substantial
- delivered quickly
- collected painlessly

The guarantee must be liberal. You've had the experience of returning something to a store and being given the third degree just to get your money back. And God forbid you lost your receipt! Wouldn't it be nice if no questions were asked, if people took your word for what happened and resolved the situation quickly and painlessly. All it takes it trust and flexibility.

Emil: *I was staying at the J.W. Marriott Hotel in Washington, D.C. I gave them a pair of jeans and a shirt to be cleaned. They returned the package and the next morning when I opened it, I realized the shirt was missing. I was going to check out later that morning, so they had time to search before I left. After hours of* *searching, the desk clerk simply said, "Mr. Bohn, you've been through enough inconvenience. How much was the shirt worth?" I told him it was probably a $35-$45 shirt. Without hesitation, he went to the front desk, got $45 in cash and apologized for their mistake. It couldn't have been easier!*

The best service guarantee promises customer satisfaction unconditionally, no exceptions; and there are companies that actually practice this rule to the letter. L.L. Bean and Nordstrom will take anything back at any time. That includes shoes after they've been well worn. Rich's Department Store in Atlanta has the same policy. There is a story circulating about a woman who went into Rich's one day with a brown paper bag. She approached a clerk, opened the bag, and said, "I want my money back." The clerk said, "There's a dead parrot in there." "That's right," the woman said. "I paid $85 for this dead parrot and I want my money back." "But we don't have a pet department, Ma'am," the clerk objected. The woman persisted, "The sign says if I'm unhappy I should bring it back and you'll refund my money. It doesn't say I had to buy it here." She got her money back!

This is one way a service guarantee can be honored. The money lost on a dead parrot will be made up in goodwill. That woman will be back to buy many other $85 items. And look at the publicity the situation generated.

The guarantee must be straightforward. A service guarantee shouldn't be so convoluted that only an attorney can decipher it. It should be written in everyday "people-ese" language and should get the point across quickly. This is especially true if the guarantee is going to be promoted in print or other media.

A clear guarantee tells customers what to expect and tells employees what to do. "Delivery in 30 minutes" can be measured and enforced whereas "quick delivery" is too vague to be meaningful to customers or employees.

The guarantee must be relevant. A good guarantee relates to your customers' priorities. The Bennigan's restaurant chain promises 15 minute service (or a free meal) at lunch, when business people are pressed for time. They don't offer that guarantee during dinner hours, when fast service is not a priority to most customers.

The guarantee must be substantial. An effective guarantee must carry some weight. When a customer perceives the company has nothing to lose, they won't be impressed with the guarantee. The same is true of employees. If they risk nothing in the transaction, they can become complacent or feel impotent about service.

How much weight should a guarantee carry? What is fair compensation to the customer for a service failure? There's no formula, but money-back pay-outs should be sizable enough to motivate customers to ask for them when necessary. It is possible, however, to go too far. Domino's Pizza started its guarantee program by promising "delivery in 30 minutes or the pizza is free." The penalty was inordinately severe. People were uncomfortable accepting a free pizza just because it arrived ten minutes late. So Domino's changed its policy. Now it's "delivery within 30 minutes or $3.00 off."

The guarantee must be delivered quickly. Just as a company should create a comfortable complaint environment, it should make it easy for customers to ask for their money back. There's nothing worse than inconveniencing dissatisfied customers by requiring them to jump through the hoops of company red tape. Furthermore, customers shouldn't be made to feel guilty if they invoke the guarantee. Employees must encourage dissatisfied customers to speak up and ask for their rightful refunds or adjustments.

The guarantee must be collected painlessly. Collecting payment on a guarantee should be quick and easy. The ideal payout is immediate—cash or credit to an account. This requires management to authorize front-line people to give instant refunds and credit.

The Service Guarantee at Work

The service guarantee is a powerful tool to help you achieve progressive customer service and provide you with a vehicle to promote it. There are many advantages to offering a service guarantee, not the least of which is that it puts you on the fast-track to service differentiation.

A guarantee forces you to think and act with a market-focused philosophy. Knowing what your customers want is an absolute prerequisite to offering a guarantee. Before you create a guarantee, take the step that few businesses take: find out exactly what your customers' expectations are. This must be done for every facet of the service you provide. If you fail to do this, you may create a guarantee that misses the mark.

British Airways conducted a market study and discovered four criteria passengers use to judge an airline's service:

1. Employees' sincerity, friendliness, warmth, care, and concern.

2. The amount of initiative employees took to try to work around the system for the passenger. In other words, how customer-focused (versus operations-focused) was the employee?

3. The ability of airline personnel to solve problems that were either routine or unusual.

4. The willingness of employees to make the extra effort when things went wrong. This included handling problems, and, believe it or not, simply offering apologies.

The managers of British Airways admitted they had never given much thought to the second and fourth service categories. What's worse, they realized that if management hadn't understood the importance of these service expectations, their line employees certainly had not.

It is interesting that the people surveyed did not mention things such as on-time performance and baggage handling—criteria the airlines love to flaunt in their ads. Obviously, the people in this study regarded those things as minimum standards of performance—and no big deal when they're done right.

A service guarantee can propel you into the progressive zone. A clearly defined guarantee raises the expectations of customers—an important part of *encouraging demanding customers* and *managing* expectations. At the same time, it increases employee commitment to meet and exceed those expectations. A guarantee defines each employee's role in delivering service and reinforces the most important words they will ever hear: *The function of every employee of every business is the acquisition and maintenance of customers.*

A service guarantee can put you in the indulgent zone. Is that bad? Yes and no. It's not bad for a short time, but no business can survive if it is constantly in the indulgent zone. Companies that have liberal return policies, however, create so much goodwill that they make a fortune on the customers who don't take advantage of them. In retrospect, it was wise for Rich's Department Store to lose money by giving a woman $85 for a dead parrot. Of course, if everyone in town started bringing in their dead pets, the store would have to get itself out of the indulgent zone by putting a condition on its guarantee. But with a little promotion or publicity, customers would accept the new guarantee as reasonable.

A guarantee generates feedback. The weakness of most companies is in the lack of a practical and accurate system for generating and acting on customer feedback. Due to the intangible nature of services, unhappy customers have little incentive to complain; far less than customers who are dissatisfied with a product. It's bad enough that most people in general don't complain when they have a problem. It's up to you to give hesitant people an incentive to complain.

A guarantee forces you to understand why you fail. Service companies don't often know their weaknesses. Creating a service guarantee can correct that problem. There are some basic questions to ask before you establish a guarantee; the answers will give you valuable insight into the strengths and weaknesses of your company.

What are the weak links in your service delivery system? What happens between the time an order is taken and the time service is rendered? Once you have identified these weak points, you have to determine if they can be overcome. For example, imagine the detail with which Federal Express had to analyze their delivery system to see if it was possible to offer their overnight guarantee. The guarantee forces you to find out, preferably in advance, what your capabilities and limitations are.

What you will discover in analyzing your service delivery are internal and external weak points. Internal factors such as ineffective employees can be rectified with better hiring and training practices, pay increases, motivation, and recognition. External factors such as outside vendors and independent contractors are less controllable, but you should be aware of their level of service nonetheless.

Once you have identified your weaknesses, you will be better able to deal with them—replace this, work around that or compensate for it. A company whose service is restricted or limited by outside factors can still offer a service guarantee. The guarantee, however, will have to be limited to those facets of the business which can be controlled.

A guarantee builds marketing muscle. The strongest argument for a service guarantee is that it is one of the most powerful marketing tools available today. A service guarantee reduces the risk of buying because it assures customers that they will be satisfied. When there is little or no risk, people spend less time laboring over buying decisions. This translates into increased sales, more repeat business, and greater customer loyalty.

The most valuable promotion a company can acquire is word-of-mouth advertising. Remember, however, that word-of-mouth advertising works both ways—for positive and negative experiences. It is important, therefore, to minimize or eliminate bad service. Many companies' biggest competitors are themselves. They spend enormous sums of money trying to attract new customers and spend considerably less time and money trying to understand how to provide consistent quality service to their existing customers. So, in effect, their marketing money is wasted.

Some executives balk at the idea of a service guarantee because their industries have many external factors affecting the delivery of service. Some managers are afraid a service guarantee will put them at the mercy of the cheating public. There's no denying that some customers will take advantage of a company's generosity. But they are by far the minority. It makes no sense for management to worry about the 1% who will cheat them instead of the 99% who make up their bottomline profits.

Every company can benefit from a service guarantee, especially if they can answer yes to the following:

Is the price of your service high? The more your customers are at risk in their buying decision, the more you need a guarantee. No one thinks twice about a bad car wash, but anyone would get upset if extensive body work were botched. Wouldn't it be great if physicians guaranteed their work!

Is the prospect's expertise with your service limited? When prospects are not knowledgeable, they will protect themselves by choosing a company that guarantees its work. For example, most people know very little about landscaping, so a landscaper with a written guarantee would have a significant competitive edge.

Are the consequences of bad service very serious? Again, the more risk involved, the greater the customer's reliance on a guarantee. Risk can take the form of money, time, reputation, aesthetics, ego, aggravation, or lost business. If you were sending an expensive Grecian vase across the country, you would spend the extra money for the courier service that guaranteed delivery. If you were to buy expensive Italian marble for your home's entry, you would want it laid by a craftsman who guaranteed his work.

Does your industry have a bad reputation for service? If it does, you have the opportunity to differentiate yourself from the competition. You also have the opportunity to change the industry rules of the game by changing the service delivery process. It only takes one maverick to start the ball of change rolling; you might as well be the one.

Does your company depend on repeat business? Every company does, but some would fail without it. A small business in a finite market must generate loyalty. Think of where a massage therapist, psychologist, fashion consultant, personal shopper, or personal fitness coach would be without a consistent following. The rule of thumb should be obvious—the smaller the potential for acquiring new customers, the greater the effort must be to maintain existing ones.

Does your company rely heavily on word of mouth? All the professions just mentioned would be mere hobbies if word of mouth didn't generate new business. Add to that list restaurants, business consultants, doctors, lawyers, chiropractors . . . we could go on and on.

You Get What You Give

A service guarantee will work only if it reflects a 100% commitment to your customers. You will have to invest time and money to increase your service capability so that it exceeds the industry average. That cost, however, is already there—only now it's being shifted from mopping up errors to preventing them.

If customers don't complain . . . you're doing something wrong. Companies that create complaining customers and offer service guarantees tap into a powerful competitive advantage. It isn't easy, but then, taking the high road always requires more effort. The return on your time, money, and emotional investment can be fantastic—industry dominance, greater productivity, higher employee morale, fewer service errors, more loyal customers, word-of-mouth advertising, a steady stream of new prospects, and a stellar reputation—everything a company could want!

SERVICE R$_x$:
Nurture complaining customers.

Chapter Eleven

Managing the Recovery Process

No company is perfect. Products are shipped late, waiters spill soup, salespeople forget to return phone calls, clerks misplace orders, hotels overcharge, airlines over-book flights and lose luggage, and so on. These things happen every day. The issue is not that they happen—we're all human—but how a company deals with them when they do occur.

Whenever there's a breakdown in reliability, there is an urgent need for recovery. One big difference between companies with excellent service reputations and those who wallow in mediocrity is the way they welcome, manage, and resolve customer complaints. Companies in the rigid and safe zones often mismanage these opportunities and leave customers dissatisfied. Indulgent zone companies know how to recover and come out smelling like roses; however, they give away the store in the process. Progressive zone companies solve problems creatively and economically.

Managing customer complaints is both an art and a science. The art is in the skills required to deal with people, their money, and their emotions. The science is in understanding the procedures of recovery. Both can be learned and, in fact, are taught by customer service consulting and training firms throughout the country.

The key ingredient to managing customer complaints successfully is your attitude. There's no greater rapport builder than enthusiasm and sincere caring. This is precisely the reason to select your customer service people so carefully. They must have the right dispositions for managing complaining customers. Grumpy, irritable people do not belong in customer service, as the following illustration depicts. It's interesting to note that this cartoon was published in the mid-1950s and is still relevant today.

Drawing by Ton Smits; © 1954, 1982, The New Yorker Magazine, Inc.

Just as a bad attitude will cut you off at the knees, so will a slow response. Time is always of the essence.

SERVICE R$_x$:
A genuine interest in the customer plus flexibility and a commitment to a quick, fair resolution will always culminate in effective problem solving.

In addition to mastering all the people skills of your job, how should you go about recovering from a service failure? Your system of recovery will, to a large extent, be determined by the procedures set up in your company. It is important for management to create a set of guidelines for front-line people to follow. Without clear parameters to work with, service representatives run the risk of either giving away the store or not being generous enough with customers. Part of developing an effective recovery system involves examining all the common service breakdowns and then asking, "What are we able and willing to do to compensate customers for these problems?"

The following guidelines for managing complaints will take you a long way toward creating a comfortable complaint environment and resolving customers' problems. These guidelines should be taken as the skeleton on which your company can hang more specific recovery procedures.

Listen

This step is so important that it cannot be overemphasized. It is essential that you practice active listening for a number of reasons. The most obvious is that you will get an accurate picture of the degree of disappointment and inconvenience your customer has experienced. The severity of the service blunder must be looked at from your customer's point of view. Your gauge for assessing the damage will be the customer's perceived wound. Here you find out the consequences of the service breakdown.

The second most important reason for being a good listener is something called "the poof phenomenon." Someone walks up to a customer service counter with a complaint. They feel like a crime victim and want justice. They are red in the face and ready to tear down the walls. What do they need most? A refund or a good listener? You guessed it, a good listener. So let them blow off steam and they'll feel better immediately. And sometimes that's all people want—someone to listen to them and take that weight off their shoulders. That's the poof phenomenon—the release of tension that comes from talking about problems.

SERVICE R$_x$:
First fix the customer, then fix the service problem.

While listening to customers, there are several things you should and should not do:

Do be empathic.

Do tactfully acknowledge their emotional state.

Do acknowledge their right to better service.

Do assure them that you will solve the problem immediately.

Don't interrupt.

Don't get defensive and make excuses.

Don't attribute blame.

Don't let other business distract you.

Apologize and Empathize

Of course, the breakdown in service may not be your fault, but remember, as an employee of the company, *you are the company*. So acknowledge that the difficulty exists and apologize. Never question the validity of a customer's complaint or become defensive. It may seem obvious that an apology should be given, but too many companies never offer one. Every disgruntled customer wants someone to accept responsibility, apologize, and correct the matter.

"Well. That's more like it!"
Drawing by O'Brian; © 1975, The New Yorker Magazine, Inc.

It is important to state your apology in the first person. Third person apologies are impersonal and unconvincing. "We're sorry this happened," is meaningless. Phrase your apologies so they show you sincerely care and are taking responsibility.

- "I'm sorry this happened."
- "I'm sorry we inconvenienced you."
- "I'm sorry we overlooked that."

You don't have to offer to put a gun to your head to show how sorry you are, but you should be apologetic. Inasmuch as you accept responsibility for the problem and its resolution, do not take the complaint personally. You are not the target of the customer's anger, although it may appear that way. Don't internalize the customers' hostilities. This may be easier said than done—it takes practice and patience. Keep everything in perspective. Managing customer complaints can be stressful work.

Empathy is important. It shows people that you care. When there's a breakdown in service, customers feel wronged and are anxious to see that you agree with their interpretation of what transpired. Quickly discover the customer's perception of the seriousness of the problem and then respond appropriately. The key words here are "the customer's perception." Their perception plays an important role in determining what you should do to correct the situation.

To get on the same wave length as your customers, you have to show them you understand their problems. Let them know that you would be just as irritated if you were in their shoes. It's helpful to say something such as, "I see how you feel about this, Mrs. Jones. I would feel the same way if this happened to me."

What do you do when you encounter someone on the phone who is being abusive? Many customer service representatives are trained to say something like, "Mr. Customer, if you don't stop talking to me like that I'll have to hang up." This response usually makes people want to scream more. A better way to handle this situation would be to say, "Mr. Customer, I really want to help you with this, but to do that, I have to know what the problem is."

Share your customer's sense of urgency about the situation. When things are fouled up, correct them quickly. Tell the customer they have been inconvenienced long enough and show them that you are committed to doing your absolute best to achieve a speedy resolution. At The Ritz Carlton, when a customer lodges a complaint with an employee, that employee owns the complaint. They have the responsibility for the resolution of the complaint, regardless of who is supposed to fix it. That means thorough follow-through. The buck stops with every employee— that is a culture in which excuses are eliminated.

Ask Questions

If your customer's story is unclear, ask clarifying questions. Gather as much information as necessary to resolve the problem, but avoid interrogation. Customers shouldn't have to jump through hoops to get complaints resolved. You are the one who must run interference.

Quickly Get Back on Track

After you've listened carefully, apologized, and conveyed concern and empathy, it's time to wrap up the problem. This could be as simple as saying, "I'm terribly sorry this happened. Let me correct it right away." Whatever you do, be sure it re-establishes the relationship and shifts the customer's frame of mind from wounded to pleased.

Solve the Problem *with* Your Customer

There are some situations in which the solution is cut-and-dried. You give your customer a refund or exchange the product. There are other situations in which a solution is more complex. In these cases, make your customer an active part of the problem-solving process.

One of the most important questions to ask in an unusual problem-solving situation is, "How would you like to see this problem resolved?" or "What do you think would be fair in this situation?" The answer will give you a wealth of useful information, not the least of which is an indication of how reasonable your customer is willing to be. You may be surprised how easy it is to please your customers. Most people are willing to be fair and reasonable, if you show sincerity and a commitment to the business relationship.

By giving your customer a voice in the service outcome, you also prove your willingness to be flexible. Furthermore, a customer with "ownership" in the solution will be more satisfied than one that was required to accept a stock solution.

There are times when an unreasonable customer or a complex solution requires some negotiating. Negotiation is an art unto itself—one that is too involved to delve into here. When negotiating, however, don't lose sight of your customer's point of view, keep them involved in the process, and always strive for a mutually-beneficial resolution. There are times when it is appropriate to ask, "Mr. Customer, assuming we cannot do X, what could we do to make you happy?"

Keep your customers informed. That means telling them why paperwork has to be filled out, why they have to go through this process, why they have to do this, that, or the other. It is demeaning when you treat customers like children, simply saying, "You'll have to do this, this, and this." Take the time to explain the system and, if possible, the logic behind it. In fact, go a step further. Take over the reins so your customer doesn't have to do all the work. You fill out the paperwork or make the necessary phone calls.

Fair Compensation

There are times when you have to say to a customer, in effect, "I'm sorry this problem occurred. Now that it's straightened out, I want to give you something extra to show you how much I value your business."

Free products, services, or gifts are important gestures of good faith. It is important for customers to know that you have no intention of letting them walk out the door if they are not happy. That is precisely as it should be. People hate to part with their money when they're unhappy. Think of how you feel when you pay a restaurant for a meal you were dissatisfied with. It's a frustrating feeling.

Compensation, like any aspect of managing a complaint, should be done quickly and by the front-line employee. It's important, therefore, for supervisors to give employees the authority to compensate customers for routine inconveniences. There is nothing more annoying to a customer than having to appeal to various corporate levels or waiting for an employee to appeal to various levels for approval of compensation. If compensation is going to be expensive and require management approval, it's the service representative's job to act as the customer's advocate by presenting the case to the ultimate decision-maker.

> Emil: *I bought a pair of dress pants from a department store. When I went to pick them up from their tailor, he couldn't find them. Without any hesitation, the salesperson told me to pick out another pair of pants—any pair I wanted, even if they were more expensive—and they would be mine.*

When the company has "dropped the ball," it's no time to be petty with the solution or compensation. Compare Emil's experience to Garry's:

> Garry: *We once bought a new home from one of California's largest home builders. We experienced a lot of problems with the*

house. Granted, the defects were covered under the warranty, but they were a nuisance and, at times, emotionally stressful. We heard through the grapevine that some homeowners had been compensated for the emotional duress their defects had caused. We called their Customer Service and asked to be compensated for all we had endured. We weren't asking for much—just a kitchen item that retailed for about $200 and probably cost the builder half of that. The customer service rep said she didn't have the authority to grant our request. She referred us to two other people, both of whom passed the buck. Finally, weeks later, we received a letter from the director of marketing who told us she had to deny our request. Her reason was definitely operations-focused. According to her, the determination of compensation was made on a subjective basis and, upon reviewing our warranty claims, she felt the problems we had experienced were "typical." Can you imagine that—coming from the director of marketing! "I'm sorry, the defective plumbing in your new $285,000 house flooded a room, soaked a downstairs wall, ruined the ceiling and uprooted the linoleum in the bathroom, but that's typical."

Obviously, sensible flexibility was lacking in this situation. One of the factors that will determine what you are willing to do is the significance of your customer to your business. You will go to greater lengths to compensate a $100,000 account than you will to compensate a $1,000 account. In an ideal world we would treat all customers equally, but the realities of the marketplace pressure every company into giving big customers preferential treatment. Those customers represent your bread and butter.

Your company's guidelines for complaint resolution will determine, to a large degree, the action you will take. As we discussed in the chapters on zones of service, some companies are rigid, some are flexible, and some go overboard in managing complaining customers. Every company has its culture and with it comes an attitude toward helping people. If you are one of the millions of people who work for rigid or safe zone companies, strive to be the exception to the rule. Become a customer-advocate. Work hard to accommodate your customers. Think of creative solutions to their problems. Bend over backwards for them in ways that don't cost the company money.

What should you give a customer as compensation? The ideal gift is something of high perceived value to your customer and low actual cost to your company. In addition, your gift should be something that differentiates you from your competitors. All of these key elements are important, but the first is absolutely essential. If you give a customer something that is meaningless, you will insult them.

> Phil: *I once had a problem with a night manager of a hotel. The problem wasn't catastrophic, but his inflexibility and offensive attitude was. I wrote a letter to the hotel's vice-president of operations—someone who should know how to respond to this kind of situation. What he did was totally inappropriate. He sent me a box of candy and a letter that defended his night manager! That was his response! There was no apology—not even an acknowledgement that I might have been offended! I would have preferred a phone call and an apology to an impersonal box of candy!*

The perfect combination of high perceived value and low cost is exemplified in the way good restaurants manage complaints. When a diner complains about an entree, the waiter takes the unacceptable item off the bill. He then offers to have the chef rush through another entree or he may offer a dessert, salad, appetizer—something to fill up his guest—on the house.

High perceived value (free food) and low cost to the restaurant is an ideal combination. This can also be achieved by giving out coupons. A coupon for something either discounted or free accomplishes two things—it brings people back and gives them something of value as a way of saying, "We're sorry."

There are two other important elements to gift giving as compensation. Gifts should be creative and customized. Ask your customers some questions so you can be creative with your generosity. Try giving an experience such as tickets to a baseball game, the theater, the circus, a bay cruise, a helicopter ride, or other novel outings.

Remember, the only way to make the gift meaningful is for it to fit the person it's intended for. You may love the opera, but don't assume your customer would love two tickets to *La Boheme*. Do some research and customize the gift.

Problems out of Your Control

Few companies can control every aspect of their service. It's a nearly impossible feat. When a breakdown in service occurs and the reason is out of your control, it may be managed differently than if you were in control. Airlines can't control the weather or mechanical problems, so they usually don't compensate passengers for delays. They will, however, help people when there are inordinate delays by arranging lodging, transportation, and meals. This is a noble gesture, above and beyond the call of duty.

There are four basic guidelines for dealing with service failures that are out of your control:

- Communicate the specifics of the situation.

- Give details on exactly what happened and when the situation is expected to be corrected.

- Keep people informed of developments.

Feed information to your customers as you receive it. It makes them feel important when they're part of the process.

- Assure customers the situation will be rectified.

Customers are more likely to be patient when they know you're working as quickly as you can to correct the problem. It also bolsters their confidence to know you have a solution at hand.

- Be honest.

There are ways to be honest without making a bad situation worse. Take the airlines, for example. When they have a mechanical problem, they don't say, "We're sorry to announce that flight 1050 will be delayed due to a hose spewing hydraulic fluid all over one of the engines." If they did that, people wouldn't want to get on the plane. Instead, they say, "We're sorry but we are having a minor mechanical problem. We expect the delay to be only 30 minutes. Let us assure you that our first priority is to get you safely to your destination . . . etc."

Follow-Up

Follow-up is always a part of problem solving and takes many forms. There is the follow-up during resolution when you make sure that your solution is implemented. This may entail baby-sitting a delivery, walking paperwork to another office, or making sure a check was mailed. There is also the follow-up after the problem is resolved—a simple phone call to make sure your customer was satisfied and that everything is back on track.

Efficient follow-up requires commitment, organization, and an attention to details. It pays to be obsessive when it comes to your customers. Write notes to yourself, tie strings around your fingers, or do whatever it takes to see the service process through to the end. This may mean verifying and double-checking any facet of the resolution that is out your control. All this is necessary, however, because there's nothing worse than a service breakdown during recovery. When that happens, there are no viable excuses. Customers just walk.

The follow-up gives you the opportunity to do two things—get feedback and cross-sell. The feedback is simply asking, "How are we doing?" "Did we resolve that problem (be specific) to your satisfaction?"

While getting feedback, it is appropriate to ask your customer about other needs. This is a low-key way of seeing if there are any sales opportunities present. For example, an office that has just received service on a leased copying machine may need more toner, paper, or other related products or services. How many copying machine leasing companies do you know, however, that follow up after a service call? Few, if any.

SERVICE R$_x$:
Turn the follow-up call into an opportunity for the customer to buy more.

The follow-up is an excellent time to take advantage of the goodwill you have just created. Remember, the most loyal customers are those who have had a problem and had it successfully resolved. Give them an opportunity to do more business with you.

Feed the Loop

It's not enough to create complaining customers, understand recovery, and devise ways to compensate customers when the company goofs. You miss a major creative destruction opportunity when you don't do something with the valuable information contained in complaints. You have to feed that data back into the service and operations loop to raise your service standards.

It takes a long time for people and organizations to change, which is why managers have to keep track of the change process. Keeping records will help you see the big picture—the most common problems and ways to avoid them. If they are unavoidable problems—and few are—then parameters must be created for repeated recovery.

To make complaints useful, you have to create a system for evaluating and categorizing them. As complaints come in, they should be evaluated to determine if they require immediate action. Not all complaints are serious enough to warrant operational changes. The less serious are filed and, as the frequency of the complaint increases, so does the impetus to make changes. The whole process—from reporting complaints to improving the system—requires open lines of communication between every department in the company.

One of the most valuable tools for improving service is to hold regular meetings between managers, front-line people, and various departments. The people who deal face to face with customers every day are a valuable resource for directing change, but don't think they alone have the answers. People throughout the organization are capable of thinking horizontally (across departments) and contributing to a conversation on how to best serve customers.

SERVICE R$_x$:
   Create a learning culture. Reward employees for ideas for improving service.

When you devise your system for collecting, categorizing, and correcting complaints, devise a parallel system for collecting compliments. People thrive on recognition. Publicizing success stories is an excellent form of recognition. At the same time, you will be providing a form of training because people learn by example.

How to Ask a Manager for Help

There will be times when you have to ask your manager how to help a customer. There is a right and wrong way to do this. The market-focused way sets a positive, helpful tone. The operations-focused way creates an "us versus them" mentality in which you and your manager conspire to deny the customer's request.

The situation is common enough. A customer makes a request or has a problem that needs special attention; you call your manager on the phone. The wrong way to ask for permission is, "Mrs. Jones is here at my counter. She wants to return her tennis shoes even though she doesn't have a receipt. I already told her we can't take them back. What should I tell her to make her go away?"

The correct way to ask for permission would be, "Mrs. Jones has a pair of tennis shoes she wants to return. She doesn't have her receipt, but claims she bought them here about two weeks ago. I want to give her a refund, but I'm not sure how to write it up. Can you help me figure out a way to give her what she wants?"

In the first case, the customer is going to leave unhappy even if she gets what she wants. In the second case, even if the store doesn't give her exactly what she wants, it is going to find a way to make her happy. This gets back to how you resolve a problem and the importance of attitude.

Attitude over Results = 33% Competitive Edge

It's all a matter of attitude. Are you predisposed to helping customers get what they want or to denying them? It's incredible—and maybe you've experienced this—there are actually front-line employees who have become so attached to company policies that they derive great pleasure from depriving customers of special requests. And when a supervisor makes an exception to the rules, these employees resent the customer for having gotten their way.

Managing Complaints on the Phone

When you deal with irate customers face-to-face, you can observe a number of clues to help you determine their personal styles. On the phone, however, you are limited to what you hear. Your only clues are three characteristics of your customer's voice: pace, priority, and tone.

Match the Pace

One of the most rapid and effective ways to create rapport with people on the phone is to match the speed with which they talk. If your customer speaks slowly and precisely, you will make him comfortable by doing the same. If your customer speaks rapidly, he will relate to you better if you also speak quickly. Think of it from your point of view. If you were a customer who spoke slowly, you would feel rushed if the person on the other end of the line were speaking rapidly. If you were speaking rapidly and the other person were speaking slowly, you might lose your patience as you hung on his every word. This can be seen in people who habitually finish other people's sentences.

The pacing technique works well and does so subtly. Without giving it any thought, your customer will feel that you like them.

Stick to the Priority

Another characteristic for you to match is the priority of the call. Some people call and immediately launch into the business at hand. Other people like to talk about the weather first. This preference for priority may not be a reflection of the urgency of the problem, it is simply a personal style. Some people like to build the relationship first. ("Do you believe this rain!") Others don't even say hello, they just cut to the chase. ("Here's my problem . . . ")

Again, the rule is to do what your customer does. If they want to chat, accommodate them for a minute or so. If they get down to business, don't ask them how the weather is. Priority will also dictate how quickly you handle the phone call. People who get right down to business will want you to manage the call quickly. This may mean taking down some information and calling back later. People who like to chat will be less rushed and won't mind a more lengthy call. If the call is long distance and is going to take time, offer to call back. It's one more thoughtful way of showing that you don't want to cause any more inconvenience.

Imitate the Tone

Like pace, matching someone's tone is another way to build rapport. Vocal tone is the presence or absence of emotion in the voice. Some people are open, warm, and emotional. Others are more flat and business-like. Although you should try to match your callers' tones, be careful not to sound like you are mimicking them.

As you listen to people, train your ear to pick out their styles in terms of pace, priority, and tone. Practice varying your vocal qualities a little at a time and see what effect it has on people. You will be surprised!

Caution: Loaded Words

You can do everything right—from your attitude to your vocal inflections—and blow it by saying the wrong thing. And you may not even know that you said anything wrong. Everyday words push more emotional buttons than you think, especially when your customer is hot under the collar.

When you say something to a customer, it is helpful to replace the negatively emotional words with positive words. For example, no customer wants to hear, "Now tell me again, what is your problem?" A more positive way to say the same thing is, "I'm sorry, would you tell me again what happened?"

The following lists will make you aware of negative, positive, and power-laden words. Practice eliminating the negative, including the positive, and wielding the powerful.

Words With a Negative Impact

Can't	But
Company policy	Why
Have to/must	Next
Necessary	Try
Required	I'll tell you what . . .
You need to	Industry jargon or slang
You don't say!	Didn't you know . . .
Old Friend	Do you understand?
Problem	What you said was . . .

Words With a Positive Impact

time-saving	value	however
reputation	ethical	situation
safe	popular	concern
guarantee(d)	economical	unable
quality	bargain	will/willing
courtesy	hospitality	Thank You
status	enormous	please
low cost	genuine	tasteful
progress	thinking	tested
excel	excellent	kind
recommended	admired	help
beauty	independent	appreciate
successful	up-to-date	understanding

Phrases With a Positive Impact

What have you considered?	I understand
Here are some options	How can I help?
How can it be corrected?	I'm so sorry

What are some alternatives?
Will you help me?
What happened?
Would you consider?
If I understand you correctly . . .

Tell me more
Please forgive me
What do you think?
When is it best?

As an exercise, write down the five most common phrases that you say to customers when they come to you with a problem. Then rewrite those phrases so they are stated positively.

Don't Confuse Features with Benefits

It is important for front-line people to be able to think the way customers think. That means you have to see things in terms of benefits rather than features. Imagine you are a service rep for a computer company. A customer calls to complain about the printer in the system you installed. Most service technicians would automatically assume the customer is upset because the printer isn't working. Sounds logical, but that's looking at it from a technical/features point of view. In reality, your customer may be upset because they cannot derive the benefit that the printer provides—the ability to print invoices, letters, and other documents. It is the interruption of the benefits that is upsetting, not the broken hardware. It's a case of *benefitus interruptus* that gives the situation a new sense of urgency.

Do Your Laundry Elsewhere

You've seen it—you're in a retail store, a customer has a problem, and instead of quickly and efficiently straightening out the situation, the clerk or manager is more concerned with finding out who created the breakdown. It's embarrassing for the customer, it makes the company look bad, and it flies in the face of smart business.

When solving a problem in front of a customer, employees and managers should never, ever argue or try to identify the guilty party. Customers should only see the unemotional process of resolving the problem. Fault finding is never relevant. It shows an operations-focused mentality. Your first priority should be your customer; your second can be coaching the employee who made the mistake, but do that later, and in private.

You may remember a scene from the movie, "The Godfather," in which the Godfather's son inadvertently let another mafia family know there was some divisiveness within the Corleone family. It was a big mistake and eventually led to an attempt on Don Corleone's life. The same principle applies in business—"Loose lips sink ships." Pointing fingers only undermines the credibility and professionalism of your company. Instead, put up a pleasant, professional appearance. Keep your dirty laundry out of the public's view.

> Phil: *I was once eating in a restaurant and the waiter was one of the worst I have ever had. When I told the manager about this terrible waiter, the manager said, "I'm really glad you told me this; we've been looking for another reason to fire this guy." I felt like asking the manager, "Wait a second, if you know this waiter is so bad, why are you still subjecting customers to him, especially me?"*

What do you do in a situation in which a customer complains to you about another employee? Simply listen carefully, thank the customer for the feedback, and then do your part to see that the problem is fixed.

Rigid Adherence to Company Policies

One of the most pervasive problems in customer service today is the mind-set people bring to the workplace. That mind-set is one of unquestioning subservience. It's one thing to be a good employee who stays out of trouble, but quite another never to question illogical company policies.

A parent-child relationship is often played out in business settings. Managers relate to their subordinates as children rather than adults and are, in turn, related to as parents. It's ingrained in the culture; the boss is always the authority figure who must be obeyed. It's no wonder so many people act as if their parents were saying, *"Do as you are told!"*

Some companies have policy manuals that make *War And Peace* seem like *Cliff Notes*. Every possible contingency is covered so that the company is protected both logistically and legally. Operations-focused companies think the alternative to an exhaustive policy manual is chaos. If their people are that inept, the company is either hiring the wrong people or not giving them enough training, or both. It's a ridiculous way to do business. Why should a company have to protect itself from its customers and employees!

If you're a front-line employee who is trying to serve customers the best you can, what should you do when a company policy presents an obstacle to giving customers what they want? Ask yourself, "How can

I solve this problem in a way that makes the customer happy?" "Is there a way to comply with the rules and give my customer what he wants?" If making the customer happy means you have to break a rule, break the rule and don't lose sleep over it. Then work on getting the rule changed or made more flexible. Customers were made to be satisfied just as rules were made to be broken.

A market-focused organization creates policies and guidelines designed to help customers get what they want. Granted, there will always be a small number of customers who will try to take advantage of liberal company policies, but those opportunists are, by far, in the minority. The majority of customers only want to be treated reasonably, fairly, and flexibly. In return, they will be honest and loyal.

Operations-focused thinking is, "Let's do everything the same way for all our customers because that's easiest for us." Market-focused thinking is, "Let's make this a memorable shopping experience for our customers so they'll come back." The Sportsman in Logan, Utah, is a good example of the latter. Jim Kofoed, an employee of the company for over 13 years, said management has given him (and every other employee) the authority to do what he wants to satisfy customers. "The company stands behind us 100%. I had a young man come in with a pair of Nike hiking shoes he had bought in Salt Lake City. The soles were falling off and he wanted to know how to get in touch with Nike. I said, 'I'll replace them for you.' He was shocked and said, 'Even though I didn't buy them here?' I gave him a new pair of shoes and charged him a couple of dollars for my shipping cost, which he was happy to pay."

If necessary, you have to try to change the rigid rules of your company so it can move toward being market-focused. To do this, make your managers aware of how the rules make it difficult for you to provide meaningful service. Point out alternatives to company policies, using real cases to illustrate your points. Experiment with bending the rules and see what happens. The more often rules are bent without consequence, the easier it will be to change them permanently.

Does it pay to put a lot of time and money into training people to recover when there is a service blunder? You bet it does! Consider that 95% of complaining customers will remain loyal if they perceive the service provider as being sincere, enthusiastic, and committed to the relationship. And it costs six times more to acquire a new customer than to keep a current customer satisfied. Dissatisfied customers tell 15 to 20 other people of their bad experience. Think of the airlines. Could they survive if they didn't recover well from their service glitches? Enough proof? It pays!

Chapter Twelve

Fostering Moments of Magic, Misery, and Truth

In the last three chapters we have talked about selling with service, nurturing complaining customers, and encouraging demanding customers. In effect, we have been teaching you how to manage interactions. It is the management of interactions that creates success or failure for a company.

Every business has ample opportunity to create a higher level of customer satisfaction. From the simple to the complex, every customer interaction is a chance to develop or cement a long-term business relationship.

In 1981 Jan Carlzon took over as chairman of one of Europe's most poorly rated airlines, Scandinavian Airline System (SAS). That year the company recorded an $8 million loss after having lost $20 million the previous year.

Carlzon quickly implemented many changes. He was a charismatic leader, and he had a sharp marketing mind. He redesigned his fleet of planes, and most important, he invested in people and service. In a nutshell, he managed the interactions his customers had with his employees.

"Last year [1985], each of our 10 million customers came in contact with approximately five SAS employees, and this contact lasted an average of 15 seconds each time. Thus, SAS is 'created' in the minds of our customers 50 million times a year, 15 seconds at a time. These 50 million 'moments of truth' are the moments that ultimately determine whether SAS will succeed or fail as a company. They are the moments when we must prove to our customers that SAS is their best alternative."[5]

In 1982, one year after Carlzon took over, SAS posted profits of $72 million. This was a year in which international airlines as a group lost over $2 billion. SAS is now one of the most highly rated airlines in the world.

It should be added that Carlzon realized that the quality of moments of truth was largely determined by his front-line people, so he delegated to them the responsibility of figuring out what people wanted and how to best give it to them.

SERVICE R$_x$:
It is not an extraordinary product or service that makes a great company, it is extraordinary people.

Moments of truth describe occurances of interactions between customers and the company. They do not, however, attach a value to that interaction. For this reason, we have added the concepts of Moments of Magic and Moments of Misery to Carlson's concept of Moments of Truth.

Anytime a customer interacts with anyone in your company, three outcomes are possible: a neutral experience (Carlzon's moments of truth), a positive experience (a moment of magic), or a negative experience (a moment of misery). Examples of each will remind you of similar experiences you've had.

Moments of truth happen all the time. You ask someone for the time and they tell you. You go into a fast-food restaurant and get the level of service you expected—no better and no worse. These are everyday, neutral experiences that are easily-forgotten.

Moments of magic are much easier to remember.

Emil: *I went to a frozen yogurt store and ordered a cup of chocolate yogurt with nuts on top. The clerk gave me the yogurt and then started to weigh the nuts on a scale. I told her I didn't want that much, I just wanted some sprinkled on top. She said, "Oh, okay, that's not very much, so I won't charge you for them."*

A pleasant surprise, no matter how small, is a moment of magic. It's the intention of the deed, not its size, that counts. The clerk could have charged an arbitrary $.20 instead of the full $.50 for the nuts. Instead, they were sensibly flexible and generous, and those two qualities are part of what creates customer loyalty.

Bill: *We contacted a cater for my father's 65th birthday party. While going through all the details of types of foods, color schemes for tablecloths, and all that stuff, the caterer asked us to tell her about my father. We told her all kinds of things, from his favorite flavor to the fact that he wishes he could have been a race car driver. The night of the party everything was perfect, but the caterer really knocked us out when she brought out the cake. It was a chocolate mousse cake in the form of a Formula One racing car! It almost brought tears to my father's eyes!*

Moments of misery are easily remembered also:

Phil: *I was walking down the street in Venice, California, with my wife and two other couples. I wanted to make a phone call, but didn't have any change. So I went into a small fast-food store and asked the clerk if he had four quarters for a dollar so I could make a phone call. He said flatly, "No." I asked him, "Does that mean you don't have four quarters or you don't want to give them to me?" He said, "I don't want to give them to you. If you want to buy something, buy it."*

Let's look at the ramifications of a moment of misery. Phil was walking down the street with five other people, four of whom lived in the neighborhood. Phil was from out of town, so he probably wouldn't patronize that store again anyway. But his friends might. Once he'd told them about his shabby treatment there, however, they would probably go to another place to do business. So in one fell swoop the clerk lost six customers.

There could have been two other outcomes to Phil's experience. A moment of truth would have been the clerk simply giving Phil change.

A moment of magic would have been the clerk saying, "Is it a local call? Here, you can use my phone."

There's a bigger picture to be seen here. It doesn't matter if the person walking in off the street is a prospective customer or not. It's not your business to analyze that. What if someone came in and said, "I'm a tourist from Ohio, can I have change for a dollar?" That's not the point. The bigger point is—you don't treat people that way. A core value of every business (and therefore, every employee of every business) should be, "Around here, we treat people with respect."

As valuable as the concept of moments of truth is, in real life, interactions with customers are rarely neutral; they are more often positive or negative. As such, they should be regarded as volatile assets that must be managed. Just like highly leveraged investments, moments of truth, magic, and misery can either make money for you or get you into big trouble.

SERVICE R$_X$:
Moments of truth, magic and misery should be regarded as fragile assets that must be managed with deliberate care.

Make the Exceptional the Routine

A complaining customer does you a favor. They provide you with feedback and the opportunity to turn a moment of misery into a moment of truth. By properly handling the complaint, you move that customer from a negative frame of mind to a neutral frame of mind. Exceed their expectation in the resolution of the problem and you will create a moment of magic.

A demanding customer also does you a favor. They come to you with a request, which is a moment of truth. You are then able to take them from feeling neutral to feeling delighted. You can create a moment of magic.

The wonderful thing about moments of magic is that they do not require a complaint, they only require a moment of truth. Think back to Phil's story about the fast-food store that refused to give him four quarters. Think of the impact if the clerk had said:

"Change for a dollar? No problem, Sir. You know, I haven't seen you in our store before. Just in case you get hungry later and want a snack, I want you to know that we bake our own cinnamon rolls here. Let me give you a taste."

Not only would the clerk have created a moment of magic, he probably would have made a sale! There was no heavy-handed sales pitch, just friendly conversation and a little generosity. In effect, he was selling with service.

In chapter one we mentioned the fact that most companies base their advertising on product features rather than service. A couple of years ago, American Express was an exception to that rule. In one of their ads they claimed that, as a cardholder, you would be extended credit even if you lost your wallet.

Emil and Phil wanted to see if American Express would live up to their promise. Emil walked up to the front desk of a hotel where he had a reservation and said he had lost his wallet. The hotel clerk wouldn't check him in, but asked if Emil had a credit card. Emil told him he had an American Express card. The clerk called American Express and put Emil on the phone. The service representative asked Emil a couple of simple questions and then gave him approval for $1,800 credit without showing proof of who he was! They went out on the limb for him. If Emil had been a crook, the hotel would have gotten paid and American Express would have had to absorb the loss. So the advertisement was true. They promised extraordinary service and delivered it, a perfect example of managing expectations.

The Power of Moments of Magic

To see how powerful moments of truth, magic, and misery can be, let's look at a hypothetical restaurant. A Gallup survey in 1987 found that good service was rarely a reason people chose to go to a restaurant *for the first time*. The two most-cited reasons were "recommended by a friend" (44%) and "curiosity" (20%).

Quality of service, however, did determine whether or not people returned to the restaurant. In the Gallup poll, 63% said they would not return to a restaurant if the service was bad. Virtually an equal number—65%—said they would black list a restaurant if the food was bad. Only 15% said they would not return if the prices were too high.

What this says, in essence, is that you can win or lose on service. Once you've provided the minimum acceptable standard of quality—in this case, good food—what makes or breaks a restaurant is service. A dining experience can be reduced to the customer's experience with waiters or waitresses, the front-line ambassadors. Statistics prove that failing to provide good service can be as deadly as failing to serve good food.

To show you just how significant an impact service providers have, let's calculate the approximate number of contacts a waiter has with customers in a year.

Imagine you're a waiter with seven tables of four people each. For each seating you have contact with those people ten times. That's 7 X 4 X 10 = 280. If you turn those tables three times each evening, five nights a week you have, 280 X 3 X 5 = 4200 customer contacts. Now assume you work fifty weeks a year, the number of moments of truth, magic, or misery you have with customers in one year is 4200 X 50 = 210,000! Almost a quarter of a million moments when your professionalism directly influences a customer's level of satisfaction.

As a waiter or waitress, if you were to have 210,000 moments of truth per year, do you think it would be the food that determined your personal success? Absolutely not. Your success would hinge on how you managed those intensely personal customer contacts. With 210,000 moments of truth to play with, however, many people might adopt the attitude, "There are so many moments of truth in a year, it won't be catastrophic if I blow it once in a while." That's a dangerous attitude.

Instead you must think in terms of getting every moment of truth right—210,000 times.

Managing Moments of Truth

Every moment of truth must be identified and managed. The key is to be aware of all the points of contact from the moment customers come in contact with your company to the moment their experience ends. If the typical customer interaction brings 17 moments of truth, then it takes all 17 to make a customer happy, but it takes only one moment of misery to lose a customer.

Bill: *I had to fly from Salt Lake City to Washington, D.C. It was a Tuesday morning and I had a speech to give Tuesday evening. At the Delta gate the gate attendant asked me if I would catch another flight that would take me to Dulles Airport instead of Washington National. She told me Delta would provide transportation to my hotel and assured me my luggage would be brought over from National. I said to her, "What you're telling me is that you overbooked the flight and you want me to help you out." She agreed. I told her, "Okay, I'll do it. And you owe me one, but let me make one thing clear. If my luggage doesn't get to the hotel on time, I'm dead. I've got a speech to give tonight and I'm not going to give it in cowboy boots."*

The woman assured me that everything would go like clockwork. Sure enough, I flew into Dulles, went to the Delta counter, and the reservationist said, "Mr. Adams, we've been expecting you. Here is your transportation voucher. That'll get you a cab to your hotel. If you want, we can deliver your luggage to your hotel or you can take the cab to National and pick it up." I chose to pick up the luggage myself.

At that point, a ticket agent came over and said, "By the way, Mr. Adams, we want you to know how much we appreciate your helping us out. Here is a free ticket, round trip fare anywhere you want to go." Bingo! A moment of magic. I was thrilled.

I went out and waited for the Washington Flyer cab to pull up. It was hot and humid outside. I got in the cab and the driver was a really nice guy. He said, "It's hot out there, isn't it? As long as you're in my hands, you'll have cool weather." He turned up the air conditioning and handed me a bag of Brach's candies.

He then gave me a choice of either a new USA Today *or a* Washington Post. *I was impressed with this guy!*

We got to Washington National Airport and found out my luggage had not arrived. The woman at the Delta counter handled the situation very well, and assured me my luggage would be at the hotel well before my speech at eight o'clock.

So far everything was fine. Delta exceeded my expectations, the cab driver continued Delta's excellent service, and at seven o'clock that night I got a call from their luggage delivery service telling me my luggage had just arrived and would be delivered to my hotel in fifteen minutes.

My luggage showed up at twelve fifteen the next morning! Five hours late! The delivery service that Delta used failed to make my luggage a priority and caused the whole day's positive experience to be ruined.

There is a redeeming end to this story. The next day I was supposed to fly from Washington to San Diego. Problems with the weather caused us to be delayed in Dallas and, in fact, Delta had to put us up in a hotel for the night. The next day a whole group of us continued on to San Diego. There we were, wearing the same clothes as the night before, in lousy moods, and boarding the plane together. Those of us in first class had the best flight attendant I have ever experienced. Susan Heflin was a dream, someone who truly loved to serve her customers. And it was a godsend that she was the last Delta employee we dealt with that day. Our last impression was our best.

When Delta contracts with Washington Flyer for taxi service, they are contracting for more than transportation; they are contracting for the type of service that Delta wants its customers to receive. How could Delta control the level of service provided by Washington Flyer? They could have a clause in their contract that stipulated service standards. In effect, Delta could tell the cab company they expect the same level of service in their cabs as Delta provides in their airplanes.

We've all done business with companies that are not thoughtful. A typical example of not managing moments of truth is what every company does when its phone receptionist calls in sick. What do you do? Chances are good that you call a temporary agency and hire someone for the day. Think about what a risky proposition that is! Here is this temporary person who knows nothing about your business, doesn't know who's who in the building, and often has little or no incentive to do the job well. This is the person you're trusting to make a good first impression!

The resourceful way to manage moments of truth is this: When the receptionist calls in sick, have someone who knows the company, but normally works in a noncustomer contact position, answer the phone. Hire a temp to take that person's job behind the scenes in the non-customer contact position. A better (long-term) way to handle this eventuality is with cross-training. Train several typists or secretaries to use the phone system so that filling in for an ill receptionist will not cause any loss of service quality.

A company also puts itself at risk when it uses an answering service. Regardless of why the service is used—to fill in during lunch or after hours—it makes an impression, not always a good one. An otherwise excellent company can undermine its image and lose customers by using an unprofessional answering service. That's why it's imperative that you "shop yourself." Call your answering service regularly to see how it is handling your calls.

If you fail to manage every moment of truth of every customer's experience with your company, you risk creating moments of misery. For an airline, a passenger's impression begins with the behavior of the skycaps and ends with the promptness of the luggage delivery service. At a fancy restaurant, moments of truth start with the person who answers the phone to take reservations and end with the valet parking attendants who get your car after the meal.

When you calculate all the moments of truth for your business, you will be astounded by the number of opportunities available for someone to disappoint your customers. No matter what that number is—five or five hundred—it takes only one person to mess it up for all the others who are trying so hard to please.

SERVICE R$_x$:
Each and every moment of truth must be managed, which means ensuring the professionalism of everyone who will come in contact with your customers.

Companies that subcontract services are responsible for the level of service provided by subcontractors. A perfect example is the sundry shop in a hotel. The shop is not owned by the hotel; it is a concession. However, the quality of service provided by the shop reflects on the hotel. Phil had a disturbing experience with a sundry shop. When he told the hotel's manager about it, the manager said, "We don't own the gift shop." Obviously, the manager was short-sighted. His attitude should have been, "If the shop has anything to do with our guests, then I care *very much* about the way it conducts business." The guests don't know or care who owns the shop. They do associate it with the hotel though.

Business today is more complex than ever. On a large scale, businesses merge; on a smaller scale, there are joint ventures, franchises, collaborations, and associations. What you do reflects on the people whom you're associated with. Customers do not differentiate between a McDonald's at one location and a McDonald's at another. If you're unhappy with McDonald's A, chances are good you won't give McDonald's B a chance. That's why franchisers insist on uniformity throughout their chains. Customers demand reliability.

Calculate Your Moments of Truth

From the examples we've given so far, you should be able to calculate the approximate number of moments of truth in your business annually. Do this by adding up all customer, noncustomer, and vendor contacts and multiply them by 250 business days in a year. You'll come up with an astronomical number of moments of truth.

We suggest you not only calculate your company's moments of truth, but do something with the number you come up with. Motivate people! Make a poster that shows everyone the incredible number of times each day—each year—that they influence the customer's experience.

Service excellence can be expressed in terms of a mathematical formula. It is the ratio of moments of magic, moments of truth, and moments of misery.

The greater the number of moments of magic in relation to moments of truth and misery, the greater your success will be. As soon as the moments of misery start to outnumber moments of truth and moments of magic, marketshare will decrease and your business will be headed for failure.

Your goal must be to manage the three types of customer experiences. When you create complaining customers, you succeed in turning your customers' moments of misery into moments of truth. When you create a demanding customer, you have succeeded in turning a moment of truth into a moment of magic.

The Quality of Experiences Affects Customer Perceptions

Figure 12.1: Service Quality is measured in the perception of the customer. One "moment of misery" can significantly affect a customer's overall experience with an organization.

Tom Peters, in his book, *A Passion For Excellence*, points out that companies at the top of the service spectrum—the companies rated highest for quality customer service—are eleven times more profitable than the companies at the bottom of the service spectrum. The message is profound: When you *don't* spend money on quality service, it becomes an expense anyway! When you spend money on service training, it turns into an investment. And that investment has a measurable return in terms of more customers, or customers who spend more money, or both. It should be obvious by now that what makes or breaks a company is people.

PART IV

*Building
a Quality Service
Organization*

Chapter Thirteen

Creating the Vision-Driven and Values-Guided Organization

We mentioned in our introduction that American business executives are constantly looking for new management fads. They want help in achieving the basics of a quality product or service, keeping people satisfied, acquiring and maintaining customers, and making a profit.

To achieve these basic objectives, management theorists have devised all kinds of notions about the behavior of people at work. If you've taken Business 101, you know them:

Management Theories X & Y: *McGregor's outlook on the nature of people.* Theory X took a cynical view, contending that people have an aversion to work and, therefore, need to be controlled. Theory Y stated just the opposite. People are motivated, committed, self-managing, intelligent, willing to work hard, willing to accept responsibility, and underutilized by most organizations.

The Hawthorne Effect. A series of experiments was conducted at Western Electric between 1927 and 1932. Researchers set out to find the relationship between changes in lighting level and productivity. What they discovered was baffling. No matter what changes were made in lighting, productivity always increased. We now understand why. The variable that caused the change in productivity was not lighting level; it was attention. People appreciated the fact that someone (even a researcher) cared about them. When you pay attention to people, they are motivated to work harder.

Managing by Objectives. MBO is a system in which managers and employees set employee goals for a fixed time frame and then assess the degree to which they were accomplished at the end of that period. MBO ties in well with strategic planning and performance appraisal, but overemphasizes the need to quantify results. It is also very traditional; that is, it is based on the organizational pyramid in which all authority rests at the top. MBO has also been criticized for placing more importance on "ends" rather than "means."

Quality Circles. Many people think the concept of Quality Circles was a revolutionary management practice introduced by the Japanese in the early 1960s and imported to the United States in the early 1970s. The fact is, Quality Circles originated in England in 1917 and were quickly adopted by many industries in the United States during World War I.

In the early 1920s, Quality Circles were called shop committees or work councils. They were formed as a means of settling grievances between labor and management. Management soon learned a secondary benefit of shop committees was "the better utilization of the practical knowledge and experience of the work people . . . for improvements of (work) processes, machinery, and organization."[6]

During the early 1920s, shop committees became the rage; employers saw them as fads to experiment with. In the five years between 1919 and 1924, the number of shop committees grew from 225 to 814.

The benefits of shop committees were exactly the objectives American businesses are still trying to accomplish today: reductions in defects and failures, increased productivity, conservation of materials, increased morale, better workmanship, reduced turnover, higher quality employees, and an improved public image, among others.

Shop committees had significant benefits to employees as well including: more job security, improved working conditions, better tools and work methods, profit-sharing, a 75% reduction in grievances, quicker complaint resolution, and higher standards of workmanship.

With all these benefits, you have to wonder why shop committees and the other effective management practices disappeared, only to be rediscovered and renamed later. The answer is short-term thinking, a lack of persistence, and a disregard for the basics.

The Reasons We Fail

There are two major reasons why many companies fail to accomplish significant change. One reason is the American way of managing. It is short-term and impatient. When overnight results don't materialize, managers use that failure as proof the solution failed. It then becomes an excuse to switch to the next short-term fix. You can't implement a change effort and then give up on it in a year or two. The fact is, every solution is a long-term solution because you're dealing with people—and people take time to change.

When it comes to organizational change, persistence is the key. It doesn't matter what management theory you subscribe to as long as you stick with it. You will get results from even the most ill-founded philosophy if it is consistently applied. Western Electric's Hawthorne experiments produced results, inadvertently, simply by changing light levels. Conversely, you will get insignificant results even from the best management theory if you give up after a year or two. The truth is that it doesn't matter what you do, just do something.

SERVICE R$_x$:
In everything—business, life, the arts—people with more dedication and persistence succeed over those with just raw talent. To achieve success, talent must be driven by dedication and persistence.

The other reason companies don't change is they fail to recognize the importance of the human side of business, taking care of people's basic needs. One of the most salient differences between managers in operations-driven organizations and those in market-driven organizations is the way they view their employees. The former still think in terms of the Industrial Age. To them, employees are *tools* to be managed along with budgets, deadlines, and piles of paperwork. In fact, managers usually give paperwork a higher priority than people. When a manager in an operations-driven company is spending a lot of time with a subordinate, you know they are dealing with a crisis.

The people-as-expendable-tools mentality prevails because we are still oriented toward production and technology. When the company needs a shot in the arm, we call in the engineers to design new systems.

When we focus on systems as the solution, the human side of the process gets shortchanged. It is the vision, values, support, communication, empowerment, creativity, training, coaching, and counseling that breathe life and energy into an organizational change effort and make it succeed.

SERVICE R$_x$:
Don't look to new technology to make people's jobs easier. Train, develop, and motivate people to take on new challenges.

There is no new paradigm of management. The ideas we're talking about have been around for centuries. They are basic concepts everyone has talked about from Aristotle, Jesus, and Gandhi to Dr. Martin Luther King, Jr., Peter Drucker, and Tom Peters.

The essence of what the great philosophers advocated is the very heart of the service philosophy we are advocating—people should be treated well. People need to be treated in ways that make them feel wanted, included, competent, and in control. Then they will be motivated to be productive, creative, and committed.

Management has ignored these basic ethical values for years because business schools focus on variables that are measurable. All the measurement, record keeping, and statistical analyses in the world won't mean a thing if you fail to care about people and meet their basic needs.

Max DePree, CEO of Herman Miller, Inc., said it perfectly:

"Many managers are concerned about their style. They wonder whether they are perceived as open or autocratic or participative. As practice is to policy, so style is to belief. *Style is merely a consequence of what we believe, of what is in our hearts.*"[7] (Italics ours)

As long as data has been collected on management science, people at work have been asking for the same things they are asking for today. Too many companies are guilty of not listening to their employees, ignoring customers, and not heeding the advice of consultants. How, then, do they expect to change, much less excel?

Rita Mae Brown once defined insanity as "doing the same thing over and over again expecting a different outcome." It's time to listen, learn, and apply what follows. The place to start is with the basic building blocks of a quality service philosophy—a vision and unifying set of core values.

Unity and Guidance

A corporate vision and its values serve two broad, far-reaching functions in an organization: unity and guidance. Together these are driving forces bringing people together and focusing their sights on common goals. A vision gives meaning to peoples' work and provides the energy and team spirit of a common purpose. Together the vision and core values serve as a guide for decision-making and create behavioral expectations of employees. A vision and core values clearly communicate to employees and the public the principles behind the company, the company's objectives, and the kind of work environment it aspires to create.

SERVICE R$_x$:
Creating a clear vision and a set of core values is an indispensable step in building a high-commitment organization intent upon being the best at everything it does.

Make the Implicit Explicit

Every company has a set of values affecting both its operations and the interactions between people in the organization. More often than not, those values are implicit. They are the unspoken rules you learn on the job; things never spelled out in the policy manual. They may be learned through osmosis, observation, or from someone whispering to you by the coffee machine. Regardless of how they're acquired, there is no denying the power these values have in shaping the work environment.

A company must make its values explicit. When values aren't explicit, misunderstandings can be costly. In 1989 Nordstrom took a public relations blow, the ramifications of which are still being felt. An employee's union charged that the Seattle-based company routinely failed to pay its salespeople for after-hours work. The union and disgruntled employees claimed salespeople were expected to attend meetings, make deliveries, stock shelves, and send thank you notes on their own time. Reporting the hours for those tasks would dilute the sales-per-hour statistics on which commissions were based. At first Nordstrom denied there was a problem, but later the company established a $15 million fund for compensating employees with grievances.

There are a lot of issues surrounding this incident, but the point most relevant to this discussion is that Nordstrom failed to make its expectations explicit. It should have told each new employee exactly how the system worked and what was expected of them. Prospective salespeople could then have either taken or refused the job, based on additional information. Making expectations explicit would have protected Nordstrom. Instead, the company tried to enforce implicit values and got into an ethical, if not legal, dilemma.

SERVICE R$_X$:
Put everything on the table and let people choose for themselves, then hold them accountable for results.

The problem is, in most companies, values remain implied. When values are unspoken, they're also unmanageable. That's why you must articulate organizational values and make them clear, controllable, and manageable.

Encourage Ethical Conflicts

When an organization creates ethical and philosophical standards, it raises issues that normally might not surface and be resolved. This stirring up of the corporate conscience is precisely where the power lies. It makes you aware of the ways your business practices conflict with your ethical and philosophical values.

Awareness is the key, and most companies don't have it. When you become aware of ethical conflicts, you have two choices. You can either adhere to your core values and make changes or you can choose to ignore the issue. Your new awareness points toward the direction you should go, which prepares you to understand and acknowledge the consequences of your decisions.

A case in point: Michael Milken and the 1989 fall of Drexel, Burnham, Lambert. Although the Drexel firm pleaded guilty to six felony counts and agreed to pay a $650 million penalty, they tried to minimize the perception of the severity of their crimes by claiming "the transgressions chiefly involved verbal agreements that were not disclosed to the firm and which no amount of diligence could have detected."[8]

SERVICE R$_x$:
One of the steps in producing a vision-driven and values-guided organization is to look at the gap between how you say things *should* be and how they actually are.

If Drexel's corporate culture had been guided by a vision and set of ethical values, there would have been no need for diligence. People "police" themselves when they are given consistent parameters for decision-making. The problem is that most companies don't operate by a set of core values. Their sole purpose is to make a profit, which explains why any day of the week you can pick up a newspaper and read about defense industry fraud, insider trading, savings and loan scandals, and a myriad of other crimes in every industry imaginable, including the supposedly noble practices of medicine and law.

The ABCs of Ethics

Is it realistic to expect to influence or change the ethics of adults? Are their values established long before they come to work for your company? There is no precise answer, but, because Milken and Drexel are not isolated cases, something must be done.

In 1988 an FBI probe uncovered fraudulent trading practices at the Chicago Mercantile Exchange (CME) and Chicago Board of Trade, the world's two largest futures exchanges. As a result, in April of 1990 the CME ordered its 2,500 members to enlist in ethics classes. It arranged for 50 two-hour classes to be conducted across the street from the Exchange. Any member who failed to take a course before the end of 1990 would be fined and possibly suspended from trading.

Every organization has the responsibility of establishing a set of core values, for many reasons. As corporate America takes on the role of educator, ethics must be included in the curriculum so we do not evolve into a society of "crooks." From a strictly business standpoint, the responsibility is obvious—business relationships cannot exist without trust. The last reason, and the one most relevant to the theme of this book, is that service quality is a direct reflection of corporate culture.

Service Is a Mirror Image of Corporate Values

The most basic value an organization conveys to its people, implicitly or explicitly, is, "This is how we treat people around here." When management treats front-line people well, it sets an example of what is expected—how everyone (including customers) should be treated. If management abuses employees, it initiates the "kick-the-dog" syndrome; everyone passes anger and frustration on to the next person lower on the totem pole, customers included. In the end, employees get even, one way or another. That's how service standards start at the top and work their way down. Service quality is a direct reflection of how management treats employees.

SERVICE R$_x$:
Employees are your best PR. Invest in them as you would an award-winning ad campaign.

You have to value your employees, otherwise you cannot expect them to value your customers.

One of the many benefits of treating people well is less turnover. Research by the Forum Corporation found a correlation between companies with high turnover and poor service quality. The cycle of poor service and high turnover has to broken. You do this by training people to do their jobs well and giving them responsibility and control.

Ford's assembly plant in Hermosillo, Mexico, is an excellent example of the pride employees take in their work when they are given responsibility. Managers started by making everyone equals; there is only one job classification for all assembly line workers. The workers do their own quality control, maintenance, and assembly. They even have the ability to stop the assembly line. During the first year of operation, the plant established a lower defect rate than most Japanese automakers.

What were the dynamics at work on the assembly line? When the workers were given control over the quality of their work, they cared more, increased their competence, and turned out a better product. This is a much better scenario than workers who have no control and are reduced to subservient drones. They become indifferent, careless, and resentful.

We've seen how morale and productivity are profoundly affected by management's treatment of employees. How does treatment get transferred to the customer? It could be as subtle as how well or poorly customers are handled on the phone. It could also be as blatant as an experience Bill had several years ago.

> Bill: *I was standing in line in a supermarket in Florida. The woman being checked out was talking to a woman behind her and complaining about what a miserable experience it was to get claims processed through a large health insurance company. She was going on and on about the numerous phone calls, the claim forms, the computer foul-ups, the rudeness of the claims processors and so on. The woman was livid, so this went on for several minutes.*
>
> *Finally, the woman who had been listening to the tirade looked the complainer squarely in the face and said, "Listen, lady, you think you've got problems, you only have to deal with them occasionally. I deal with them every day—I work there! You only call in once or twice a day. I'm there 40 hours a week. So don't talk to me about your problems!"*

As unbelievable as this may sound, it's true. Here was a customer service employee who hated her customers and her company. Uncommon? Not at all.

In May of 1990 there was an amusing article in the *Los Angeles Times* about an underground newspaper that circulated around the offices of the 20th Century Insurance Company. There were seven issues of the 20th Century RagTime over the past six years, each with mock interviews and other spoofs taking shots at what editors consider stodgy management practices. The centerpiece of RagTime is an advice column written by Myra Atkins, a fictitious mailroom overachiever. "Dear Myra," one letter began, "Isn't charging employees for parking the same as giving us a pay cut?" "Yes," Myra replied.

At first, some 20th Century managers were amused by the paper, but after observing the reaction at the executive level, they realized the publication was not to be openly enjoyed. In fact, management discouraged the paper and made a concerted effort to root out its creators. To catch the scoundrels, managers spent hours pouring over videotapes from security cameras. Employees claim that desks were searched, hallways staked out, and suspects questioned. Management failed to uncover many solid clues and continued to accuse the paper of being "illegal and libelous." Meanwhile, employees anxiously look forward to the next issue. It is interesting, but not surprising that the president and other executives of the company refused to be interviewed for the article.

One of the many questions that arise is, why didn't these two insurance companies notice their employees were so unhappy? And if they had noticed, why wasn't something being done about it? Chances are good that there are more than a handful of disgruntled employees. Think of the negative impact those people have on co-workers and customers. Now imagine how much greater their productivity and service would be if they were satisfied.

SERVICE R$_x$:
Companies must establish "on the table" cultures in which employees can air their grievances without risk. It is hypocritical to encourage customer complaints, yet repress ones from employees.

If service is a mirror image of culture—and our experience as consultants and trainers supports this—then how can Nordstrom, with its disgruntled employees, manage to provide such exemplary service. Nordstrom is not an exception to the rule. We believe the complaining employees are, however, an exception and that the majority of Nordstrom people are satisfied with their jobs and the way they are treated. In fact, there have been demonstrations in support of the company at some of Nordstrom's California stores.

High turnover, low morale, unethical behavior, and poor service must be eliminated if a company is to provide service in the progressive zone. Competitive companies of the future need to develop highly trained, highly committed work forces that have a stake (emotional and financial) in the success of their organizations. To accomplish this ideal, corporate structures, attitudes, and training standards must be transformed for high performance.

The High Performance Model

Figure 13.1 represents the dynamics of a high performance organization. On the left side are eight boxes representing the various elements that work together to drive a company forward. Notice these are not departments within an organization. Departments don't make a company successful. The eight elements are the intangibles that fuel the efforts of the people within the organization:

1. A strategy to get you where you're going.

2. Effective leadership

3. Effective communication

4. An emphasis on teamwork

5. An emphasis on quality service

6. A clear focus on results

7. Meaningful reward and recognition systems

8. Effective organizational structure

The large arrow represents the energy that provides directional thrust in the high performance organization—a vision and a set of core values. This direction shows people where the company is headed and how to get there. By working within established guidelines, the company moves forward ethically to achieve its goals of profits, results, fulfillment, and social responsibility.

The model of the typical organization is not as ideal as figure 13.1, but looks more like figure 13.2. In figure 13.2 there is the traditional hierarchy, full of conflict. There are always employees trying to move forward with the organization. At the same time, there are layers of managers and supervisors playing the role of cops and constantly pressuring employees to rigidly conform to policies and procedures.

The natural tendency for people when they are being pushed is to dig in their heels and push back. What develops is tension between employees, supervisors, and managers. That tension causes a lot of energy to move perpendicular to the direction of progress, thereby slowing down the company's forward motion. What supervisors and managers need to create is movement forward rather than control. This is part of the paradigm shift they need to make.

High Performance Model

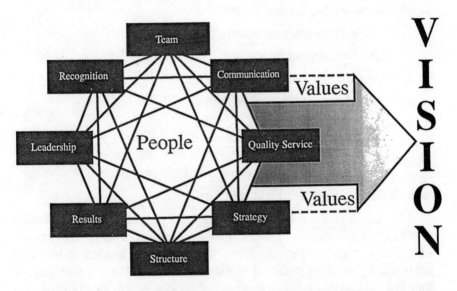

Figure 13.1: The High Performance Model focuses on establishing a compelling vision of the future, using shared values as the signposts to guide day-to-day behaviors, operating with critical success factors in mind, and having people at the core who can "make it all possible."

The principles of forward momentum versus control apply to many aspects of our lives. Dale Murphy, and many other great hitters in baseball, often threw their bats after a hit. It wasn't intentional. They held their bats so loosely that they sometimes slipped out of their hands and wound up in left field. The reason Dale held his bat loosely was so that he could put more energy into the forward motion of his swing.

When you stop pushing down on your people to control them, you will give them the freedom, authority, and self-confidence to excel.

Then, and only then, will they be able to set your company apart by virtue of its progressive service. To effect this change and create a culture in which your company will thrive, you must avoid the common pitfalls of organizational change:

- A lack of commitment and leadership from top management.
- Lack of modeling from management. ("Do as I say, not as I do.")
- Short-term focus and impatience.
- Viewing the change effort as a program, not as an ongoing process. (The "flavor-of-the-month" syndrome.)
- Absence of planned communication and feedback.
- Inadequate attention to new skills and knowledge required to sustain the changes.
- Burdens of bureaucracy from above.
- Trying to force-fit someone else's solutions.

Figure 13.2: The typical organization is designed to keep people in line. In the effort to maintain position, all the energy and momentum is consumed internally.

The High Performance Organization

In the 1990s, we will begin to see many changes in the way employees work, the way managers manage, and the way people are promoted and compensated.

In the evolution of business operations, especially in production, technology has reached a plateau. To bring about or manage change, companies can no longer find the solutions in technology. The solutions lie in transforming the organization into one that is more responsive by virtue of its structure. New ways of decision-making, grouping jobs and people, delegating responsibility, and sharing of power are some of the high performance strategies that will keep an organization in step with or ahead of the times. Many of these changes are already in motion in corporate America.

Many people have been advocating the inverted pyramid as the corporate structure that will emphasize the importance of the customer and improve service. One of the many problems with a pyramid—whether it is right side up or inverted—is that every layer is separated from other layers, except for the ones immediately above or below it. And there are still a lot of people separated from the customer and each other.

Another problem with the pyramid is the inherent assumptions about promotion. In most companies, the basis for promotion to manager is technical competence. The reason for this is the old guild system. You learned a trade and moved up through the ranks from apprentice to journeyman to master craftsman. As you moved up through the skill levels, part of your job was to teach the neophytes.

Nowhere is this more apparent than in the sales department. Top producers are routinely promoted to sales manager, where they sometimes confirm the Peter Principle—that people eventually rise to their level of incompetence. Everyone knows that sales skills and managerial skills are not the same skills. When you promote a top salesperson to manager, you run the risk of losing a great salesperson and installing an ineffective sales manager.

All that is changing. Not only is there little room left in middle and upper management, but large organizations are paring away managerial layers. The streamlined organizational chart of the future is no longer a pyramid. The answer, one that is beginning to be implemented in corporate America, is the flattened structure that represents a network of interdependent resources.

This flattened configuration lends itself well to lower overhead, increased responsiveness to customers, faster product development, greater internal harmony, and higher profits. Keep in mind that this flattened model does not represent the best way to structure an organization. There is no "best" way. There is, however, a "wrong" way.

Figure 13.3: The flattened organizational structure allows people to work in concert and direct their energy toward achieving a common goal. Managers and supervisors become coaches and counselors working along side of their people as the role of "enforcer" is "replaced" by core values.

Any structure that inhibits the company from performing at its best and utilizing the talents of its people is the wrong way.

The best way to become a high-performance company is to create a philosophical context from which a corporate structure can be designed. Designs will also take into consideration internal requirements, marketplace needs, economic and political forces, and company resources.

A large corporation—we'll call them Acme—had a division called Corporate Information Systems (CIS). CIS were the people who provided data processing services to all the operational divisions within the company. Up until recently, CIS had a captive audience and were giving other divisions poor service. CIS could get away with delivering poor service because they were a corporate function serving the company. One day, however, Acme changed its policy. It gave CIS one year to "clean up their act." If, at the end of the year, the other operational divisions were not satisfied with the level of service they were getting from CIS, the other divisions were free to seek those services from outside vendors. Suddenly CIS had to tow the line and justify their existence. They had to treat each operational division as a customer! CIS realized the expectations of the other divisions was not low price, but quality service. It put a new perspective on performance when CIS had to sell themselves to their own company!

SERVICE R_x:
When there is a shared sense of purpose, people are *expected* to accept responsibility for producing quality.

High Performance Innovations

Self-managed teams, skill-based pay, cross-training, and pushing decisions down to the lowest levels are some of the innovative changes being made in high performance organizations.

SMTs are groups of people within departments who are responsible for a cluster of jobs. Instead of a department supervisor overseeing eight or ten people who work on a related function, a self-managed team supervises itself. Group members have the responsibility of assigning tasks, setting objectives, evaluating performance, hiring new people, assessing training needs, and attending to other operational details. Self-managed work teams are the way of the future for increasing quality, improving service, and garnering greater commitment.

Traditionally, promotions lead you up the corporate ladder from front-line employees to supervisor to manager to assistant vice-president to director to executive vice-president and so on until you are the president or CEO. As we mentioned earlier, there's no more room left at the top. There are too many managers and far too many people who are qualified to be managers. How, then, will people be promoted in the high performance organizations of the future?

In an organization of self-managed teams, the people with the most technical ability will be kept on the front lines to do what they do best. Supervisors and managers, therefore, will be the people with organizational and leadership skills, the human resource experts who know how to ask the right questions and listen in order to bring out the best in the technical experts.

People will no longer be promoted vertically; they will be promoted laterally. Skill- or knowledge-based promotions and pay increases are some of the systems gaining in popularity. With the former, you are trained to perform more than one job in your department. Once you have mastered additional skills and can perform other jobs, your pay will increase to reflect your increased value to the company. With knowledge-based pay, you remain in the same job, but your pay increases as you become more of an expert at what you do. The more you know, the more you are worth to the company.

Skill-based pay is an example of cross-training, in which people learn to perform more than one job. Cross-training is essential in service organizations, especially small companies. When employees are able to fill in for one another, there are fewer interruptions in service when someone calls in sick. Cross-training prevents the system from breaking down due to a missing link. It also enhances teamwork and responsiveness to customer needs.

In a company with self-managed teams and a flattened organizational structure, everyone takes on more responsibilities. Decision-making is pushed down to the lowest possible level. Managers are asked to devise strategy. Supervisors are required to do jobs that managers formerly performed. Self-managed work teams are assuming responsibilities supervisors once held.

Companies that push decision-making to the point closest to the customer are more flexible, efficient, and easier to do business with.

Emil: *I dropped my truck off at Axtell Chevrolet in Logan, Utah, to have the oil changed and a new bumper installed. When I returned for the truck, I was told they had not installed the bumper because it hadn't arrived yet. I was also told that, while they were changing my oil, they noticed the seal on my transfer case was leaking badly. Without calling me, they had gone ahead and replaced the part.*

"The service manager said to me, "Mr. Bohn, I know you're busy and often out of town, so I took the liberty of fixing this problem so you wouldn't have to bring the truck back." I was thrilled. I really appreciated that.

I talked to the owner of the dealership about this new policy. He told me he has authorized his mechanics to make needed repairs without permission if the repair cost is reasonable. And if the customer resists the additional charge, the service manager has the authority to delete those charges from the bill.

"Sorry Ma'am I don't make the rules around here . . .
Oh, yes I do make the rules around here."

If you're asking yourself how a manager can give a mechanic the responsibility of deleting charges from a customers' bill, you're not alone. There is a vast group of you out there who need to change the way you view your job and your attitudes toward employees.

The Need for Paradigm Shifts

Charles E. Exley, Chairman and CEO of NCR, was quoted as saying, "I've been in this business for 36 years, I've learned a lot—and most of it doesn't apply anymore."[9] What does apply is flexibility. Flexibility in the things you do, the things you learn, and the way you welcome change and make "paradigm shifts."

A paradigm is a model or a way of looking at the world. The way you see a situation is determined by your frame of reference. The things that shape your frame of reference are every experience you've had—those things that make you the person you are today, including your upbringing, education, self-esteem, personal experiences, and business background.

At this point in your life, you have attitudes and ways of looking at all kinds of things: customers, bosses, employees, power, responsibility, and commitment, to name a few. A paradigm shift takes place when your perspective changes due to new information or an external demand. Managers and supervisors need to make paradigm shifts when their companies change from being operations-driven to market-driven. Those shifts include changing the way you define your role:

FROM:	TO:
Boss	Leader
Cop	Coach
Director	Resource person
Operations	Quality Service
Parent	Peer
Technical Expert	Communicator

A paradigm shift sometimes requires practice. Your new mind-set may not come naturally and, like anything new, will require a commitment and frequent reminders. Some paradigm shifts are so dramatic that they need no assimilation at all. People who have near-death experiences often see the world differently after the event. For many, that shift stays with them for the rest of their lives.

To show you how quickly a paradigm can change, imagine this experience a friend had in New York City:

Star: *I was on a train headed home late one night. At the other end of the car was a man with two children—about nine and seven years old. The kids were completely out of control. They were yelling, screaming, crying, running up and down the aisle, and, in general, disturbing everyone. I had just spent a long day at the office and was tired and irritable. I automatically made a judgement about this man's inability to discipline his children and thought he was rude to not care about their disruptive behavior.*

Finally, I got fed up with it all. I got up and went over to the father to ask him to keep his children quiet. As I was about to speak, the father looked up at me and said, "I really don't know what to do with them. We just left the hospital and their mother passed away." In a fraction of a second my attitude turned around 180 degrees and I asked, "Is there anything I can do to help?"

An instant paradigm shift—and a powerful lesson in keeping an open mind. All too often we look at situations and make assumptions, only to discover later that our assumptions were wrong. It's difficult to withhold judgement, but part of being an enlightened person is the ability to be open to possibilities you hadn't thought of.

For managers, the most difficult paradigm shift is giving up power. Many managers got to where they are today by being hard-driving tyrants; and a manager's worth has traditionally been measured by the number of people being managed. The work environment of the future, however, will measure managers' worth by how productively and independently their people work. Down-sized companies will push a lot of responsibility to lower levels, which means managers must loosen or completely give up their grip on power. In the high-performance organization, managerial power will be redefined to mean the ability to capitalize on change, develop people, absorb information, model desirable behaviors, and, in general, be an effective leader.

SERVICE R$_X$:
You manage *things*. You lead *people*.

The Role of a Leader

What do leaders do that is different from supervisors and managers? What will it mean when your role shifts from being cop, task master, rule enforcer, and technical expert to leader, resource person, and coach?

As the person at the helm, a leader takes a long-term view. Looking at the big picture means three things: keeping the corporate vision alive, managing the work environment, and anticipating the future. This requires a leader to wear many hats: crusader, ring leader, politician, saint, and visionary.

Keeping the vision alive is done by modeling the behaviors you expect in others and articulating the values attached to the vision. This requires goal clarification, establishing priorities, and enlisting others in support of the vision. It means being a cheerleader of sorts, a crusader who keeps the vision alive and in the forefront of people's minds.

Managing the work culture requires a manager to act as a facilitator and coach. The social environment includes demands from customers, suppliers, corporate staff groups, and other entities inside and out of the company. A leader works with all these people to 1) get his people what they need to excel and 2) achieve a smooth transition to the new corporate structure.

If self-managed teams are going to work, some people must be willing to pass influence and power along to the people who are doing the work. Since few people are inclined to give up power, it is the leader's job as facilitator to help everyone understand that humility is a virtue and that the sharing of power is necessary for achieving the company's vision.

Leaders are patient. They realize that people change slowly. Employees are used to being treated as children by managers who are used to acting as parents. When changes are being ushered in, employees need some time and experience before they can trust and commit themselves 100% to the new order.

People must be weaned from old habits, one of which is to try to pass "monkeys" back to management. Leaders must realize this and be patient. They know that if employees are going to take the initiative and accept more responsibility, they need training, coaching, support, understanding and clarity.

The third broad responsibility of a leader is to be a visionary. By looking at the big picture, a leader anticipates changes in the marketplace, responds to customer demands, and keeps abreast of new technology—all of which moves the organization forward toward its vision.

Leaders must have unwavering faith in the company vision and core values. In the face of resistance, criticism, and challenges, a leader must stand firm. The Wright Brothers failed to fly on their first 147 attempts. People were skeptical, to say the least. The prevailing wisdom of the day was that if people were meant to fly, they would have wings. The Wright Brothers were true leaders. They had a vision and they stuck with it. Their commitment was uncompromising, a true stretch to accomplish "the impossible."

The transformation from an operations-driven company to a market-driven, high performance, vision and values-driven organization is a giant leap. Like all leaps, it is accomplished with small steps. It is a long-term commitment—one that requires careful planning and occasional outside help. It requires the use of strategic planning sessions to clarify values, create a vision for the firm, and map out the change process.

An understanding of individual and organizational change will take you a long way toward developing a necessary virtue—patience.

Chapter Fourteen

Implementing a Quality Service Change Effort

To most people, change does not come as any surprise. We've grown accustomed to and dependent on our high-tech world in which today's fantasy is tomorrow's best selling electronic gadget. The fact that you can be playing a round of golf and receive a cellular phone call as well as a fax transmission is fascinating, but not surprising to most people. Technology is advancing so rapidly that we expect science fiction to become fact, virtually overnight.

Watching the world around us change or taking advantage of new technology is less stressful than embarking on personal change. Being creatures of habit, most of us avoid personal change. However, change is like aging—everyone goes through it sooner or later. The healthiest attitude is to accept the fact that continual change is a natural part of our fast-paced world.

The key to welcoming change is to stay informed. This means keeping abreast of changes in your field as well as being knowledgeable about as many other things as possible. It means being well-read, keeping abreast of world events, and embracing new technology.

"Would you like your cart phone with or without a fax machine?"

> **SERVICE R$_X$:**
> **Knowledge is the antithesis of fear of change.**

Like anything else in life, your perception of change is influenced by how you view it. You don't always have to like it, but you should at least understand it. If you fight it, you postpone the inevitable. When you create it, however, you also create opportunities. If you manage it, it will not manage you. Control the controllable and keep everything else in perspective. Don't sweat the small stuff.

Organizational Change

The most difficult change of all, involving people and technology, is organizational change. The complexity of organizational change is exponentially greater than individual change. If you consider the difficulty of one person to change and then multiply that by the number of people in your company, you can see why any organizational change effort is a long-term process.

There are three ways a company can react to change. Figure 14.1 illustrates the common paths that are typical outcomes of organizational change.

Organizations that only react to change—and do so inflexibly—are destined for failure. Typically, they are rigid zone companies that resist change and hold tenaciously to present modes of thinking. Their executives and managers defiantly refuse to move away from the secure past toward the pressures of new challenges. As a result, these companies find change difficult to manage. Managers spend a lot of time explaining why it isn't their fault the company is failing.

The less successful, but still viable organizations of the 1990s will be those that respond flexibly to change, but rarely anticipate it. Safe zone companies in this category will spend a great deal of time coping with the rapidly changing environment of the '90s, with little energy left for looking ahead. Internally, their people will react to change perfunctorily—with compliance and minimal support.

The high performance, progressive zone organizations of the future will be those that have mastered the art of change. They are the companies that respond to change proactively, not reactively; that is, they make change happen. Leaders of progressive zone companies not only accept and enthusiastically support change, they also work at systematically anticipating the future. Progressive zone companies, especially companies with flattened structures and self-managed teams, quickly and decisively allocate resources for new options that enable them to meet challenges and set industry standards, rather than following the standards set by others.

To meet the demands of the marketplace, corporate change is inevitable, but positive growth as a result of change is optional. A well-planned and implemented change program will provide your organization with a blueprint for initiating, managing, and capitalizing on change. By controlling every step of the change process, your company will create dedicated leadership, a team spirit, superior performance, increased sales, truly differentiated customer service, and increased bottom-line profits.

The most effective change efforts place an emphasis on high involvement. Virtually everyone in the organization contributes to the process of change. People are more likely to take responsibility for and ownership of a transformational process they have helped develop.

Three Possible Paths of Organizational Change

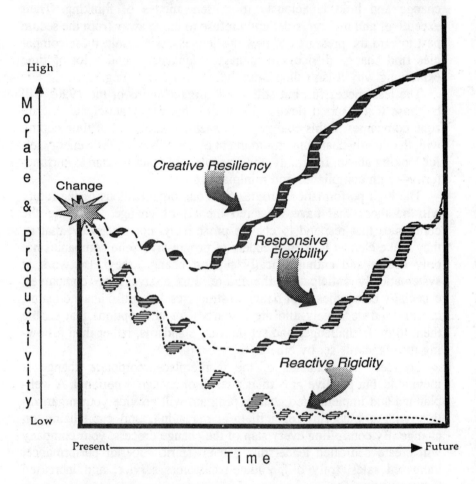

Figure 14.1: Organizations that choose the path of creative resiliency increase productivity and build morale over time.

When implementing a quality service philosophy, you have to establish two levels of responsibility for the program. First, you promote the ideal that everyone is responsible for excellent service and the acquisition and maintenance of customers. Second, you create an executive design team that is ultimately responsible for the design, implementation, measurement, and effectiveness of the change effort.

SERVICE R$_X$:
Promote *responsibility* for excellent service in every employee, then make the executive team *accountable*.

The following five-step process for the implementation of a service program or any other change makes the art of dealing with people and organizational change more of a science. The five basic steps are:

1. Setting the Stage.

2. Diagnosing the Situation.

3. Designing Solutions.

4. Implementing the Plans.

5. Evaluating the Results.

Setting the Stage

It is important to set the stage for any kind of transition. Setting the stage simply involves introducing the new philosophy and practices in a way that makes them as nonthreatening as possible. This is one of those times when management must act as a public relations firm. Executives and managers have to carry out coordinated steps that are designed to communicate the right messages and positively position the upcoming changes within the organization. Change should be portrayed as an ally. Help interpret the change for your people by selling its benefits.

Every change effort needs an effective communication plan, a way to manage messages. Typically, senior executives have a meeting and discuss various issues. When they leave the meeting and return to their areas, people ask them what happened in the meeting. What you get is a lot of people giving different accounts of what transpired, so the organization gets mixed messages.

Transformational Development Process

Step 1. Setting the Stage

- Brief Executive Team on change process
- Set Direction—Vision and Values
- Select/Train Transition Manager and Design Team
- Design and Deliver Management Training Program
- Design Communication Plan
- Plan Vision roll-out

Step 2. Diagnosing the Situation

- Conduct Organizational Assessment
- Data Feedback
- Develop Gap Analysis

Step 3. Designing Solutions

- Development of Strategic Plans
- Development of the Strategic Training Plan
- Continuation of employee ownerhsip and commitment processes

Step 4. Implementing the Plans

- Implement Action Plans
- Begin Training Plan
- Evaluate results to this point

Step 5. Evaluating the Results

- Progress Monitoring and Evaluating
- Fine-tuning based on Evaluation
- Start New Diagnostic Phase

© Maxcomm Associates, Inc.

Figure 14.2: The Transformational Development Process includes five steps. Even though the steps appear to be sequential, they often overlap and occur simultaneously.

The smart approach is to admit this happens and control it. At the end of a meeting, the president should say, "Here are the five key messages to disseminate to your people . . . " Managing communications will give your company more faith in the people who are running the show because they're sending consistent messages. It also creates a model that will be emulated by other levels of the company.

You want to ensure that everyone understands the rationale behind the change effort and views it as a positive challenge to be welcomed rather than a threat or imposition to be resisted. Setting the stage in a coordinated way helps you accomplish the following:

- Minimize disruption.

- Gain organizational commitment and maximize employee "buy-in."

- Use communication networks to focus on short- and long-term successes.

- Surface, address, and manage all expectations, fears and questions about the change effort.

- Set the direction for the organization.

The last item—set the direction for the organization—is a very important step. As we discussed in the last chapter, every market-driven, high performance organization is driven by a vision and guided by a set of core values. The vision and values are created as part of a strategic planning process. Strategic planning is the discipline of clarifying and achieving a consensus on the purpose, direction, and objectives of your company. A strategic plan usually projects out five years and defines the business you are in, how you intend to make money, and how you want to position yourself in the future.

When strategic planning is done well, it accomplishes many things:

- Senior management gains a sense of direction and purpose.

- The objectives to be attained become clear.

- The action plans required to achieve the objectives become apparent.

- Everyone involved in the planning process learns what is needed for success.

The corporate vision and core values that come out of strategic planning can also be called the statement of intention or "The Willed Future." The willed future describes the organization in relation to its marketplace and the environment. The willed future becomes the basic operating document of the company. It is the combined ethical, strategic/philosophical and operational values with which all future decisions will be consistent.

SERVICE R$_X$:
The corporate vision and core values become the conscience of the organization and the guiding force that keeps everything in alignment.

The vision and set of core values are created by top executives and then taken to the organization for challenge. The purpose of the challenge is to allow people to show top management those areas in which the lofty ideals of the vision and values are not being upheld in the daily operations of the company. This company-wide feedback is indispensable in fine-tuning the vision and core values, bringing them into step with reality and encouraging company-wide involvement and ownership of the ideals.

After the corporate visions and values have been challenged, rewritten and refined, they are rolled out for the entire company to commit to. Like any incentive program, the new company philosophy should be rolled out with some fanfare. Make a big deal of it. Print posters or T-shirts and create other novelties to acknowledge and recognize the change.

Unlike most incentive programs, however, this one has to be permanent. Many companies shortchange their customer service programs by understaffing or underfinancing them. The change effort must be taken as seriously as building a new factory or revamping a product line. The investment and commitment must be there; the quality service philosophy must become a permanent way of life. Too many companies stop being market-driven after the party's over. Others usher in their new service consciousness with training. They bring in high-priced trainers, consultants, and keynote speakers—but the changes never get out of the classroom.

An organization can only become a high-performance company when it has 100% commitment to the effort. Part of the commitment—and one of the core values—is open communication. Establishing an "on the table" culture in which anyone can say anything to anybody is important in the accomplishment of the next step of the process. Only when people are willing to be completely honest, without fear of retribution, will they come forth with the type of information needed to diagnose the situation and make long-lasting changes in the organization.

"Improve our Customer Service . . . sure, great idea. Now, who wants to be Santa Claus at this year's Christmas party?"

Diagnosing the Situation

After you articulate a new vision and create a set of core values, the next step is to assess the gap between where your company is today and where you want to go. A common mistake many companies make is to assume they know what the problems are and how to solve them. All too often people look at symptoms and think they see the underlying problem. Jumping to conclusions may produce a fine solution, but it may not address the real problem.

To avoid wasting time and money, look for problems, not solutions. The way to do this is with an in-depth organizational assessment that analyzes the technical and people aspects of the business in relation to its vision and values. This is a time-consuming and highly specialized undertaking—one that, more often than not, is best left to objective, outside consultants. By using interviews, surveys, file and document audits, observation, and participation, management consultants can analyze all the major facets of your company, including:

- Readiness for and acceptance of change
- Leadership effectiveness
- Major functional systems and departments
- Task/Value analysis
- Employee attitudes and motivation
- Communication effectiveness
- Organizational style and culture
- Customer service quality
- Product quality and delivery systems
- Recruitment, selection, orientation and training of employees
- Strategic planning systems
- Budgeting and financial management systems
- Sales/Marketing trends and concentrations
- Organizational rewards and performance review systems

After all the pieces of this detailed analysis have been put together, you will have a vivid picture of your company's present strengths and weaknesses. The gap between where you are and where you want to be will also become apparent. From this insight you will be able to make solid, informed decisions about which things to change and how to change them.

Setting the stage and diagnosing the situation guarantee that your actions will move the company consistently and directly toward its new vision. Without the in-depth analyses in these two steps, your planning and program implementation could end up being done by the seat of your pants and would be, at best, educated guesses as to what needs to be done.

Designing Solutions

The next step in the transformational process is to design practical, results-oriented solutions. These activities are designed to close the gap between the status quo and the vision of the future. The solutions stem directly from the development of the strategic training plan, your road map to an integrated training system. By following a coordinated plan you will provide your people with the critical skills they need to serve the company and achieve its objectives.

Part of the organizational assessment performed by outside consultants includes the analysis of various factors that bear directly on the strategic training plan:

1. Conditions within your company, in your marketplace, and in your industry that suggest training needs.

2. The present skills and backgrounds of all employees.

3. The skills and knowledge necessary to take on future job responsibilities.

4. The resources available to develop and implement an integrated training system.

Based on an analysis of these factors, the strategic training plan outlines the training required. It spells out what competencies have to be acquired, how they will be taught, who the instructors will be, in what order the competencies should be taught, the time line for training, the instructional materials needed, and the overall training budget.

Implementing the Plans

The next step is assigning responsibility. People have to be made responsible and accountable for every aspect of the change effort, including training. Assigning accountabilities ensures a commitment to the implementation process.

In general, people don't rush to change their behavior, especially when it means increasing their workload. So it isn't unusual for a group of executives or managers to agree to a program and then leave it hanging. That's why the people who play major parts in implementing a change effort must be intimately involved in its design. Without that involvement, they won't feel the degree of ownership they need to sustain a high level of motivation.

Another important part of this step is the preparation of a detailed, step-by-step schedule for the implementation of the action plans. At this point, training begins and measures of effectiveness are developed.

Evaluating the Results

To monitor how well you're doing, it is necessary to constantly evaluate the effectiveness of the change effort throughout the five-step process. Unfortunately, many companies ignore this phase and miss the opportunity to gain insight and refine their efforts.

A major evaluation is made in the five-step process, both in the beginning—with an organizational assessment—and at the end, by measuring the effectiveness of specific solutions. Every step of the way, however, you still have to ask, "How will we know when we've solved this problem?" "What will our success criteria be—in specific, measurable terms?"

It is often assumed that the results of a successful solution will be obvious. This can be true, but it isn't always. Even in cases where the solutions are obvious, it is productive to determine exactly what worked. Training can't be improved with guesswork, you must have concrete success criteria.

During the implementation process, employee performance and perceptions are measured so that training can be adjusted as necessary. This requires open communication and feedback as well as a system for observing and measuring behavioral changes.

It's important to realize that the five-step process doesn't end when the trainers walk out the door. It is an ongoing process in which evaluation uncovers further problems needing solutions. This continuous feedback and refinement process is what drives high-commitment organizations to higher and higher levels of performance.

The People Side of Change

Conventional wisdom dictates that attitudes must change before behaviors. We disagree. It is more effective to change behaviors first. For years management consultants have been hired to improve productivity in the workplace. Many of them conducted training programs that focused on the attitude and relationship-side of problems. Their rationale was that people would be more productive when they were not in conflict with their co-workers.

There is no documented evidence that this works. In fact, the literature on the management sciences is full of research supporting just the opposite. When you help people achieve results, you also resolve relationship problems. When people become more functional, competent, productive, and in control, they get along better with their peers. In addition, relationship issues surface in a context that makes them easier to solve. They become a specific, "I have a difficult time working with you when you . . . " as opposed to a vague, "I don't like you."

SERVICE R$_x$:
Show people how to achieve results first and new attitudes and relationships will follow.

On a personal level, there are three types of change, two of which are desirable. Involved change occurs when you participate in its creation. Informed change exists when you are passively aware of it. Imposed change happens when it is thrust upon you. When you push people, they push back.

For managers, the key to ushering in change is to make it as involved as possible. Involved changes requires that you:

- Use your employees' input to the extent possible in your decision-making process.

- Listen carefully to your people. Consider their opinions and feelings as well as the facts.

- Get input from those who will be affected before a decision to change is final.

- Tell them why, if you do not use their input.

- Give credit where credit is due.

Communication is an important element in any change effort. Show you care by letting your people know about a change as far in advance as possible. Paint a picture of how things will look after the changes and explain the reasons they are being made. Take the time to be sure your people understand. Ignorance and misunderstandings only promote anxiety.

Empathy also plays a significant role in helping your people change. It's important to know your people as well as possible. This means knowing why some of them may resist the change and others will welcome it. If you can anticipate how each person will be affected by the change, you can do what's necessary to smooth out the transition and capitalize on individual differences.

A Psychological Model for Change

In some respects, organizational change is similar to personal change. It requires a combination of steps that psychotherapists have been using for years. People can't concentrate on a corporate vision or a higher purpose for themselves if they're in pain. Pain is caused by things that aren't working—unresolved, frustrating problems. It's important to help people resolve the problems causing their pain. They have to get rid of the frustration, anger, resentment, feelings of incompetence, and fears before they can move forward.

In daily interactions with employees, a manager's job includes leadership, training, coaching, and counseling. Helping people adjust to change is an ongoing process—one that will be aided by understanding the dynamics of change. Keep in mind the following steps therapists believe are necessary for change:

1. Capitalizing on the past. This means pointing out the positives. Helping employees realize their past successes, accomplishments, and strengths. Highlighting other aspects of their work and home life that have worked well for them. Leveraging the power of praise while avoiding the temptation to flatter. Using the strength of the past as a foundation to allay the fears of the future.

2. Reaching resolution with the past. Taking the past negatives and not only putting them in perspective, but putting them to rest. Resolving issues around work, conflicts with people, inadequacies that need to be eliminated, and so on.

3. Alleviating the symptoms. After the past has been resolved, the present must be dealt with. This means replacing old attitudes and behaviors with new ones—starting with behaviors and results. Arranging for needed training. Setting up performance criteria so that success is easily attained. Successes make people feel competent. Increasing performance demands incrementally. Constantly attending to people's basic needs.

4. Painting a compelling picture of the future. Part of moving out of the past and present and into the future is having a clear picture of where you're going. Just as it is the CEO's job to provide leadership for the company, it is every manager's job to provide leadership for their people. This means setting the stage—helping them see the big picture and their own starring roles.

> **SERVICE R$_x$:**
> People cannot concentrate on a vision of the future when they are in pain. Get rid of as much pain as possible, then you'll be able to look clearly into the future.

The Canvas Versus the Jigsaw Puzzle

A lot of organizations, with the help of consultants, spend all their time trying to get rid of the pain. You have to do more. Think of a business as a jigsaw puzzle in which some of the pieces are missing or out of place. If you do nothing more than get rid of the pain, all you've done is put your puzzle back together. Then what's the most you can ever have? The same picture as before. This limits your imagination, creativity, and productivity.

Putting the jigsaw puzzle back together is just a part of the solution. You have to change the picture. A good consultant will provide a canvas on which a new picture can be created. Company personnel gain a vision of the future when they pick up the brushes and paint the new picture for themselves. The vision, the picture, acts like a magnet pulling people toward a common goal, away from their pain.

> **SERVICE R$_x$:**
> Stop obsessing over the present by creating a compelling vision for moving into the future.

Resistance—What to Expect

No matter how you slice it, influencing change in an organization is not easy and will not take place overnight. You can have the most insightful techniques and still hit a brick wall. That happens because the only other thing as predictable as change is the fact that people will naturally resist it.

Why is change so difficult? Where does so much resistance come from? The reasons people resist are fairly obvious.

Uncertainty. The mere fact that they are expected to do something new makes people feel awkward and anxious. The new behaviors are not yet integrated, so changing the old ways comes slowly. This is true for any endeavor. Try changing your morning routine. Or you might try, even briefly, doing things left-handed if you're a righty and right-handed if you're a lefty. It's not easy. Not only will you resist the change, but you'll find it awkward. Attitude and behavioral changes are just as difficult to implement as physical ones.

Uncertainty is natural. If people don't feel awkward, they're probably not trying to change. When Phil taught hotel reservationists to sell the most expensive rooms first, they felt awkward; he told them they would feel awkward for a while. Expecting the awkwardness made it easier and less embarrassing for them. Knowing that the awkwardness was normal and temporary also made them more willing to work through it, that is, to vary their behaviors before their attitudes changed.

Loss of Control. Whenever you ask people to do something differently, typically their first thoughts are, "What do I have to give up?" "What is this going to cost me?" "What's in it for me?" or "What did I do wrong?"

These are common questions you have to address. It's important to reassure employees that the rug isn't going to be pulled out from under them. By encouraging them to participate in the design of the change effort, you will increase their sense of control, decrease their skepticism, and avoid resistance to change. This is especially true for people whose commitments to the company are questionable.

Spell out what is expected of employees in terms of time and training for the change effort. The best way to present any new program is to sell the benefits. Focus on what people will gain, not on what they may have to give up.

The Difference Effect. Changing a habit means giving up the past. It has been said that all change is initially met with grief. That grief may stem from thoughts such as, "Gee, this job used to be pretty easy. Now it's going to get tough," or "They're going to make a tough job even more difficult."

The difference effect often stems from a fear of the unknown, something we all have. People resist change until the need hits them squarely over the head. Therefore, it is a manager's job to hit, but to hit gently and with guidance. And always share the venture into the unknown. Present the change as "we are changing," not "you must change."

Concerns about Future Competence. It's a strange phenomenon, but when you ask people to do things differently, they suddenly worry about their ability. They also feel isolated. It doesn't matter that everyone is going through it, employees still assume they shouldn't ask each other for help. It's as if they assume the training they're being given is all the help they were going to get, and to reveal ignorance after training would be interpreted as a sign of incompetence.

One of the most important elements in any change—whether it be organizational, individual, physical, or psychological—is support. The most successful self-help programs (Weight Watchers and Alcoholics Anonymous) work when others fail because people are provided with support groups. People who lack support groups find it much more difficult to motivate themselves.

Part of your change effort must include the creation of a team culture. Make it clear to your employees that everyone is on the same team working toward the same goals. Change your management style from "hands-off until there is a problem" to "stay in touch and intimately involved." The 1001 questions arising every day should be answered, which means you and every other department in the company must be readily accessible to anyone—a true network.

Resource"less"ness. Unfortunately, most companies see a major shift in customer service quality as an expensive proposition. Immediately they assume they don't have the resources. Nothing could be farther from the truth.

Revamping the customer service philosophy *is* an investment because most executives cannot plan and execute major changes by themselves. Outside help is needed, but it doesn't have to be long-term if management will pick up the ball and run with it after the consultants leave. There must be a permanence and persistence to the new philosophy and training, and that's where executive commitment comes in.

SERVICE R$_x$:
Don't make customer service training the flavor-of-the-month. Quality service is a full-time, life-long, company-wide commitment.

The resource issue really comes down to one of attitude. You already have the people who can implement the changes, you just have to trust them to figure out how. You have to delegate and then get out of their way so they can do the jobs they were hired and trained to do. When mistakes are made, on any level, they should not be regarded as breaches of trust, but simply as honest mistakes. If something doesn't work the first time, assume it's because of unfamiliarity, not because of mutiny.

Part of trust is taking the advice of your line people—asking them to let you know what customers want. The people who are closest to customers know best how to serve them. You also have to trust your new customer-driven philosophy and overcome the short-term, operations-driven mentality.

More Work. One aspect of change that frightens people is the quantity of change they're asked to cope with immediately. Most companies heap changes on employees. Instead, changes should be phased in slowly. It's better to phase in the changes than to have the whole program die of gluttony. People have their saturation points; beyond that, they panic and resist. When changes are implemented in steps, they're also easier to manage and measure. After all, the whole idea behind implementing change is to work smarter, not harder.

Regression. We know that old habits are not easy to break. What happens to most people who quit smoking? Within a short time, they start smoking again. The same thing can be said of dieters. They revert back to their poor eating habits, which is why diets don't work. *People* (make them) work.

The cure for regression is day-to-day coaching and counseling. If you understand the dynamics of change, you will be able to keep your people on track, motivated, and satisfied.

Commitment and Responsibility

Personal Responsibility

There is a sense of responsibility that some people bring to everything they do. That responsibility is an attitude that whatever they do, it should be done conscientiously and to the best of their ability. Even though everyone shares that responsibility, not all of us acknowledge it. An analogy will help you see this more clearly.

When you grow up in a household where your parents are loving and supportive, it's easier to become a well-adjusted, productive member of society. If you grow up in a less nurturing or downright abusive environment, it's much more difficult to become a well-adjusted and productive member of society. That does not, however, relieve you of your responsibility to become a "good citizen." It just means the obstacles you have to overcome are greater.

The same principle applies to your attitude and performance at work. If you are fortunate enough to work in a company that recognizes the importance of the customer and encourages and rewards independent thinking and creativity, then it is easier for you to do your job with excellence. If, on the other hand, you work for an organization that wallows in mediocrity—one that doesn't care about customer or employees and doesn't encourage people to excel—you are not relieved of your responsibility to excel. Even if you aren't recognized for doing so, you still have the inherent obligation to provide your customers with the highest quality service you can deliver.

SERVICE R$_x$:
An organization is comprised of people. It can never be something that its people are not.

A friend of the authors, Janet Ackerman, worked for an insurance company. Four months into the job she advised them she was pregnant. Out of anger, they demoted her to the PBX switchboard. There she was surrounded by two women who hated their jobs. Janet decided, for her unborn child's well-being, not to let their negative energy affect her emotional state. She mustered up all her self-control and went out of her way to be pleasant to her co-workers and to every customer that called—no matter how nasty they were. In time, her pleasant disposition began to change the environment. The two women lightened up, customers became more pleasant, and one day a senior manager stopped by to say, "I don't know what's been going on down here, but we've been getting all kinds of compliments about you people!"

Quality people know that quality is its own reward. That reward is an inner satisfaction, not the anticipation of external recognition. External recognition may come, but not immediately. In fact, we believe that quality work is always rewarded. It may take a while, but someone will always acknowledge and recognize your attitude and ability.

Jim Knutsen is a manager for the Sport Chalet in San Diego. Having experienced his remarkable customer service, we interviewed him to find out what motivates him to provide such extraordinary service and to train his staff to do likewise.

"Job satisfaction," Jim said. "Being able to be my own boss. Working for a company that gives you basic policies and guidelines, but pretty much turns you loose to use your own judgement. With a job like this, the more you put into it, the more you get out of it. I get a lot of personal satisfaction from doing 'the impossible' for people. It makes me feel good when a customer says, 'You're my last resort. Everyone else has turned me down; no one will even suggest to a way to solve this.' I then tell them I'll use all my resources to solve the problem. It's a great feeling. It's kind of like the medical field; people come in with problems and I solve them. They walk away happy and I feel good. It's personal satisfaction—a job well done."

We asked Jim if there was anything else that motivated him. "Yes, I figure somewhere down the road someone may recognize me and say, 'Just the man I'm looking for.' I treat every potential customer as a potential boss. One of them may say to me, 'If you like doing this, how about doing it for an even bigger operation.' Reputation is also important. It means everything."

And the payoff? That "person somewhere down the road" always comes along. People who work earnestly always rise to the top—if they are persistent.

One obstacle to employees doing their best is the misconception that they have less authority and responsibility than they really have. Many employees are so afraid of breaking the rules that they become corporate robots. And, by the way, most managers are under the impression that they have given their employees more responsibility than the employee has assumed.

Look around at the people who succeed. Who are they? Are they the people who rigidly follow the rules and never ruffle feathers? Are they the ones who dare to be innovative? Aren't they the free-thinkers who take risks to better serve the company and its customers? They are the people who say, "Why not . . . ?" instead of "Yes, but . . . " or "I can't . . . "

Become a Catalyst

The difference you make in serving your customers can act as a catalyst for more widespread organizational changes. Think about what a catalyst does in chemistry—it lowers the energy barrier between two chemical reactants and speeds up their interaction. You can serve the same purpose in a social sense. People pick up cues for appropriate behavior from those around them. There may be a lot of co-workers who are willing to serve customers better, if only someone would set an example and show them it's okay to do so.

Any movement—improved customer service, total quality, pro-democracy, anti-nuclear energy, saving whales or dolphins, fighting drugs, preventing child abuse, or the anti-apartheid movement in South Africa—needs a catalyst to lower the barriers to change. Change is a process that comes slowly. Once people are of the same mind, however, a catalyst is created. Synergy develops and a company can transform itself into a market-driven, high performance service organization. It takes personal responsibility and company-wide commitment. Managers play an important role in creating and maintaining that commitment.

SERVICE R$_x$:

Act "As if."

It is sometimes easier to beg forgiveness than to ask permission. Regardless of your corporate culture, assume responsibility and work to please your customers. You are less likely to get into serious trouble if you break the rules to *keep* a customer than if you follow the rules and *lose* a customer.

Commitments Eliminate Excuses

When you set out to implement a change effort, naturally you want to optimize your chances of success. That means you have to eliminate the excuses people may use to skirt their responsibilities. To do so requires a formalized process of commitment.

There are two levels of commitment—promises and declarations. A promise is a written commitment to accomplish a goal that is within reach. A declaration is a written commitment to accomplish a goal that appears out of reach. For example, in 1962 President John F. Kennedy declared that the United States would be the first country to put a man on the moon by the end of the decade. At the time, the United States didn't even possess the technology to achieve this goal. That kind of commitment to a monumental leap is what we call a declaration. A promise is a lower level of commitment—one that involves an attainable goal, based on existing evidence.

People make promises all the time and, in general, they're not significant. The real challenge is getting people to make declarations. It is the sum total of the achievement of many declarations that pushes an organization to make the quantum leap.

It's no small task to get everyone in an organization to commit to the change effort. It's even harder to get them to commit to written declarations. That's why employee involvement at all levels is so important. A sense of ownership of the vision and values will encourage people to make declarations and accept responsibility and accountability for their roles in the process of change. It takes extensive communication, a nurturing of team spirit, and the defining of individual responsibilities.

The only way to manage performance is to be able to measure it. Every position in the organization must be analyzed in terms of critical job dimensions (those aspects subject to increased productivity or change). Determine who is responsible and whether it's 100% or shared responsibility. Once you have broken the job accountabilities down into concrete, measurable terms, determine what additional training the person will need to accomplish a declaration.

When your company takes on new tasks, often the questions are asked, "Who wants to be responsible for this? Who wants to be responsible for that?" The tasks often go to people who volunteer. The right way to assign projects, however, is to capitalize on competencies. Ask, "Who is competent to do this?" Assign tasks to those who are most capable and let people with less competence assist those of greater competence.

Support the Change Effort

Management's support of the change effort is absolutely essential if the implementation process is to succeed. As a manager, you don't have to agree with the changes—although it is better if you do—but you must align yourself with the change; otherwise your subordinates will not commit themselves.

Supporting the party line doesn't mean you can't disagree with it. Most companies welcome feedback from their managers; however, if you disagree, it should be discussed privately with your superiors, not with the people you supervise. Until you succeed in changing the system from the top, it is your job to support the system. If you succeed in changing the system, then you and your superiors can implement the changes together.

Realize now that it will take your company between three and five years to completely change its service quality, philosophy and image. The complexity of your organization is one factor that dictates that time frame. The most significant determinant of change, however, is the degree to which your program is managed. A carefully managed change effort will show bottom-line results faster than a program that has a half-hearted or no management commitment.

SERVICE R$_x$:
There is no such thing as a short-term, successful, customer service effort. That is an oxymoron. The only way to truly change the service culture in an organization is to commit to the long-term.

The high-performance, market-driven organization will only work if you have a work force that is competent, challenged, and committed. Add to that the qualities of flexibility, resourcefulness, and responsiveness and your company will be in the progressive zone of service. To make it a reality, you must invest in your people systems.

Chapter Fifteen

Managing the People Systems

There is no denying that it is easier to manage an operations-driven company. All you have to do is hand new employees the company policy manual and say, "This is our bible—memorize it. If you follow our procedures, everything will be fine. The only time you'll get in trouble is when you break the rules."

The Japanese take this practice to an absurd degree. Mitsubishi Trust and Banking gives its new people a brief list of "do's" and "don'ts" to get them started. It warns them to respond with a quick "yes" when a superior calls, to stand up immediately to receive instructions, never to scratch their heads or cross their legs or arms in front of customers or superiors, never to smoke while talking with a superior, and never to criticize the company or its management.

Needless to say, that kind of structured, controlled, and repressive (almost military) environment would never work in America. It would only produce resentment, rebellion, and mediocrity.

SERVICE R$_x$:
Rigid adherence to rigid rules produces mediocrity.

The role of management in a market-driven organization is less well-defined and, therefore, requires the types of paradigm shifts we discussed in chapter thirteen. Hard-and-fast company policies become flexible guidelines. Suddenly there is room for interpretation and independent thinking, which calls for new roles for managers and employees.

SERVICE R$_x$:
Progressive customer service is the result of hiring the right people, training them properly, leading them, providing them with thoughtfully conceived guidelines and empowering them with freedom, authority, and responsibility to make decisions on behalf of the company.

Invest in Your People

Imagine you are the owner of a major league baseball team and you have just signed contracts with some of the best players available. Would you send your team out on the field to play the first game of the season without spring training? Of course not. Once the season started, would you stop the training and coaching? Not if you wanted to develop a winning team.

Now imagine that, as a manager, you're shopping around for a new computer system. How would you go about researching it? You'd spend time and money conferring with consultants, researching systems, gathering bids, and selecting a vendor. Finally, you would make a decision and buy the best system for your needs. After the system was installed, you would spend more money on service contracts, supplies, and professional training for your staff. Once the computer system was up and streamlining your operations, how would you typically train a new employee? If you're like a lot of managers, you would provide on-the-job training supervised by someone who also received on-the-job training—someone whose training skills are, *at best*, adequate—and possibly inadequate. In other words, at this point you would have stopped investing in professional training. Now if your new employee were to leave after six weeks, would *he* deserve the blame for not working out? Most managers would say yes.

Here's another perspective. You've got a computer system. You have office equipment. You may have trucks, conveyor belts, fork lifts, airplanes, and manufacturing equipment. You have all these systems and you also have employees. The key is to think of your employees as a "system" that requires the same care in *selection and maintenance* as any other resource in your organization. That is what is meant by Managing the People Systems. When an employee fails to work out, everybody is responsible—management as well as the employee, although a bad employee does occasionally slip through the selection process.

SERVICE R$_x$:
Maintain your people systems meticulously. High employee turnover is a symptom of being operations-driven. When your people systems fail, your whole business fails.

When your phone system develops a problem, you lose your ability to communicate for a day. When your alarm system breaks down, it hurts you if someone tries to break in one night. When your computer system has bugs, you lose the ability to enter or retrieve data. All of these breakdowns may cost you money. When your people systems fail, however, the consequences are far more grave. You absolutely must protect and capitalize on your investment in people by spending the time and money necessary to provide initial and ongoing training, coaching, counseling, and leadership.

Managing the Market-Driven Organization

To adequately discuss the skills of an enlightened manager of the '90s, we would need to write an entire book. Instead, we have chosen a handful of areas in which to share our insights. The skills and techniques that follow are people skills. It is precisely these skills managers need to properly select, train, measure, and develop their people.

Stay Close to Your People

Staying close to your people is a management style characterized by involvement rather than detachment. Staying close to your people means, literally, walking around and keeping your finger on the pulse of the people you supervise.

Think of all the times during the day when you walk from one part of the building to another. How many employees do you pass without stopping to say a word? Now think of all the managers in your company. Multiply all those numbers together and you'll see there is a tremendous number of opportunities for managers to stop and ask, "How are things going?" You can consider these as internal moments of truth.

Managers often think they need a business-related reason to stop by to chat with someone. Being sociable and caring is reason enough. Think of what would happen if you chatted with your employees for no apparent reason other than for the benefit of the relationship. You would create a completely different working environment—one that would be reflected in better service.

> **SERVICE R_x:**
> **The best managers are like the best generals—they work (or fight) alongside their people in the trenches, not from behind their desks.**

Sitting in your office and doing paperwork is managing, but it is not *leading*. The primary job of a manager is to lead. You lead people, you manage things (budgets, paperwork, logistics, etc.).

Let's take it a step further. Managers are often looking for specific behaviors in their people—behaviors that improve customer service. Let's assume employees have been trained, behaviors defined, and measurement criteria established. Staying close would allow you to go up to people and ask them how they're doing on a specific task. This is the perfect opportunity to observe front-line operations and see if there is a need for coaching, counseling, or further training. At the same time, you could praise their performance of the previous day (or some time in the past).

Set Behavioral Objectives

Although it's done all the time, it is unfair for a manager to judge someone's behavior on a criterion that you have not previously discussed. Conversely, it is unfair to set goals and then not measure results. The two go hand-in-hand in terms of motivation, fairness, and morale. If you're not going to measure results, don't set goals, and vice-versa.

"Sam, I understand you're what we call a 'front-line employee.' I just wanted to see what one of you looks like. Thanks for coming up."

When you stay in touch with your people and keep tabs on measurable behaviors, you first have to set the objectives they will be striving to achieve. Setting behavioral objectives is like setting goals. Admittedly, the difference is a fine line. The former targets specific, observable *behaviors*; the latter targets results to be achieved.

Behavioral objectives must:

- be obtainable
- be measurable
- have a time frame attached to them
- match the results to be accomplished

Matching behaviors to goals is absolutely essential and often overlooked. An example of how *not* to do this occurs often in the hospitality industry.

> Phil: *I was doing some consulting work for a hotel. I asked one of the reservation managers if she ever did performance evaluations. She said she did. I asked her what they were comprised of. She reached in her desk drawer and pulled out a stopwatch.*

"What do you do with that?" I asked. She said, "When it comes time for an evaluation, I look over the person's shoulder and wait for the phone to ring. When it does, I start the stopwatch. When the call is over, I stop it. If the call was more than so many minutes, it was a bad call. If it was less than so many minutes, it was also a bad call. If the call fell within the acceptable time range, it was a good call."

I waited for the rest of the explanation, but none was forthcoming. She explained that she does that periodically over the year, takes the average of the calls, and that's what constitutes the performance evaluation."

What questions did this performance evaluation neglect to address? It failed to take into consideration the quality of the call and the outcome. Was a room sold or not? Did the reservationist sell the most expensive or the least expensive room? Most important, was the customer *happy* when the call was completed?

Reservationists are expected to sell rooms; however, their performance is often measured by how long their phone calls last. The behavior measured—length of calls—is not operationally related to the objective of selling rooms. In fact, rushing a call is counterproductive.

The proper way to measure is to identify the goal—in this case, selling a room *and* serving the caller. Next define the behaviors likely to attain that goal. Give reservationists the training they need to do the job effectively. Then develop a measurement tool that keeps track of desired behaviors, not the lengths of calls.

The front desk manager's narrow performance evaluation is a typical example of operations-driven thinking. To be fair, there was some value to measuring call length. It could have been used to allocate manpower to answer the phones. After all, if the phones are too busy, it is management's job to hire more help, not the reservationist's job to rush the calls. The way the manager originally used the measurement, however, was off the mark. We certainly can't blame her. In an operations-driven organization, she was just doing her job as she understood it.

To match behaviors to goals, you have to start off with the outcome you're looking for, then work backwards and figure out what behaviors will achieve those outcomes. In addition, keep these tips in mind:

- Sell the benefits of the new behaviors to your employees.

- Show your employees how they make a difference in the company. Make them feel included and wanted in the change process.

- Give employees a voice in the goal-setting process. Participation fosters ownership and responsibility.

- Keep employees within their comfort zones so they will feel psychologically safe and in control.

- Provide training if needed and ongoing coaching. In all cases, model the expected behavioral change.

- Create an expectation of success. Remember the power of self-fulfilling prophecies. People function poorly when they don't feel competent or when supervisors doubt their competence.

SERVICE R$_x$:
Set behavioral objectives in a participative rather than dictatorial way. Employees will be more likely to attain their goals if they have a role in defining them. People support what they help to create.

Performance Evaluation and Evaluating Performance

There are two ways to tell employees how they are doing—formally, in periodic performance evaluations, and informally, on a day-to-day basis.

A performance evaluation is the formal process of sitting down with someone and reviewing their accomplishments since the last performance evaluation. These evaluations become a permanent part of employees' records and affect job retention, promotions, salary increases, bonuses, and so on. A performance evaluation is a time-driven rather than event-driven evaluation. It should take place no less than three times and no more than five times per year. Quarterly seems to make the most sense in the majority of cases.

A performance evaluation is a time to build an employee's confidence, not to destroy it. Examine the typical performance evaluation session and you will see why so many managers fail to make their people feel competent. The employee walks into the manager's office at a prearranged time for a one-hour meeting. In the first three minutes, the manager talks about the things the person has done well. The next 57 minutes are spent talking about those areas that need to be improved. Even if the person is a top performer, managers always seem to give the impression there is significantly more that needs improvement than is done well.

In our research into the competence of people inside organizations, we have found that a lack of confidence is usually a reflection of management's inability to make the person feel competent. Granted, some jobs require more of a learning curve than others, but, as a general rule, people are competent.

The simplest way to change your performance evaluation procedure is to end the meeting on a positive note. Reverse the order and save the accomplishments for last. A better way would be to provide ongoing training and coaching during the year so there are fewer items on the "to be improved" list.

Evaluating performance, on the other hand, is a continuing process that is also called coaching. This is part of staying close to your people. You constantly look for opportunities to give feedback that will improve your people's skills and build their confidence. Coaching is event-related, not time-related. What a manager looks at in evaluating performance is the process—that is, a person's continued improvement, not overall accomplishment.

The Power of Praise

As a manager, you need tools for leadership. One tool you need is a way to reinforce desired behaviors. Those behaviors may be making more sales, developing self-management, being creative, taking risks, or providing quality service. No matter what the goal, if you use praise generously, you will discover it has a remarkable power to motivate. In fact, if you use praise effectively, you will never need to reprimand your people.

Criticism and reprimands are counterproductive. Granted, the "One Minute Reprimand" has gained a lot of popularity in recent years, but it misses the mark. It is far more constructive to praise, train, coach, and counsel.

There is always something to be praised. Even if you're dealing with a problem, no behavior is all bad. Find one aspect of the person's behavior—even if it's in the past—and praise it. The idea is to make that person feel competent. Then you can gently point out how to change certain things.

Praise works. You can't, however, go out and start praising people and expect to see an immediate change in their behavior. Not because the praise would be ineffective, but because you would probably evaluate subsequent behaviors incorrectly. It is important to understand the concept of regression toward the mean. If you don't, you run the risk of drawing the conclusion that praise does not work.

Regression Toward The Mean

In physical science and human behavior, one of the many laws governing the occurrence of a series of events is regression toward the mean. The mean is an average, which, statistically, is where the majority of cases fall. The theory of regression (to fall back) toward the mean states that every time there is an exceptional case—one that is significantly above or below average—the next case is more likely to be closer to the mean. For example:

Imagine you are an avid golfer who plays every day of the week. Your average is 100 for eighteen holes. On Monday you shoot an 80. According to regression toward the mean, the odds are in favor of you playing worse the next day; that is, you'll probably shoot closer to 100. Let's say on Tuesday, however, you shoot a 120. On Wednesday, the odds again favor you shooting closer to 100—your average—which will be an improvement over Tuesday.

The reason for this statistical pattern is the law of averages. With an average of 100, most of your scores over a long period of time cluster around 100. The odds of playing significantly better or worse are low, so when you do, the odds "predict" that you will play closer to 100 the next time.

Now imagine you've hired a golf pro for a week. To try to help you improve your game, he reprimands you every time you do something wrong. On Monday you shoot a 120. On Tuesday, if you play better, will it be due to the pro's reprimands or to the natural tendency to play closer to your average?

Now you see the dilemma in training and coaching employees. The way to evaluate performance is to compare a person's behavior to their average. The average gives a more realistic perspective—it shows you the big picture.

Another example is a hole-in-one. If you were to shoot one on the first hole, would you assume your score for the remaining 18 holes will be an 18? That would be as absurd as a new salesperson who closes a big sale the first week on the job and makes a $2,000 commission, then goes and tells everyone he is earning $100,000 a year.

All this leads us back to the point. (Regression toward the mean dictates that we will not digress too long.) The best way to get positive behavior is with positive strokes. Praise is far superior to reprimand as a motivator. In situations where reprimands were previously used, enlightened managers now use praise, coaching, and counseling.

If you praise an employee's exceptional performance on Monday and then observe that the performance has declined on Tuesday, don't jump to the conclusion that praise doesn't work. Tuesday's performance may be worse than Monday's, but it may still be above average. Make a paradigm shift—when observing, evaluating, and responding to behavior, remember the law of regression toward the mean and you will be a more insightful, realistic and patient manager.

SERVICE R$_x$:
If you wait until you get perfection before you reward people, you'll never get exceptional results. Praise the small victories on the road to high performance.

Managers are like parents. If parents waited for perfection when teaching their children to walk, we'd all still be crawling on the floor.

Praise in the workplace brings into play at least two dynamics. First, you praise the *progress* that people are making; they appreciate a pat on the back. That feeling is addictive—they want to perform better so more praise will be forthcoming.

Second, when you praise one person, you indirectly motivate others. When people overhear someone being praised, they think to themselves, perhaps unconsciously, "Gee, I'd like to get some of that. I've got to work harder."

How you praise people is very important. Always be specific. It is meaningless to generalize and tell someone, "You're really great with customers," or "You're doing a terrific job." Too vague and too unbelievable. The praise is more likely to be effective if you give yourself and the praise credibility. Speak directly to the behavior you want to reinforce. "Joan, I like the way you split your attention between many customers when we're busy so that no one feels ignored."

Most of us listen to criticism, but distrust compliments, especially when the compliments border on flattery. For this reason, it's wise to phrase your praise modestly and realistically. Avoid absolutes and exaggerations such as "always," "best," "smartest," and predictions of future greatness.

Training professionals once advocated "positive strokes for positive behavior plus negative strokes for negative behavior equals positive behavior." That has changed. Praise is so powerful that, used effectively, it eliminates the need to criticize or reprimand. The way to use praise effectively is to recognize achievement only when it is deserved and meaningful. Like flattery, empty praise is meaningless.

SERVICE R$_x$:
Catch your people doing things right!

Training, Coaching, Counseling, and Encouraging Creativity

In a very real sense, the skills used by parents are the same ones employed by managers. Employees have to be nurtured, taught new skills, and dealt with patiently. For a moment, put yourself in the role of a parent. You've just caught your child drawing on the kitchen wall. What do you do, assuming you don't want to squelch your child's creativity? A reprimand won't work. Here's the perfect opportunity to praise, coach and counsel.

The act of drawing on the wall is not one behavior; it is several behaviors, only one of which is negative. So you have to break the overall behavior down into smaller increments. First, you praise your child for their creativity and talk about what a beautiful picture they drew. Then you take the negative approach—where the picture was drawn—and you train your child to express their creativity in a more acceptable location. You take out a pad of paper and show them that they can draw just as well on it. In fact, you point out some additional benefits to drawing on the pad. You tear the page out, tape it to the wall, and explain that it never has to be thrown away, whereas the picture drawn on the kitchen wall will have to be removed eventually. The picture on the paper can be hung on the refrigerator or in their room. In addition, that picture can be folded, put in an envelope and mailed to Grandma, who might send them something in return!

What have you done with the child? You have praised the positive, coached, and counseled.

What is the difference between training, coaching, and counseling, and how do they fit into your repertoire of management skills?

Training. After you have hired the best people, you must educate and provide them with the skills they need to be competent, productive, and effective. Don't assume people know how to do basic, "unskilled" tasks such as answering the phones or dealing with customers. You have to make your performance expectations clear.

Coaching. Once people have the skills required for a particular job, their skills occasionally need reinforcing or fine-tuning. It's a manager's job to stay close to employees to make sure the new skills are internalized and to diagnose and treat skill problems when they arise.

Every professional athlete—even the ones at the top—has a coach. Coaches can't play as well as star athletes, but they serve as objective observers—people who can stand back, see strong and weak points, and suggest ways to do things better. Think of a collegiate athlete who has the raw skills, but upon turning pro becomes a superstar with the refinement of high-level coaching.

Counseling. This is a good example of one function of a manager in an organization comprised of self-managed teams. SMTs are proven to increase efficiency, but they are also the source of conflicts. People problems arise, which is where the manager as communicator comes in. If members of the team are unable to resolve a problem themselves, the manager must act as a resource to help.

In other contexts, counseling becomes necessary when you have an employee with adequate skills, but little motivation. People often need encouragement or someone to listen to personal problems. Hence, the manager's role as a "people-technician"—someone who is able to recognize, diagnose and treat people problems when they arise. If you can't help someone with a problem, at least act as a resource to find someone who can.

Figure 15.1 shows the appropriate actions to take with different employee needs. Those employees who perform well and are highly motivated should be constantly rewarded and challenged to achieve higher levels of performance. Employees who are well-trained and able to perform a job, but lack motivation, are in need of coaching and/or

Types of Employees and How to Help Them

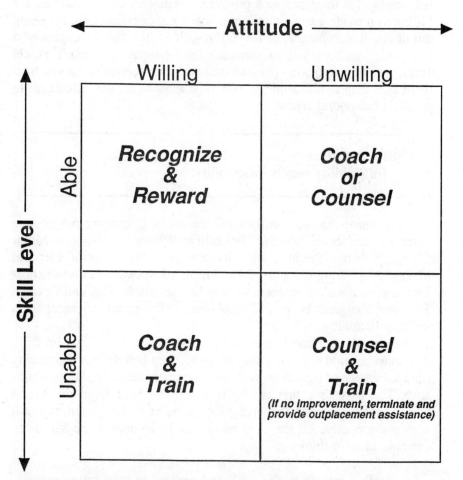

Figure 15.1: This model allows for easy identification of employee needs and how best to meet those needs.

counseling. Employees who are motivated, but lack the skills necessary to perform well, need coaching and/or training. Last, but not least, employees who are not able to perform well—and lack the motivation to do so—should be trained and counseled. If these rehabilitation efforts fail, give the employee outplacement assistance and terminate the relationship.

When you have a problem with an employee, it is helpful to determine how much of the problem is attributable to the employee and how much is due to management. Supervisors and managers are often responsible for their people's problems. Managers can be blamed for failing to provide adequate training, coaching, or counseling, for being out of touch with people, or for ruling with an iron fist. Managers who rule with iron fists fail to stimulate their people. You can't expect employees to give quality personalized customer service when you treat them as if they're all identical. You must account for the differences in people's behavioral styles.

SERVICE R$_x$:
Inflexibility begets inflexibility.

Two words that constantly come up when discussing progressive customer service is sensible flexibility. Whether it is Ford Motor Company being flexible with its warranty period or a clerk at McDonald's giving extra Big Mac Sauce, all we want as customers is for the people we do business with to be reasonable, fair, and flexible. The same thing can be said of employees—all they ask of managers is sensible flexibility.

As management consultants, we constantly see managers who think they must be rigid with their subordinates. They believe that demanding rigid adherence to rigid rules will give them consistent, quality performance. The only time that is true is when you have hired the wrong person, given someone the wrong job, or failed to lead, train or coach someone properly. All three mistakes may be evident in the following example of rigid thinking.

Emil: *I was in a city park and walked up to a refreshment stand. There were two windows. I went to the window on the right and ordered a Coke. The guy behind the counter said, "I'm sorry, I can't take your order from this window." As I started to walk away, he went over to the other window and said, "But I can take your order from this window." I was puzzled, but he explained the system after he gave me my Coke. He said each employee had been assigned a cash register by a window and instructed to take orders only from his window. After hearing that, I wondered why there wasn't a ridiculous rule forbidding him to stand in front of someone else's window!*

Rigid adherence to rigid rules yields nothing but mediocrity. From a management standpoint, there are three false assumptions that lead to this mediocrity. First, management assumes all customers are the same. Second, they assume all employees are the same. Third, they assume that all the customer service situations that arise are the same and can be accommodated by identical employee behaviors.

In reality, there are a myriad of combinations of customer types, employee styles, and service situations. No one has succeeded in writing a company policy manual that can address all those possible combinations so the answer must be sensible flexibility.

You want your employees to use the intelligence you hired them for and the training you provided. If you give them freedom, authority, and responsibility, they will do the best job they can for your company and your customers. If you don't give your people freedom, authority, and responsibility, your company will be providing, at best, service in the safe zone.

Ken Blanchard relates the following:

My friend Howie loves ice cream. He went into one of those 33-flavors places and walked up to the counter. A young woman asked him what he wanted and he said he hadn't quite decided yet. While he was thinking, an older woman came up behind the young clerk and whispered something in her ear. When Howie looked up to place his order, the young woman said, "You'll have to take a number."

There was nobody in the store! Howie said, "You have to be crazy, why would I have to take a number?" What do you think she said? She said, "It's our policy." Howie said, "There's no one in here. This is the stupidest thing I've ever heard of!" The young woman went quickly to one of the last lines of defense. She lowered her voice and said to him, "Please don't get me in trouble." She looked over at the older woman. "She's my boss."

Howie decided to go along with her request. He took a number; it was 30. The present number was 27. Imagine the poor clerk behind the counter. How could anyone maintain their self-esteem. There's no one in the store and she has to say, "28, 29, 30. Can I help you?"

Howie said, "I'm no longer hungry!" As he was leaving the store, he went over to the boss and said, "Do you see how absurd this was?" She looked at him angrily—perhaps she had been reprimanded by her district manager. She said, "How can you expect my people to do what I want them to do when it's crowded if they won't do it when nobody's here?"

It's easy to get upset with people like that, but you have to realize it isn't entirely their fault. They're victims of the system. The rigidity starts at the top of the organization and works it way down.

"It doesn't matter if you're the only one here.
The sign says to take a number if you want service."

As the manager of service providers, how can you avoid such pitfalls? First, stop fixating on rules! If you are obsessed with your company's policy manual, you'll never be able to justify creativity, resourcefulness, and independent thinking.

SERVICE R$_x$:
Stop fixating on the policy manual. When you're thinking about the rules, you're not thinking about your employees. When your employees are thinking about the rules, they're not thinking about your customers.

Sensible flexibility also relates to a manager's ability as a leader to communicate with all types of people. That means knowing how to read people and then being flexible enough to change your personal style to be compatible with their behavioral style. We call this behavioral flexibility. Behavioral flexibility means talking to people the way they want to listen. It also means leading people in a way they want to be led.

Encouraging Creativity

If you look at what made the United States a leading industrial nation over the last 100 years, it was creativity and innovation. Good old Yankee ingenuity. Creativity used to be highly valued, rewarded, and encouraged. To a large degree, that has changed.

"That's a good idea Smith, but you're not in that department, so don't make waves."

Creativity in American business is now given much the same treatment as customer service—lip service. It is a recognized value, but few corporate cultures promote it. The creative person in the corporation is an outcast. The only time we value a creative contribution is when there's a significant problem needing an innovative solution. Then we call in a creative person—usually a consultant. Once the problem is solved, we either get rid of that person or use them to implement the solution.

Just as an awareness of service is slowly growing, so is a rediscovery of the value of employee creativity and input. Participative management, in which employees at every level have input into the operations of the business, is once more gaining popularity. For example, General Motors' plant manager Patricia M. Carrigan has developed a dynamic partnership between management and the UAW and workers on the assembly line. She utilized such innovations as:

- Self-Managed Teams

- Pushing crucial decisions as far down as possible.

- Teaching workers about the plant's financial operating principles.

- Training employees in communication, decision-making, leadership, and other skills.

- Helping supervisors understand their changing roles—from bosses to coaches.

This is just the tip of the iceberg. Carrigan took many other forward-thinking management concepts and put them into action. As a result, the Bay City, Michigan, plant turned a $2.2 million profit in 1987 instead of the projected $3.5 million loss. "When you let responsible adults act their age," she said, "you'd be surprised at the results you get . . . People feel good about themselves when they're given the chance to run the business."[10]

SERVICE R$_x$:
Just asking for creativity will not get it. You have to encourage and reward it.

Every worker is capable of contributing a bright idea. Albert Einstein once said, "It is not the quality of a man's ideas that make a genius, it is the quantity of ideas put into action." He believed that virtually everyone, at some time in their life, has a profound idea. The difference between geniuses and the rest of us is that the rest of us never implement our ideas. In fact, we rarely even write them down. It's happened to you: You're sitting at dinner when a brilliant idea drifts into your mind. Instead of writing it down, you say, "Please pass the salt," and the idea vanishes forever. Not only is the idea not implemented, it isn't even shared with another person.

> **SERVICE R$_x$:**
> Genius is realized in the implementation of ideas, not just their conception.

As a manager, you're like a farmer shaking a fruit tree. If you want the fruit of creativity, you have to be willing to accept the good and the bad that falls your way. You can't judge the fruit before it hits the ground. Once it hits, you find the unripe, inappropriate, and useless as well as the well-formed, sweet samples. Creativity, by its very nature, is a process of trial *and error*.

Nurturing Creativity by Avoiding Idea Killers

"Don't be ridiculous."

"We tried that before."

"It costs too much."

"It can't be done."

"That's beyond our responsibility."

"It's too radical a change."

"That's not our problem."

"We don't have the time."

"That will make other equipment obsolete."

"We're too small for that."

"Let's get back to reality."

"We've never done that before."

"It would be too hard to sell."

"Let's form a committee."

"Why change things? They're still working."

"You're two years ahead of your time."

"You can't teach an old dog new tricks."

"We've done fine so far without it."

"Has anyone else ever tried it?"

"We're not ready."

"It isn't in the budget."

"If it were a good idea, we'd already have done it."

"We'll be the laughing stock."

"We're doing the best we can."

"It won't work in our industry."

"That doesn't apply to us."

In addition to nurturing creative people, you also have to accept their quirks. As a group, they tend to be self-motivated, unconventional, less likely to follow rules, and more willing to take risks. If you want the genius of absent-minded professors, you have to be willing to put up with their lack of decorum.

SERVICE R$_x$:
Dare to be different. Avoid the mental bandwagon. Stimulate the creativity of your employees. Encourage them to share their ideas—no matter how outrageous. You never know where the next multi-million dollar idea will germinate.

The best eyes for seeing the needs of your customers belong to your front-line people. Even if you don't get a multi-million dollar idea, employees often see the answers to everyday problems before you do. In 1988, Motorola's Employee Involvement Groups generated 63,000 ideas for the company, 21,000 of which were acted on. If the lines of communication are open, employees will tell you more than you ever imagined about how to meet and exceed your customers' expectations. *This* is why you should nurture and support creativity.

The Importance of a Creative Culture

People are very much influenced by those around them. Although this is an unusual analogy, consider two periods in the history of art. Renaissance Italy was a culture that adored creativity. As a result, many of the greatest works of art in the world were produced in Florence during the 15th century. The people with money—bankers and civic leaders—wanted to create a community that would be known as a second Athens. They rewarded creativity and achieved that status. In contrast, creativity was scorned in ancient Egypt—instead the ancient Egyptians valued uniformity and conformity. As a result, for nearly 3,000 years, the works of art produced in Egypt showed little variation.

SERVICE R$_x$:
People become what they do. Give your people more responsibilities and encourage their creativity, and they will become responsible, self-starting, and creative.

The Selection Process

Imagine you are in a restaurant. Your choices of waiters are Attila the Hun or Kermit the Frog. Attila the Hun has the memory, speed, and efficiency of a machine. Unfortunately, he also has the personality of a machine . . . or worse. Kermit is not as efficient or quick, but he has an endearing personality. He jokes with you, entertains the kids, and, in general, makes the dining experience more enjoyable. Who would you rather have as a waiter? Most people would choose Kermit the Frog. Most people would rather leave a tip for someone they liked than for someone who only delivered perfect service.

Every job requires personal attributes above and beyond the mere ability to perform tasks. The key to recruiting quality service employees is to find people who embody the personality traits that comprise quality service.

SERVICE R$_x$:
When selecting customer service personnel, the top priority must be the applicant's personality.

Service-excellent companies are very selective in their hiring process. When Nordstrom opened a new store outside Washington, D.C., their people conducted 3,000 interviews for 300 job openings. That's the kind of ratio you encounter when applying to medical school! Years ago,

"Would you mind flashing your most sincere smile for me please?"

Nordstrom received one good applicant for every five interviews. Now they consider themselves lucky if the ratio is 1:20. It is obvious that building and developing your people systems takes as much time and care as any other important capital investment.

What Is the Right Stuff?

The first step in finding excellent employees is not through composing a classified ad. You must first define exactly what to look for in the ideal customer service employee.

What do customer service representatives do? What are the activities that make up their days? What are the behavioral qualities needed to thrive in that position? These are some of the questions that need to be answered in order to identify a list of attributes to look for in applicants. We have compiled a list of five qualities people should possess if they're going to work with the public—especially the complaining public—on a daily basis.

You can't simply ask someone, "Will you be thick-skinned when an irate customer is screaming at you?" or "Are you motivated to serve our customers in a quality way?" You have to look for evidence in the person's work history. For every behavioral quality you think is important, you need to devise questions to reveal the presence or absence of those qualities in your applicant's work history.

Five Qualities for Service Survival

Motivation To Serve the Customer. A service position requires a person to have a strong desire to serve customers. This includes the ability to listen to requests and complaints *with empathy* and make an extra effort to help customers. In some situations, serving the customer means following-up after a sale or after a problem has been resolved. In general, service personnel must derive satisfaction from helping people.

The typical activities required under this category are:

- Showing empathy for a customer's situation.
- Practicing active listening skills.
- Taking action to solve a customer's problem.
- Resolving customer complaints quickly and thoroughly.
- Calling or writing to customers regarding products or services.
- Taking responsibility for following-through on promises.

Questions to ask in an interview:

1. Tell me about a difficult customer you had to deal with. Why were they difficult? How did you resolve the problem?

2. Have you ever had to go out of your way to make a customer happy? If so, what was the situation? What action did you take? What was the outcome of your service?

3. Can you remember a customer who was making an unreasonable demand? What was the request and what did you do about it?

Ability To Handle Stress. There's no denying that service positions are high stress jobs. The stress may be caused by time pressures, difficult customers, large quantities of work, and other reasons.

The typical activities required under this category are:

- Answering to the demands and complaints of supervisors.
- Handling customer complaints, some of which may be unreasonable.
- Assisting several people at the same time.

- Working under tight time constraints.
- Completing customer transactions in a set period of time (typical for phone reservationists).
- Meeting deadlines and performance goals even though the work flow is unpredictable.

Questions to ask in an interview:

1. Under what conditions do you work best? Give some examples. (Look for problems in working under stress.)
2. What kind of stress did you feel in your last job? How did you deal with it?
3. What are the highest pressure situations you've been under in recent years? How did you handle them?

Empathy For Customers. Empathy is one of the most important qualities for service personnel. Empathy is the ability to recognize and show concern for a person's feelings or point of view. To do their jobs well, service providers are required to accurately assess a customer's situation and take action based on that assessment. Perceptiveness and sensitivity, then, are important related abilities.

The typical activities required under this category are:

- Allowing customers to interrupt tasks and still providing 100% attention to their needs.
- Listening respectfully to customers and acknowledging their emotional states.
- Apologizing to customers when they have received poor service or had some other problem.
- Conveying care and enthusiasm for solving their problems.

Questions to ask in an interview:

1. How do you feel when you're involved in a task and repeatedly have to stop to answer customers' questions?
2. On a scale of one to ten, how would you judge yourself in terms of patience?
3. Do you consider yourself a "people person"? If so, relate a story that illustrates that quality.

4. When dealing with customers, what aspect do you enjoy the least?

5. Relate an instance when you became angry over poor service you received.

Personal Excellence And Initiative. Excellent people do things with excellence. These are people who set high standards for themselves. They are the ones you want to hire. The best service people are not content with mediocrity; they strive to exceed customers' expectations and make the company shine. They are willing to go beyond their job descriptions and initiate action to get things done right the first time. People with an inner drive for excellence always work for their personal fulfillment.

The typical activities required under this category are:

• Taking action on a customer's behalf without having to be asked.

• Questioning the way a process is conducted and making suggestions to the company for improving the delivery of service.

• Willingness to work extra hours to accomplish a task.

• Insisting their work and the work of their subordinates is accurate, timely, professional, and done with pride.

• Doing something that is out of the parameters of one's job title for the benefit of the company or its customers.

Questions to ask in an interview:

1. How did you get your last job?

2. What have you done in the past to make your job(s) easier or more rewarding? Give some examples.

3. Tell us about something you did on your own to help out a customer.

4. On a scale of one to ten, how would you rate yourself in terms of attaining perfection? How would you rate yourself in terms of aggressiveness?

5. Would you rather change a system or work within it?

6. Have you ever been involved in any work-related activities besides your job? For example, have you served on any committees or teams? Explain the purpose and outcome.

Problem-Solving Ability. One of the most important talents a service provider must have is the ability to evaluate and solve problems. This takes resourcefulness, sound judgement, knowledge, and a calm, logical approach to customer complaints.

The typical activities required under this category are:

- Asking relevant questions and/or observing a situation accurately.

- Using company resources wisely and creatively to satisfy customers.

- Working beyond the initial customer contact to solve a problem or get results.

- Changing procedures or policies to accommodate a customer.

- Tracking results, following-up on promises, and communicating with company departments and customers when necessary.

- Making service decisions that could cost the company money.

Questions to ask in an interview:

1. Describe a typical service encounter in your last job.

2. Now describe an unusual service encounter. What was the problem? What were your options for handling it? What did you do?

3. What is your attitude regarding company policies?

4. What would you do if a customer wanted something that was against company policy?

5. As a customer service representative, how did *you* define your job at _____(last Company)?

The Judgement Call. As you can see, the data you collect from these questions can only be analyzed qualitatively. As a result, you will use them in addition to, not in lieu of, other measurements and hiring criteria. When asking questions to elicit behavioral answers, it is important for interviewers to draw on all their skills, especially those of observation and, dare we say it—intuition. How an applicant answers is as important as what is said. Sometimes the only clues that someone is misrepresenting themselves are body language, long pauses, voice inflection, and lack of eye contact.

The Changing American Workforce

There are many changes taking place in the workplace, the most critical of which is the caliber of the entry-level worker. The American educational system is failing everyone—students and employers alike. The national high school dropout rate is averaging one out of five students, with higher averages in many southern states. By the year 2000, below-average skills will be good enough for only 27% of the jobs created between 1985 and 2000, compared to 40% of the jobs in the mid-'80s. 41% of new jobs will require better-than-average skills, up from 24%.[11]

Who is going to apply for these highly-skilled positions? Too many high school graduates can't even read or perform simple math computations. In one study, 58% of Fortune 500 companies surveyed reported having difficulty finding employees with basic skills. In addition, it is estimated that 65% of the American workforce is intermediately literate, meaning they read at a 5th to 9th grade level. Twenty-three million Americans are functionally illiterate. Their reading and computational skills are extremely low, but they function in jobs despite their handicap.

Clearly, the challenges of the workplace are not going to be met by such an unskilled workforce. If basic skills are such a scarce commodity, how will firms find employees who can think for themselves and be trusted in decision-making positions?

The answer is that corporate America must invest in the development of the their employees. Large companies must take over where schools have failed. U.S. corporations spent $30 billion in 1989 on formal training. That training was both general and job-specific, with classes in all kinds of subjects, from remedial reading and math to "advanced" topics such as decision-making and finance. IBM alone, on any given day, is training 22,000 of its employees worldwide. That's seven million student-days per year—the equivalent of a major university—at a total annual cost of $1.5 billion. All of this expenditure is necessary to keep up with increasingly fierce global competition. The conclusion is that you must nurture and train your employees.

In April of 1990, *Time* magazine ran an article on Lech Walesa, the founder of Poland's Solidarity union. At the end of his visit to the United States, he was quoted as saying, "We have heard many beautiful words of encouragement. But, I must tell you that the supply of words on the world market is plentiful, but the demand is falling. Let deeds follow words now."

Appendices

Appendix One

Service R_Xs

Introduction

SERVICE R_X:
> Make quality service a core value, not a marketing ploy, because that is what quality service is.

SERVICE R_X:
> Treat your people like responsible adults.

SERVICE R_X:
> The behaviors exhibited by managers and the way they treat their employees speak volumes about corporate values.

SERVICE R$_X$:
Management has to model what they advocate—
"Walk the talk."

SERVICE R$_X$:
A company's level of service is a mirror-image of the
way management treats employees. That treatment is,
in turn, a reflection of the ethical values and corporate culture created by top executives.

SERVICE R$_X$:
Compassion is an ethical value.

SERVICE R$_X$:
Treat your customers as adults. When you uphold
company policies and procedures, do it by intelligently explaining the reasons to your customers.

SERVICE R$_X$:
Never make an exception for one customer if it hurts
your ability to serve other customers the way they
expect to be served.

SERVICE R$_X$:
Operational and philosophical values are strategic
and situational. Ethical values are absolute.

SERVICE R$_x$:
Service should be everyone's responsibility . . . and someone's accountability.

SERVICE R$_x$:
You can't shoot an arrow and then draw the target.

SERVICE R$_x$:
Services are the things you do for your customers. Service is how well you do them.

SERVICE R$_x$:
Every time you lose a customer you strengthen your competitor's position. The gains and losses are not about money, they are about power.

SERVICE R$_x$:
Make superior service the reflection of a market-focused philosophy that is a permanent, cherished, company-wide culture. Service must be deep in the foundation of your company, not a glossy new facade.

Chapter One—Differentiation in the 1990s

SERVICE R$_x$:
The best sales presentation is delivering excellent service.

SERVICE R$_x$:
Keep your customers. It costs six times more to acquire new customers than to keep existing ones happy.

SERVICE R$_x$:
Be more demanding of the personal service you receive everyday.

SERVICE R$_x$:
There are three things you can do when you are unhappy with your environment. You can leave it, adapt to it or try to change it. When it comes to poor service, you have to change it.

Chapter Two—Marketing as a Philosophy, Not as a Department

SERVICE R$_x$:
The function of every business is the acquisition and maintenance of customers.

SERVICE R$_x$:
Therefore, the function of *every employee* in every business is the acquisition and maintenance of customers.

SERVICE R$_x$:
Give people a reason to take pride in their work. Make them customer-focused.

SERVICE R$_x$:
Delete the phrase "It's company policy" from your vocabulary. If the reason for the policy is a good one, explain it to people. If it isn't, give your customers what they want.

SERVICE R$_x$:
Always include the customer in your decision-making process. If your focus is not on the customer, then change your focus until it is.

SERVICE R$_x$:
Don't make policies that punish good customers to protect you from those who might cheat you.

SERVICE R$_x$:
TRUST your customers. It's little things like trust that make a big difference in a business relationship.

SERVICE R$_x$:
Be a customer advocate. Find ways to say yes to your customers' requests.

Chapter Four—The Rigid Zone of Service Quality

SERVICE R$_x$:
Spend ten minutes with an employee of any company and you'll have a pretty good idea of what it's like to work for that company.

SERVICE R$_x$:
Never, ever, invoke company policy as a reason for doing or not doing something for a customer. Always give customers what they deserve—an explanation.

SERVICE R$_x$:
You get what you give. Managers have to treat their employees with respect if they want customers to be treated with respect.

SERVICE R$_x$:
The minute you start acting like a monopoly, you're guaranteeing that you won't be one in the future.

Chapter Six—The Progressive Zone of Service Quality

SERVICE R$_x$:
In a progressive company, policies are flexible guidelines, not hard-and-fast rules.

SERVICE R$_x$:
In the race for quality service, there is no finish line.

SERVICE R$_x$:
The difference between a good service company and a *great* service company is the great company *anticipates* its customers' needs.

SERVICE R$_x$:
Be innovative. Strive to set new standards of quality service in your industry.

SERVICE R$_x$:
Cater to your customers to the extent that they become so demanding that you are the only company willing to meet their needs.

SERVICE R$_x$:
Managers teach their employees to give poor service by watching them too closely and failing to convey trust. Instead, provide training, trust your people, and give them the freedom and authority to make decisions and take risks without the fear of punishment for mistakes.

SERVICE R$_x$:
It is a manager's job to eliminate all excuses for poor service or poor job performance. Create an excuse"less" culture.

SERVICE R$_x$:
> If *you* take responsibility for other people, they'll never take it for themselves.

SERVICE R$_x$:
> People thrive on responsibility. Give it to them.

Chapter Eight—Selling Quality With Service

SERVICE R$_x$:
> Not trying to sell something to someone who needs it is just as bad as trying to sell something to someone who does not need it.

SERVICE R$_x$:
> The best sales presentation is quality service.

SERVICE R$_x$:
> Be sincere. Your attitude during the service process—not necessarily the outcome—affects your customers' loyalty.

SERVICE R$_x$:
> As much as it is nice to try to relate to your customers, you have to realize that their perspectives are often much different than yours.

SERVICE R$_X$:
Serve your customers in a manner that will:
1) conform to your core values
2) manage their expectations
3) exceed their expectations to keep them happy without creating a financial burden on the company or affecting other customers.

Chapter Nine—Encouraging Demanding Customers

SERVICE R$_X$:
Be a demanding customer. If you don't ask for it, you won't get it.

SERVICE R$_X$:
People do not buy *things*, they buy *expectations*.

SERVICE R$_X$:
Carefully manage your customers' expectations; then exceed them.

SERVICE R$_X$:
Set the quality service standards in your industry. That is where the competitive advantage lies. Avoid being the one playing catch-up to your competitors.

SERVICE R$_x$:
Your company does not set service standards. *Your customers set service standards.* Your company only determines how well it will respond to customers' requirements.

SERVICE R$_x$:
Create an environment in which your customers are continually guiding your service efforts.

SERVICE R$_x$:
The best market research measures perceptions, not choices. Whenever possible, give customers a blank canvas on which to paint a picture. Avoid closed-ended, multiple-choice questions.

SERVICE R$_x$:
The best market research is a real salesperson asking a real prospect to buy. If there is a sale, what made it possible? If there was no sale, why not?

SERVICE R$_x$:
Market research is not something you do once in a while. It is something you do continually. The company that takes its finger off the pulse of the marketplace risks losing marketshare.

SERVICE R$_x$:
When doing market research, it is not enough to find out what *you* are *not* doing for your customers. The most effective sales strategy is to find out what *your competitors* are not doing for their customers.

SERVICE R$_x$:
Create services that your customers *notice* when you deliver those services to them and *miss* when they go elsewhere.

SERVICE R$_x$:
Encourage demanding customers.

Chapter Ten—Nurturing Complaining Customers

SERVICE R$_x$:
As a customer, there are two things you should do if you want to receive good service. Complain when you don't get it and reward it when you do. People can only meet your expectations when they know what your expectations are.

SERVICE R$_x$:
One out of 27 people will complain when there is a problem. That's less than 4%! The other 96% will not complain to you, they will complain to their friends and family. In fact, they will tell between 8 and 20 people of their dissatisfaction. The 95% of those who were dissatisfied will not do business with you again.

SERVICE R$_x$:
There is a 33% swing between losing customers and keeping them, depending on how you treat them in a complaint situation.

SERVICE R$_x$:
Your company must always be interested in what customers think. Do more than listen to complaints. Solicit them. See them as opportunities for improvement. Resolve them with enthusiasm. The importance of a positive complaining environment cannot be overemphasized.

SERVICE R$_x$:
Create a comfortable environment for satisfied and dissatisfied customers to voice their opinions. Every suggestion is an opportunity for your company to learn and grow.

SERVICE R$_x$:
The customer is not always right, but the customer is always the customer, even when they are wrong.

SERVICE R$_x$:
The primary function of every employee of every business is the acquisition and maintenance of customers, even when they're wrong.

SERVICE R$_x$:
People should never spend their entire careers in collections; they'll end up hating customers! People should be rotated through collections, not deposited there. When employees hate customers, they treat them like they hate them.

SERVICE R$_x$:
Include the collections department in all sales and customer service training. Give them a sense of participation in the acquisition and maintenance of customers.

SERVICE R$_x$:
Use a service guarantee as one of the ways to nurture complaining customers.

SERVICE R$_x$:
Service guarantees force your company to gain control of its service quality, nurture a positive complaint environment, increase marketshare, and boost profits.

SERVICE R$_x$:
A service guarantee assures customers that their reasonable expectations will be met or exceeded.

SERVICE R$_x$:
Nurture complaining customers.

Chapter Eleven—Managing the Recovery Process

> **SERVICE R$_x$:**
> A genuine interest in the customer plus flexibility and a commitment to a quick, fair resolution will always culminate in effective problem solving.

> **SERVICE R$_x$:**
> First fix the customer, then fix the service problem.

> **SERVICE R$_x$:**
> Turn the follow-up call into an opportunity for the customer to buy more.

> **SERVICE R$_x$:**
> Create a learning culture. Reward employees for ideas for improving service.

Chapter Twelve—Fostering Moments of Magic, Misery, and Truth

> **SERVICE R$_x$:**
> It is not an extraordinary product or service that makes a great company, it is extraordinary people.

SERVICE R$_x$:
Moments of truth, magic and misery should be regarded as fragile assets that must be managed with deliberate care.

SERVICE R$_x$:
Each and every moment of truth must be managed, which means ensuring the professionalism of everyone who will come in contact with your customers.

Chapter Thirteen—Creating the Vision-Driven and Values-Guided Organization

SERVICE R$_x$:
In everything—business, life, the arts—people with more dedication and persistence succeed over those with just raw talent. To achieve success, talent must be driven by dedication and persistence.

SERVICE R$_x$:
Don't look to new technology to make people's jobs easier. Train, develop, and motivate people to take on new challenges.

SERVICE R$_x$:
Creating a clear vision and a set of core values is an indispensable step in building a high-commitment organization intent upon being the best at everything it does.

SERVICE R$_x$:
Put everything on the table and let people choose for themselves, then hold them accountable for results.

SERVICE R$_x$:
One of the steps in producing a vision-driven and values-guided organization is to look at the gap between how you say things *should* be and how they actually are.

SERVICE R$_x$:
Employees are your best PR. Invest in them as you would an award-winning ad campaign.

SERVICE R$_x$:
Companies must establish "on the table" cultures in which employees can air their grievances without risk. It is hypocritical to encourage customer complaints, yet repress ones from employees.

SERVICE R$_x$:
When there is a shared sense of purpose, people are *expected* to accept responsibility for producing quality.

SERVICE R$_x$:
You manage *things*. You lead *people*.

Chapter Fourteen—Implementing the Change Effort

SERVICE R$_x$:
Knowledge is the antithesis of fear of change.

SERVICE R$_x$:
Promote *responsibility* for excellent service in every employee, then make the executive team *accountable*.

SERVICE R$_x$:
The corporate vision and core values become the conscience of the organization and the guiding force that keeps everything in alignment.

SERVICE R$_x$:
Show people how to achieve results first and new attitudes and relationships will follow.

SERVICE R$_x$:
People cannot concentrate on a vision of the future when they are in pain. Get rid of as much pain as possible, then you'll be able to look clearly into the future.

SERVICE R$_x$:
Stop obsessing over the present by creating a compelling vision for moving into the future.

SERVICE R$_x$:
Don't make customer service training the flavor-of-the-month. Quality service is a full-time, life-long, company-wide commitment.

SERVICE R$_x$:
An organization is comprised of people. It can never be something that its people are not.

SERVICE R$_x$:
                Act "As if."

SERVICE R$_x$:
There is no such thing as a short-term, successful, customer service effort. That is an oxymoron. The only way to truly change the service culture in an organization is to commit to the long-term.

Chapter Fifteen—Managing the People Systems

SERVICE R$_x$:
Rigid adherence to rigid rules produces mediocrity.

SERVICE R$_x$:
Progressive customer service is the result of hiring the right people, training them properly, leading them, providing them with thoughtfully conceived guidelines and empowering them with freedom, authority, and responsibility to make decisions on behalf of the company.

SERVICE R$_x$:
Maintain your people systems meticulously. High employee turnover is a symptom of being operations-driven. When your people systems fail, your whole business fails.

SERVICE R$_x$:
The best managers are like the best generals—they work (or fight) alongside their people in the trenches, not from behind their desks.

SERVICE R$_x$:
Set behavioral objectives in a participative rather than dictatorial way. Employees will be more likely to attain their goals if they have a role in defining them. People support what they help to create.

SERVICE R$_x$:
If you wait until you get perfection before you reward people, you'll never get exceptional results. Praise the small victories on the road to high performance.

SERVICE R$_x$:
Catch your people doing things right!

SERVICE R$_x$:
Inflexibility begets inflexibility.

SERVICE R$_x$:
Stop fixating on the policy manual. When you're thinking about the rules, you're not thinking about your employees. When your employees are thinking about the rules, they're not thinking about your customers.

SERVICE R$_x$:
Just asking for creativity will not get it. You have to encourage and reward it.

SERVICE R$_x$:
Genius is realized in the implementation of ideas, not just their conception.

SERVICE R$_x$:
Dare to be different. Avoid the mental bandwagon. Stimulate the creativity of your employees. Encourage them to share their ideas—no matter how outrageous. You never know where the next multi-million dollar idea will germinate.

SERVICE R$_x$:
People become what they do. Give your people more responsibilities and encourage their creativity, and they will become responsible, self-starting, and creative.

SERVICE R$_x$:
When selecting customer service personnel, the top priority must be the applicant's personality.

Appendix Two

Nine Phrases to Avoid at All Costs

As a consumer, there is only one thing more frustrating than being refused good service—being given a meaningless and arbitrary reason for poor service. Trying to argue with someone who is giving one of these reasons is equally frustrating.

We know that you, as a service provider, would avoid using any of the following phrases with a customer. You know how offensive they are; you also know how it feels to be a victim of their cold injustice. It's reasonable to assume that anyone who dislikes being given a pat answer would not *do that* to someone else. Right?

As for the past, we won't ask if you've ever said one of the following. That's too personal. If you have, hopefully you have learned from the experience. After reading this book, you will avoid the following phrases at all costs!

"I'm sorry, it's company policy."

"If I do it for you, I'll have to do it for everyone."

"We'll do it *this* time."

"It's not my job," or "Someone else handles that."

"I just work here; I don't make the rules."

"I can't do that."

"It will never happen again."

"It says so right here on the computer!"

"Well, I'll get the boss, but he's just going to say the same thing I said."

These phrases accomplish one thing and only one thing: They turn away business. They say, in effect, "We don't want to give you what you want. Go to our competitors." And that is exactly what your customers will do.

Notes

1. Otten, Allan L., "People Patterns," *Wall Street Journal*, May 16, 1990, B1.
2. The Forum Corporation, One Exchange Place, Boston, MA, 02109, 617-523-7300.
3. This ratio of one to twenty-seven may be on the conservative side, but we are comfortable using it to make our points. Tom Peters goes as far as saying he believes one out of every 2000 customers complains.
4. Adapted from Hart, Christopher W.L., "The Power of Unconditional Service Guarantees," *Harvard Business Review*, July-August, 1988.
5. Carlzon, Jan, *Moments of Truth*, (Ballinger: 1987), 21-29.
6. Mitchell, Ron, "Rediscovering Our Roots: A History of Quality Circle Activities in the United States From 1918 to 1948," Reprinted from *IAQC Conference Transactions*, 1984, 27.
7. DePree, Max, *Leadership Is An Art*, (Doubleday: 1989), 24.
8. *Los Angeles Times*, May 5, 1990, D2.
9. Wilke, John R., "NCR Is Revamping Its Computer Lines In Wrenching Change," *Wall Street Journal*, June 20, 1990, A1.
10. Moskal, Brian S., "The Sun Also Rises On GM," *Industry Week*, Sept. 5, 1988, 100-102.
11. Statistics from Hudson Institute study entitled "Workforce 2000" conducted for U.S. Dept. of Labor. Reported in a special supplement on education in the *Wall Street Journal*, Feb. 9, 1990.

Index

A

Advertising
  product-oriented 40
  service-oriented 40
Annual Growth
  Market-Focused vs.
    Operations-Focused 110
Aristotle 9
ATM Machines 47

B

Behavioral Objectives 288
Blanchard, Ken 2
  bank story 48
  ice cream story 299

C

Carlzon, Jan 172, 225
Change
  alleviating pain 274
  commitment 282
  designating accountabilities
    271
  difficulty of 262
  five-step process 265

  in general 261
  Involved vs. Informed 273
  organizational 262, 264
  organizational assessment
    269
  resistance 275
  responsibility for 264
  The People Side 272
  The Willed Future 267
Coaching 296
Comment Cards
  follow-up 186
Commodity
  defined 28
Complaining Customers
  collections 191
  comment card, follow-up
    186
  comment cards 185
  encouraging them 177
  preferential treatment 190
  problem customers 194
  right or wrong 189
  statistics 176
  tension management 179
  toll-free numbers 186

Corporate Structure 252
Corporate vision 243, 259
Corporatization of America 29
Cost of Losing a Customer 35
Cost of New Customers 33
Counseling 296
Creative Resiliency 263
Creativity 295, 301
Cross-training 255
Customer-focused
    defined 19

D

Differentiated product
    defined 28
Differentiation
    indulgent zone 115
    progressive zone 108
    rigid zone 91
    safe zone 98

E

Evaluating performance 292
Evolution of a Business 55
Excuse"less" Culture 105
Expectations
    caring 144
    confidence 144
    five qualities of business
        transactions 143
    indulgent zone 111
    managing 147
    perceived value 155
    physical impression 144
    relative 145
    reliability 143
    responsiveness 144
    rigid zone 86

F

Function of every business 51

G

Good Customers/
    Noncustomers 191

H

Hawthorne Effect 239
High Performance Model 249

I

Idea Killers 303
Indulgent zone
    defined 111
Invite Creative Demands 156

L

Leadership 258
Levitt, Dr. Ted 28, 51

M

Management style
    indulgent zone 114
    progressive zone 105
    rigid zone 90
    safe zone 97
Managing by Objectives 240
Managing Expectations
    advertising 147
    ambiance 149
    attitude 149
    consistency 153, 168
    customer contact 152
    giving new ideas 159
    pricing 153
    promises 153
    setting service standards
        160
Market Research
    customer comment cards
        164

direct mail 162
focus groups 165
keeping in touch 162
nuances of 166
observation 165
surveys 164
Market-focused
defined 19
Market-Focused Model 68
Marketing/sales focus
indulgent zone 114
progressive zone 108
rigid zone 91
safe zone 97
Minimum level of acceptable
service 143
Moments of truth 226
calculating 230
managing 231
motivation 234
Money Equals Power 20

N

Naisbitt, John 33
NBD Phenomenon 170

O

Obsessed With Your Boss? 60
Operations-focused
defined 19
Operations-Focused Model 66
Organizational change
five step process 265

P

Paradigm Shifts 256
Performance evaluation 291
Perot Systems
philosophical values 10
Philosopher General 16

Pitfalls of organizational
change 251
Power of Praise 292
regression toward the mean
293
Progressive Zone
creative destruction 101
defined 99
sensible flexibility 100
trust cycle 105
Pushing decisions down 255

Q

Quality Circles 240
Questioning
closed-ended 128
open-ended 128

R

Reactive Rigidity 263
Recovering from mistakes 205
Recovery
asking for help 216
compensation and gifts 211
independent thinking 221
noncontrollable problems
213
procedure for 207
the poof phenomenon 207
Responsible Flexibility 263
Rigid adherence to rigid rules
299
Rigid Zone
defined 83
Role of advertising 33
Role of service 33

S

Safe zone
defined 93
Sales/service

Selection 305
    five qualities for service
        survival 307
Self-managed teams 254
Selling With Service
    common listening faults
        131
    defined 119
    feedback 132
    feedback, nonverbal 132
    feedback, verbal 132
    getting paid for service 135
    know your customers 133
    listening skills 129
    non-manipulative 125
    questioning 127
    six principles 125
    tension management 179
Sensible flexibility 298, 301
Service
    defined 18
    Law of Supply and Demand
        37
    mirror image 246
Service Guarantees 194
    benefits of 199
    qualities of 197
Service Standard Meetings
    161
Staying close to your people
    287

T

Tension Management 179
    Internal Tension 180
    Need Tension 183
    Relationship Tension 181
Theory X & Y 239
Thinking
    long-term 62
    short-term 3, 62
Training 296

Treatment of people
    indulgent zone 114
    progressive zone 104
    rigid zone 88
    safe zone 96
Trusting Your Customers
    Ford Motor Company 62

V

Values 243, 246
    ethical 7
    indulgent zone 114
    operational 13
    perceived 155
    philosophical 10
    progressive zone 103
    rigid zone 86
    safe zone 96
    strategic 11
    who gets to break the rules?
        14

W

Warm body syndrome 88
Why Is Service So Bad 40

Z

Zones of Service Quality 75,
    80
    Indulgent 111
    Progressive 99
    Rigid 83
    Safe 93
    Self-Test 76

BE ON THE CUTTING EDGE OF SERVICE IN TODAY'S MARKET!

ORDER FORM

YES, I want _____ copies of *The Quest for Service Quality: R_Xs for Achieving Excellence* at $24.95 each, plus $3.00 shipping and handling per book. (Utah residents please include $1.56 state sales tax per book.) Canadian orders must be accompanied by a postal money order in U.S. funds. Allow 30 days for delivery.

☐ My check or money order for _____ is enclosed.

Please charge my ☐ VISA ☐ MasterCard

Name _____ Phone _____

Address _____

City/State/Zip _____

Card # _____ Expires _____

Signature _____

**Check your leading bookstore
or call your credit card order to:**
800-767-5212

Please make your check payable and return to:
**Maxcomm Associates, Inc.
1333 East 9400 South, Suite 270
Sandy, Utah 84093**